Winning the Mind Game

Negotiating in Business and Life

by

Paul M. Lisnek, J.D., Ph.D.

Library of Congress Card Catalog Number: 96-77198

ISBN 0-916990-39-7

DEDICATION

To the Loving Memory of two special friends who still greatly influence me:

Ken Fischbein, a dear friend for over 30 years, taken much too soon, and whose wit, wisdom, compassion and acceptance are unmatched; he set the standard for friendship. I thank Joan and Al Fischbein for giving the world Ken, and wish Sarah and Alex the vision to live life as fully as did your dad.

James Rogner, a kind and gentle man of spirit, humanity and music, whose wonderful smile warmed every heart he touched.

I cherish having had these friends in my life. Their spirits continue to radiate hope and guidance and I cannot imaging having lived without knowing them.

TABLE OF CONTENTS

ACKNOWLEDGEMENTS

I emphasize in this book that each of us negotiates all day long, every day, throughout our lives. I would therefore need to thank and recognize everyone with whom I have come into contact in my life as each person has taught me something about the art and science of negotiation. With that global word of thanks, I must acknowledge a few very special people without whom this eighth book of mine would never have been completed. They provide the support, stability, and balance in my life.

First and foremost, my parents, Sandy and Seymour Lisnek, never cease to be the source of my every inspiration and desire to achieve. I can never repay the love and support they have afforded me throughout my life, but I hope they see this book as a small token of *their* accomplishment in raising a not so bad kid. The support of my brother Rick and his Judy, and their David, Michael, Danielle and Jaclyn is so very important to me that these words can never properly express my appreciation (but enough about me, how's the business going?). My thanks as well to family members: the Jorbins and Jacobs and our favorite leader, Dave Jorbin.

Writing only gets done because my staff, Vice President Anne Brody Elovic and administrative assistant Richard Anton do everything else! To Angie "Granny" Nikolas and Christina Sofiaskis for sustaining my energy with the world s best banana pancakes!

Writing is only a part of my life. I am most grateful to those with whom I work. To Chris M. Salamone, Executive Director of the National Institute for Legal Education, with whom I am priviledged to plan and execute the finest pre-law preparation educational program in the nation and the highest quality high school summer experience, the National Law and Leadership Foundation. To Anthony Salamone for showing both Chris and me the way through his many years of business and education savvy. My colleagues Steve Friedland, Joe Chaney, Mike Flynn, Mike Kaufman, Mike Mosca, Eve Brensike and Meredith Frimpter make the programs a memorable experience for every student.

To Julie Eichorn, President, and Joe Crosby, Vice President of Paragon, true professionals training other professionals in the most sophisticated approach to marketing and sales available. I thank Richard Gabriel, President of Decision Analysis, for the excellent work we do together in our trial consulting practice in complex and high profile litigation. To Ron Rosenblum, my colleague in the law.

Most significantly, this book would not exist without the careful guidance, input and editing of Virginia McCullough, truly one of the country's finest writers. She is a writer's writer as she insures that my words make sense, remains organized and has a style appealing to most people. Virginia, I thank you for making this book happen and keeping me going when neither the spirit nor flesh were willing in those stress filled times.

Finally, we all count on the friends and significant people in our lives to get us through difficult times, enjoy the happy times, and just plain be there when needed. No one can have a better support network than I have getting me through life. I admire those friends whose love for life inspires me: Raymond Massey, Larry Bushong, and Byron McCoy. Among the most special people in my life: Rev. Arnold Pierson and the spirit of his beloved Katherine, Steve Pearson, Michael Mendelson, Cindy Raymond, Barry and Mattie Litwin, Bob Anderson, Jan and Kelsey Freese, Michael and Sidney Menefee, Robert Bell, Al Menotti, Steve and Hester Rubin, Marlene, Mike and Izzy Brown, Marcia Moulton, Tim Jones, Kathy Morris, Christine Anderson, Gregory Adamski and Karen Conti. And to Brian and Gummo Lozell, my sincere appreciation for your never-ending support and good faith. You have shown what trust and caring mean in their finest sense . . . . and they mean more than an ocean full of sea monkeys. Umhmmm.

From my television world, appreciation to those at Continental Cablevision including Terry Cantwell, Liz Braham and Jim Serpe, and NBC News' Mimi Mouakad, David Bohrman, Art Lord and Stu Dan. Also, I so appreciate dear friends and Broadway s finest, Kaye Ballard and Myvonwy Jenn.

And to you, the reader, without your desire to become a better negotiator, there would be no need for this book. But because you have chosen to grow in the art and skill of negotiation, then your commitment to reading and putting into practice the theory offered here makes the book a most worthwhile endeavor. Thanks, again—and enjoy the world of negotiation!

Paul M. Lisnek
June, 1996

INTRODUCTION

Negotiation: A Practice As Old As We Are

FROM THE DAY HUMAN BEINGS FIRST STOOD ON TWO LEGS and used even rudimentary language, we began negotiating. Maybe the first negotiated agreements involved who got the biggest cave. Can't you just picture one of our distant ancestors saying, "Okay, you can have the biggest cave, we'll take the one with more light." Sound like anyone you know? Later, groups and individuals moved on to settle more complex issues, such as who owns which piece of land and what items they would receive for the goats and sheep they traded with neighboring clans. Indeed, when you look at the history of violent conflict on our planet, you'll see that negotiation existed, but *effective* negotiations were — and are — often absent. Even today, armed conflict can start because negotiations, as the phrase goes, "broke down."

Similarly in our own lives, we negotiate from the moment we awaken to the minute we go to bed. Will we hit the snooze button one more time and risk being late for work or an appointment? Will we drive today, or use public transportation to save money? Will that choice make our decisions about our after-work plans more difficult because we don't have our car available? Should we see the movie we just saw all over again because our good friend hasn't seen it yet and really wants to go tonight? And on and on — so go the negotiations of our life. The first step is to increase your awareness of the existence of negotiation in nearly everything we do.

Eventually, almost every global or national conflict, as well as the conflicts in our own lives, are solved with negotiation. The scope may be different, but the process is the same. Reasonable heads tend to argue: Why don't we negotiate before we get to the point of impasse, which can jeopardize relationships and even our safety or that of others? Fortunately, most individuals, partners, and businesses do exactly that—they negotiate before communication completely breaks down. However, we often wish we had acted sooner than later, or for better than for worse, or at least preserved a friendly atmosphere.

In recent years, we've seen negotiators brought into a situation in which individuals are held hostage or a person is threatening suicide or another form of violence to him or herself or others. We've heard about the government, by Presidential directive, help parties negotiate labor settlements. Remember the government's efforts to bring baseball back to the American scene? That was (believe it or not) an exercise in negotiation.

The goal of this book, *Winning the Mind Game: Negotiating in Business and Life*, is to help you understand the importance of negotiation in your daily life. It provides the communication tools you need to negotiate before conflict results in bad business deals, damages relationships, or triggers a stalemate—problems that just won't go away.

As you read through the book and study the principles and complete the forms included to assist you through your own negotiations, you will have a mixture of the following:

- Some "ah ha" experiences that will bring immediate changes.
- Slow, but steady absorption of information that leads to a new way to view your interactions with others.

- Practice in using your new skills in a variety of situations.
- A shift in the way you view yourself and the way you achieve your goals—whatever they may be.

COMMUNICATION IS THE KEY

Some people think that the best negotiators are those who put their best offer out first and refuse to budge at all from their opening position. Ah, how naive the thought. Many people think of negotiation as either a way to win something or as a way to lose something. They think it involves savvy, street-smarts, or even the ability to be sneaky and "put something over" on others. Still others think they need to lie their way to resolution. Each of these positions is wrong.

You will learn that negotiation is a complex process grounded in psychology. Success requires a knowledge of how other people think and a respect for and understanding of their positions.

Let me be clear up front. This book is not about dishonest or unethical negotiation. On the contrary, individual integrity and mutual respect form the foundation for successful negotiation. It is about flexibility and understanding. People who define their life mission as "get them before they get you," need to learn that they lose more than they could win if they worked toward a simple shift in attitude.

This book is for those who want to achieve their goals in a spirit of congeniality, with a recognition that everyone must believe that they have won in the negotiation process and that winning is possible for all parties. We should be able to walk out of every negotiation with head held high and with the knowledge that we can look at the other negotiators in the future with a sense of self respect and esteem.

This doesn't happen by itself, however. It doesn't mean that there isn't great tension and points of conflict. Rather, it starts with communication. We can assume that the cave people who spent the night in the bigger cave were satisfied and didn't resent those who preferred the one with more light. Each group might have had good reasons for negotiating for what they preferred in this situation.

A modern equivalent of this simple division of shelter might be two roommates who negotiate a division of available space. Perhaps one pays a few dollars more to secure the bigger bedroom. Or, the one who agrees to the smaller space is entitled to use most of the hall closet. I know of a group of six house mates who hold weekly sessions to pay bills and settle any disputes that might come up. No matter what the outcome, they can't achieve anything without communicating with each other.

As you will see, communication is not simply talking a lot or talking a little. Look at it this way: Talking is sending a message; communication is processing and interpreting that message — a much more meaningful process.

This is putting communication in somewhat simplistic terms, and we will discuss the ramifications of this statement throughout the book. But, always remember that stringing a bunch of words together in a speech — or in a sentence or paragraph — is not necessarily effective communication. Effective communication will show in negotiation, often as achieving the outcome you intended or desired.

It's also important to remember that we can't *not* communicate. Whether or not one intends to send a particular message, and whether the receiver perceives the intended message, communication has taken place on some level. Think of all the "miscommunication" you've experienced, those encounters in which you say, "That's not what I meant," or your think, "What's this person doing—trying to confuse me?" Communication has taken place whether you like it or not.

As you learn to become a proficient and effective negotiator, you'll also become increasingly aware that you are always dealing with a unique individual. Individual personality and character are involved every time, and you'll learn the importance in communication, and hence, negotiation, of those factors that make each person unique. If you think that age, sex, nationality and cultural background, or socioeconomic status are not crucial factors in negotiation, then think again. You'll explore just how important these demographic and sociological assessments are, and you'll learn how to consider them when you communicate and negotiate.

In Part One of this book, you'll learn about communication styles and nonverbal communication in negotiation settings. Keep an eye on the fact that the concepts you will learn will likely apply in most interpersonal interactions you have in your life, including—and far beyond—negotiation. Whether you're buying a house or negotiating a fee or a salary raise or agreeing on vacation plans with your partner and/or children, you are communicating and negotiating.

THE WHY AND HOW OF NEGOTIATION

We negotiate to reach certain goals. It s a simple concept: You have a goal, and the other person with whom you negotiation has a goal. Each of you has a position and each has a desired outcome. Because we are sometimes fuzzy in our thinking, we are often unaware of what our goal or position is as we begin to negotiate. But, part of clear communication is examining and naming a goal and identifying a position.

In addition, in most negotiations each person has firm positions and fluid ones. There may be areas that are open to compromise, but in some situations these areas are few. The more skilled we are at negotiating, the greater our ability to find the fluid areas and move beyond the firm ones. To paraphrase the Reverend Jesse Jackson's well-known theme, skilled negotiators find "common ground."

It's important to think about this concept of common ground, because we see examples all around us where people are looking for areas in which they can agree or at least compromise. Some of these attempts are successful and others are characterized by fierce struggles. In our country's ongoing debate over health care reform, there are constant attempts at compromise—most politicians, despite the bad rap they get, are good at reaching compromises in order to settle an issue and move forward.

On the other hand, one of our country's most divisive issues, reproductive choice, is characterized by the inability to find even a shred of common ground. To many observers—and activists—it appears to be a hopeless issue. However, sooner or later, some accommodation will be reached—even it appears to tear at the fabric of our cultural life along the way.

But the "stuff" of life is often far more mundane and when people are open to others and to the process, they can successfully settle disputes over which cave they live in or which restaurant they go to on Friday night. (If the similarities between life as caveperson and the natural instincts of modern day humans appear similar at their root, you should not be surprised. We haven't come all that far in our development; but we are more strategic and psychologically aware in our approach today).

In Part II of this book, we'll examine the way we can take what we know about communication within negotiation and apply it specifically to the process of negotiation. We'll look at the dynamics that occur between people as they work towards a mutually acceptable arrangement. Choosing place and time, obtaining information, learning the other's position, supporting your own position, and so forth are all part of setting up negotiations. We have developed structures to negotiate and the more informed we are about them, the better we will become at using them. Since negotiating styles vary from culture to culture, we must consider the wide variety of settings and structures in which we find ourselves.

If you doubt the importance of structures and settings, consider how you would react if your male boss wanted to negotiate your annual raise in the locker room at the neighborhood health club. If you're a man, you may have experienced such a negotiation structure—although you may not have liked it much. You can decide to accept the setting or negotiate for a different one. If you're a woman, you would probably have been confused or even offended. Confused because you know that he knows that this is an impossible setting; you may be offended because you are effectively being shut out of the negotiation.

You may receive the crudely sent message that there will be no negotiation about your raise. Recently, a woman charged her boss with sexual harassment because, among other things, her boss suggested that they discuss her raise at the Holiday Inn down the road. You may be pleased to learn that she won her case.

Consider the setting involved in negotiating a bank loan or closing a real estate transaction. You have an expectation of a conference room, neat files, and a closed door. You don't expect to sign a loan or close on a house in the bank's crowded lobby. Expectations of all parties involved are important—you may soon discover that you need to develop skills in this area. Perhaps you have entered negotiations in inappropriate settings and which used structures that have worked against you, or have made others uncomfortable.

Preparation will be discussed as a most crucial area in negotiation. As an attorney and business owner, I know that adequate preparation can make the difference between a win-win negotiation and a drawn out interaction that can result in losses for everyone involved. You'll learn how to prepare yourself to negotiate, but you'll also learn what to look for in cases where someone negotiates on your behalf.

Let's face it, no one wants to hire a lawyer who comes into the conference room without the necessary information to negotiate a contract or a settlement on your behalf. In this case, the other party's attorney is well-prepared—facts, figures, papers, and definable positions. Who do you think is in a position to negotiate a better deal? You are paying the fee, and you are entitled to a prepared negotiator.

In Part III, you'll learn important negotiating techniques such as staying on point, determining the relevance of information presented, and handling the competitive tone that often enters the atmosphere at the negotiation table. You'll "sit in" on some negotiation sessions, and plan some of your own. When you put the information together—and practice using it—you will find yourself at ease when you negotiate in your own life.

Too often I hear people say, "I can't negotiate well because I'm so nervous and tense." Some people literally freeze up and can barely present their points. I've found that more often than not, these people are frightened and nervous because they lack confidence in their skills. Have faith. When you systematically apply the ideas in this book, you will find your confidence level soaring.

IF YOU COMMUNICATE WITH OTHERS, THIS BOOK IS PROBABLY FOR YOU

- You're a business owner negotiating fees with your clients, terms with customers, or salaries with employees.
- You're a therapist or other professional negotiating a payment schedule with a client who is short of money this month.
- You're a parent negotiating with the principal of your child's school about security and safety issues, or perhaps negotiating with your children over their rights and responsibilities at home.
- You're setting up a trust fund, adopting a child, buying a house, trying to get a tree removed from a neighbor's property, and are looking for an attorney to represent you.

- You're an adult in a family of four trying to divide up the housework.
- You're a union steward handling contract violations.
- You're a representative of management's position at the union contract negotiation table, or a representative of the union putting forth the position of the members.
- You're a student applying for financial aid—or for a college loan from your grandmother, parent, or uncle.
- You're getting married next year and neither set of parents approves of the wedding plans and some family members threaten not to show up for the ceremony.
- You have five roommates in a large house and problem solving sessions are regularly scheduled.
- Your life partner has left and now you have property to divide and joint bills to pay.
- You and your partner are moving in together and you are negotiating everything from chores to money to where to hang your favorite painting.

Is the message clear? This book is for people living in a hectic and complex society. It is for men, women, young people, business owners, employees, professionals of all kinds, home owners, life partners, and parents.

For many years now, I have shared what I know about negotiation with my colleagues in the legal and corporate worlds, workshop participants, and people who have come to my motivational talks and lectures. I bring a unique perspective to this work because I am a lawyer with a doctorate in communication. I recognize the importance of the psychological component of negotiating. You could say that I have spent the majority of my career in law and, for the past several years, as a speaker and trainer helping people integrate knowledge from many fields in order to create and achieve goals. Now, I look forward to sharing what I have learned from life with you.

In my first book, *Quality Mind, Quality Life* (Meta Publications,

1995), I discussed negotiation as one skill among many that is necessary to bring quality into our lives. However, many people urged me to expand and elaborate on the information I presented about negotiation. I took these emphatic requests seriously and I now offer you the result.

It is my firm belief that we are evolving (granted, sometimes it seems like very slow progress) toward a society in which negotiation will be increasingly respected and, most important, used to settle conflicts and differences before ugliness, alienation, and violence force solutions. Mediation centers are supported in many communities as an effective way to stop clogging our court system with disputes that could better be settled through negotiation. In the corporate world and in private organizations and associations "consensus" management is becoming an ideal for which to strive.

Throughout this book you'll hear the terms "competitive" and "cooperative" applied to people's negotiation styles. Some people consider cooperation a positive concept and competition a negative one, at least much of the time. Don't be confused. As styles, we often use strategies from both worlds. But as a process, let me be clear on a point that distinguishes me from others who teach in this field. I believe strongly that we live in a society that is by its very nature competitive. Most of us just naturally want to win at what we do, whether that means winning at the card table, on the basketball court, in our careers, or when we're making a purchase. Competition is the drive that makes us want to win and it never goes away. Even when a particular negotiation gets to its final moments, where all parties cooperate to achieve an agreement, that sense of competition, of wanting to do as well as possible for yourself or a client, never goes away. Hedrick Smith wrote in his book, *The Power Game*, "We are a nation of game players...preoccupied with winning and losing...competition is our creed." Although a statement about politics in Washington, D.C., nothing could be more on point when discussing the process of human negotiation.

Most people enter every negotiation with the attitude that they want to get the best deal they can for themselves. This isn't selfishness; it's self-interest, and there's nothing wrong with it. In fact, if we all learned to negotiate our positions more clearly and in a skilled way, we would find ways to balance the competing interests in our own lives and in society in general. But we do it with the intent of getting all we can in the end.

It's important to note that competition, and hence, negotiation, is basically a psychological process. Consider Brian negotiating a salary for a new job with his potential employer, Mr. Gummo. Brian may actually feel good about a salary offer below his salary demand if Mr. Gummo makes it clear that he has made every effort to get Brian his requested salary. On a psychological level, Brian sees a boss who will fight for him and that may carry weight in Brian's decision to take the job.

We try to get inside the minds of others and they in turn attempt to get inside our mind, too. In effective negotiation we understand that each individual brings his or her entire previous experience to the negotiation setting. The ability to understand other people is paramount to successful negotiations. This is why I refer to successful negotiation as winning the mind game—and we are always players in this very human endeavor.

I believe that there has never been a time in human history in which the ability to negotiate has been more crucial. Negotiation becomes increasingly complex on a global level with each new crisis we face. That's the big picture. Most of us, however, are involved in personal issues that affect us every day. Fortunately, our needs (sometimes of crisis proportion to us) can be usually addressed with efficiency and effectiveness. Developing your negotiating skills means improved quality of life, stronger relationships, and a better sense of control over your destiny. If these are goals worth pursuing—which means we might as well do the best we can in this lifetime—then read on!

PART I

CHAPTER ONE

Can We Talk? – Oops – Communicate

ARNIE HAS HAD IT. HE'S SICK OF WORKING FOR HIS PRESENT lousy salary and it's time that he demand more money. Maybe not the perfect worker (but then again, nobody is), what should Arnie do? A bit confused himself, Arnie affirms (under his breath), "I'm just going to walk into Sandra's office and demand a raise." He folds his arms across his chest, sits back in his chair and convinces himself that this is the right thing to do.

What Arnie wants to do may be understandable in the heat of the moment. We've all probably felt like Arnie does now. He sits, holding his paycheck in hand, and he's just put in an 11 hour day. It's natural, if not particularly smart, that Arnie wants to *demand* more money. His reaction is duplicated all over the country, if not the world, every day.

However, what Arnie proposes to do falls into the category of talk, talk, talk. On some level, Arnie doesn't understand that we often don't get what we need and want simply by demanding it. Sometimes we go over and over in our minds the justifications for wanting what we want when we want it. Can't you just imagine Arnie feeling so certain that his request is just too reasonable to turn down? Why he doesn't even have to ask—a simple demand is enough, because any fool can see he's right. Then why are we always so afraid to take the step?

What is missing in Arnie's "plan?" It's easy to say "almost everything," but specifically, we can list the areas in which Arnie needs education. He has missed some of the most important elements of effective communication. Perhaps the most glaring omission is preparation. Has Arnie done his homework? Do any of us actually take the time to learn all we need to know before we make decisions that effect our lives? In this case, Arnie needs to:

- gather the facts about his salary and the financial status of the company for which he works,
- consider the timing of his "demand" for a raise,
- assess the personal communication style of his boss, Sandra, and her ability to negotiate, and
- adequately create a plan outlining what he wants and what will ultimately satisfy him.

Throughout this book, we'll look at these areas, all of which are too often overlooked in negotiation. You'll learn, step by step, how important each bit of knowledge is when creating an atmosphere for effective negotiation. Maybe Arnie will learn something and get his raise after all—but maybe not. We'll see.

Before we can help Arnie, we need to explore a few basic concepts that operate in all communication transactions and in every negotiation. First, we must understand the other person's values, beliefs, background, and so forth.

DEMOGRAPHICS—THE POWER OF SEVEN

Seven key demographic factors affect how each of us communicates. When we choose to play negotiator, we need to explore and be aware of these factors before beginning to negotiate for anything. The factors are:

- **Age:** There are generational differences in the way people communicate—just look around you and you'll see that this is true. Most young people alter the way they talk when they are communicating with their grandparents. Similarly, age peers speak a different language with each other than they normally use in a mixed age group. These differences are subtle, but if you pay attention, you'll notice these fine distinctions in communication and therefore, in negotiation.

Arnie's boss is quite a bit older than 35 year old Arnie. She was raised at a time when people didn't routinely pepper their speech with crude profanity. Arnie's language with his peers in quite a bit different from that he uses at work. But when his temper gets going, he can forget who he's talking to and get a bit salty in his speech. He's so angry right now that we can only hope he won't rush in to confront the more refined Sandra. Who knows what he'd say? Even Arnie can't be sure. You may be able to relate to how Arnie is feeling at this moment.

- **Sex:** Men and women have learned to communicate primarily by watching members of the same sex. They model behavior and it is clear that the two sexes often have differing styles of communication. In addition, individual style is more important than the stereotypical male and female styles. For example, many women report that some men are condescending and try to charm them during the negotiation process. Men often say that women bring in issues that to them seem superfluous or off the point during negotiations. In the proverbial "battle of the sexes," these are differences of substance.

Historically, power structures within our society have set up a situation where one communication style is considered "right" and the other "wrong." But this isn't the case. Communication styles may be different, but one is not better than the other. The secret is in awareness of, and sensitivity to, differences and a recognition of the importance of adaptation to whatever you get.

- **Socioeconomic status:** There are numerous ways an individual's perception of social or economic status can affect communication. There are those who believe that having a large income or living in an up-scale part of a community automatically gives them an edge over those whose incomes are lower. And the lower-income person may believe the same thing!

Socioeconomic status may lead to "one up/one down" positioning in negotiation. This means that one person attempts to look good in the negotiation by putting the other person down. But remember that this doesn't need to occur. We've all witnessed professionals such as lawyers or doctors and others who talked down to potential clients and patients, only to have the people leave and never come back. In these cases, communication was unsatisfactory and neither party may be able to explain exactly what happened. But I know one thing, the person who is aware of the dynamics is in a much better position to make the negotiation work, while remaining respectful to the other party.

- **Education:** People with less formal education may not have the same confidence about their knowledge of the situation at hand, whether their lack of confidence is justified or not. Those who have a great deal of education may exhibit more confidence in their knowledge, whether their self-assurance is justified or not. This psychological attitude is only one example of the way in which our education affects the way we communicate—and negotiate. Remember, the effective negotiator needs more than book smarts. Practical intelligence plays a big role here.

- **Information Processing:** This is a rich body of material because it recognizes that people think differently from each other and we often tie someone's need to learn in one way as being a sign of intelligence. We don't do others a favor when we deliberately ignore their ability—or inability—to understand the concepts the way we might wish them to be presented. The most practical way to make the point is to highlight what we often experience to be true; a math whiz has a style of communication different from that of an artist.

One kind of information processing isn't better than the other; it's just different. For now, you can assume that there are numerous ways people process and understand information. Our mission is to understand how we and others process information, and how we can best communicate across various types of information processing modes.

• **Nationality/Culture:** In some cultures, business negotiations proceed after a long evening of dinner and entertainment. In other cultures, the wining and dining takes place only after the business transactions are over. Remember the labored negotiations that took place in Paris between the parties involved in the Vietnam War? It took months just to determine the kind of table that would be used when the talks began. Cultural differences had to be considered before any negotiating could begin. Incredible as it seems, the slaughter continued while the shape and size of the table were being carefully considered. After all, rectangular tables have clear positions for leaders, but round tables present a bit more difficulty in determining where the leader sits. Even the seemingly small details can have significant impact on the process.

• **Religion:** Religious beliefs will often affect an individual's openness to positions that may challenge his or her underlying convictions. For this reason, it is important to know if religion is an important factor in the person's character. You may need to express your position so as not to challenge the religious (or other) filters worn by the other negotiator. Some of the toughest communication problems occur when basic religious beliefs become involved. One need only read a newspaper and watch the television news to see this point come to life.

Beginning today, notice how these seven factors shape the character of the people with whom you communicate. Make this one of the first "assignments" you take on as you learn to improve your negotiation skills. Poor Arnie doesn't have a clue so far, and there's no telling what kind of blunders he could make as he states—or maybe shouts—his immediate demand for a raise.

COMMUNICATION IS TRANSACTIONAL

Arnie has overlooked another important piece of information. He is under the mistaken impression that his demand for a raise will be received as reasonable and certainly within the realm of the possible. After all, we all see ourselves as rational and reasonable. However, communication involves a sender and receiver and each negotiator is both at all times. In other words, we send and receive communication on many levels and we have both an expectation and a need to be understood by the other person. If we don't consider the above seven demographic factors we can experience significant barriers to communication.

Communication also includes a channel, meaning that there are different modes of communication we routinely use. We can be face to face and communicate orally, and nonverbal factors enter in; we can communicate over the phone, which includes fewer nonverbal cues; and we can communicate in writing, a mode in which nonverbal cues are absent (although we "hallucinate" to fill in the missing pieces but more on that later).

Face-to-face interactions are the most complete, in that the possibility for immediate feedback is present and both verbal and nonverbal communication is sent and received. Any time the possibility for immediate feedback is removed, as in written communication, there is an increased possibility for misunderstanding. (There are situations in which written communication has some advantages. These will be discussed later in the book.) Candidly, the ultimate success we have in communication and negotiation depends on our awareness of and accuracy in reading all of the information being transmitted to us by the other person.

Let's break down the process of communication into its transfer elements. First, there is "encoding." You want to communicate information to your parents about their insurance policies. You gather the facts and present them in a way you believe they can understand them. You are "encoding", or translating, the information. When you encode, you are taking the individual's background and experiences into consideration — again, recognizing the importance of demographics. Encoding is the process of relating messages to others so that we can be understood.

The receiver of the message "decodes," or translates the message in a way that fits or is compatible with experience, that has meaning in relation to his or her experiences. (That's where the seven demographic factors come into play). There is an alignment of information with that accumulated experience. You tell your parents that their insurance is inadequate to meet their probable future needs. You suggest ways to improve it. If their experience with insurance companies is generally negative, they might decode the message based on anger and fear. "I won't give those jerks another penny," Dad says. "Don't even suggest it."

Now we have a classic communication problem. Your father has not received the information in the way you intended when you sent it. Now dad is defending his internal meaning, in this case, his experience with insurance companies. He is also adding another element in the transaction, that of creating a challenge.

If you begin defending your position — "Oh yes, we *will* look for other policies" — we have two people firmly defending their own interpretations of information. But, understand that the shared goal might not be so different here. The miscommunication may result from assumed meanings and intentions.

You can't assume that your parents will relate to your belief that the insurance is inadequate when you first approach the subject. In fact, it might be better to assume that the underlying meaning will be different. Then, by using other techniques these interpretive differences can be smoothed, soothed, patched, or mended—use your own demographic factors and language style to decide which term you like best.

NEW IDEAS, NEW TECHNIQUES

Enter a new and ground-breaking system that can revolutionize communication and negotiation. Called Neurolinguistic Programming, or NLP for short, this system involves deep understanding of human beings and what makes us tick; it's the process of developing rapport with others. NLP presents a series of techniques that can add new dimensions to our communication transactions. If you enter negotiations with others and have a basic understanding of human nature, you will gain confidence and greater understanding of the underlying process.

Let's start with a basic premise: In any given situation, reality occurs only once. Now what does that mean? In simple terms, this means that once an interaction is over, only the memories remain. These memories are tainted or biased by past experience. Furthermore, they are now shaped to fit our view of the world; this world view is sometimes called a "map."

Judy has an interaction with a customer, Ms. Danielle, in her golf supply store. Ms. Danielle wants faster service, and Judy is getting to her as fast as she can. Both sender and receiver hear the words and once the words are spoken, each brings her experience to the transaction. This can't be any other way, because human beings aren't blank slates every new day. Each day we bring everything we are to all our relationships.

Judy is doing what she thinks is her absolute best to serve all her customers. Ms. Danielle has been ignored in two other stores that very morning, but how would Judy know that? Each woman's conviction is influencing her actions. Judy, as a business owner, must dig below the reality that is presented if she is going to satisfy this woman's needs. Just as we've all witnessed, Judy's response can either alienate the person for all time, or her response can effectively "disarm" the customer and soften her response. Each moment has a reality of its own, and each moment is constantly shaped by experience.

This example illustrates—and admittedly simplifies—the assumptions by which NLP operates. There are a set of presuppositions about people that must be understood before NLP techniques can be properly used. Let's examine these and clarify some important NLP principles.

1. Communication is redundant.

We are always communicating—we can't *not* communicate, even when we aren't speaking. Verbal communication constitutes about 10 percent of our total face-to-face message. The other 90 percent is made up of the manner in which we say the words and our nonverbal cues: facial and body expressions, tone and pitch of our voices, the way we dress, and so forth. These accompany all face-to-face transactions.

2. Meaning lies within the receiver.

Some people mistakenly believe that the meaning of what they say is what they as sender think it is. They believe that meaning lies within them. However, meaning lies within the *recipient*. It is this person who reads the meaning. This should be obvious, because most of us have sent a message with the best intentions, only to have it produce a negative response. Therefore, consider all messages you are sending from the perspective of the receiver and prepare your communication with that person in mind. After all, nothing guarantees that your message will be understood as you intend it. It only makes sense that you take time to calculate the very best way to shape that message for the person for whom it is intended.

Arnie is a good example of this common misconception. He believes that it is his demand that carries the meaning. Sandra is a mere responder and will certainly understand the obvious logic in what he says. But there is no way to predict how Sandra will receive the information. Let's say that her father routinely made demands and intimidated everyone in the household. Thirty years later, she is still turned off by anyone who makes demands. In addition, she views a person who makes demands as lacking respect for her position of authority. In other words, Sandra will not have the ability to listen beyond Arnie's style.

Arnie's words do not contain meaning, but Arnie's style does. He has lost the battle for underlying reasons that actually have little of nothing to do with him. But how is he to know? He'd need to watch for the clues and understand how Sandra needs to have requests related to her. The challenge and burden for effective negotiating rests with Arnie. It is he who wants to get something from Sandra and his awareness of the negotiating process will be key to his success.

3. **People act and respond to their map of reality, not to reality itself.**

Two people see the same war scene in a movie, the same accident on the street, the same menu in the restaurant. Their reality is based on their individual world view. The accident is terrible to Corey because he has never seen a car wreck before; his companion, Aaron, has been badly injured in an automobile accident, so the car wreck on the street looks fairly minor because the passengers in the car walk away with barely a scratch. Leo looks at a violent war scene and is disgusted to the point of nausea; Seymour, viewing the same scene, is taken back to his own World War II experiences, which he occasionally admits were among the best years of his life. Shelly thinks the prices on the menu are outrageous; her companion, Helen, thinks they are low. Different experiences, different reactions.

Sounds simple, but we often forget this basic information when we enter a negotiation. And we end up feeling so misunderstood. We may think, "How can that be? Why would my friend think these dinner prices are high?" Hey, this person just came from a small town where the three restaurants compete for business and prices are low. In short, we all would like to say,

"It's my world and welcome to it!"

Always remember that we rely on our view of the world to relate our reality. So does everyone else. In addition, we must discern what is known first hand from what is assumed to be true, simply because it fits this map. Can we really assume that prices are either low or outrageous? How could anything be more relative than that?

4. People make the best choice available to them at the time of the decision.

We must see ourselves as functional people—no one is broken. Our job is to figure out and understand how others function. If this sounds very different from the common view of the world, which holds that most people are dysfunctional (usually others, of course) and that mistakes are littered everywhere and others are usually at fault, then you're right— this concept is different. And as you absorb it, you will find that it can bring radical change in the ways you interact. We are not perfect by any means, but with our human limitations and weaknesses, we do quite well on our walk through life.

NLP has a basic respect for each individual. NLP philosophy assumes that whatever action is taken is done with a positive intent and for some useful reason. While the old thinking might say, "this person messed up," NLP explains that the person acted with the best of intents and made the right choice among those available at the time, given the circumstances. This will become more clear as we go along, but it is an extremely useful philosophy to understand when you negotiate. Even if it sounds confusing, don't reject it. Keep an open mind. Give your opponents in negotiation more credit than they may deserve.

Sure, in any given situation there may have been other options, known *unconsciously*, but not as part of *conscious* reality. But given what is known, people make the best possible choice in a particular situation. In NLP thinking, it is important to create a choice even when one doesn't appear to be possible.

It is important to seek out new options in the face of a dilemma posed by the perception of only two roads of action (two options do not present choice, they present a dilemma). If one choice is perceived, there is no choice. The decision-maker is much like a robot, acting out the only option. Again, when two options are available a dilemma is created. True choice exists when there are at least three alternatives; when we have less than three opinions we lack a situation for true considered choice. Real choice simply does not exist until we expand the options.

5. People have all the resources they need to go through life successfully.

Reserve judgement here—read on. Resources are always available, but we may not know how to tap into them. In other words, we may not have the skill to gain access to the resources we have. When we do know what resources we have we can call on them any time we need them. When given the proper techniques, we can all uncover these resources and options and perceive their value to us. We don't need more resources, we only need better ways to uncover them. Resources are people, places and experiences. For Arnie, the teachings of his parents, Katheryn and Carl, his work as a counselor, and his travels through Europe and the Far East provide a wealth of insight for the current negotiation. His past massages the ties to the present and future negotiations.

6. There's no such thing as failure; there's only feedback.

Have you ever tried to tell other people what is wrong with their attitudes or behavior? Did a person ever perceive your words as criticism? When that happened, did it feel like failure to you? This is a common situation. But, if we look at this in a different way, we can see that there was no failure; what we have is feedback that can inform our actions in future situations. We all love to be given feedback when we have done something well. I recall the wonderful line Bette Midler delivers in the movie "Beaches." She's just finished a performance and says to her friends, "Ah, but enough about me . . . what do you think about me?"

When we eliminate the concept of failure, we are more likely to undertake new and different actions. We're more likely to try again or take on something entirely new when we look at the results as feedback, not failure. When we talk about feedback instead of failure, we've effectively eliminated the pass/fail judgment to which most of us have become accustomed. What a freeing concept! Learn to use it and you'll see your life improve immediately.

7. **Anything can be accomplished if the task is broken down into small enough parts.**

This process is known in NLP as "chunking down." When we think about chunking down, we ask, "What is a smaller component of this issue?" This helps us clarify the steps we need to take to accomplish the task—from entering graduate school to feeding 100 people in a homeless shelter to negotiating Arnie's raise.

There is also a process called, "chunking up." In this process, we generalize the issue to a higher level in a positive way. We do this to move away from specific details that may bog us down. This process might help us to move to a higher analysis of a situation. If I'm asked to argue a First Amendment case, I will chunk up to the larger constitutional question—the principle involved. I'll not bog myself or others down in the specific detail of what is being challenged or censored. See the ability to group up or break down concepts as a strategic opportunity available in negotiation and all communication situations.

8. **Every behavior has positive intent and function.**

Most of us spend far too much time defining — and debating — problematic behavior and its potential destructiveness. NLP assumes that every action is done for a positive reason. If my stomach is jumping around as I look at my watch and realize that I could be late for a speaking engagement, this is a positive reaction. The jittering stomach—and the anticipation of it — helps me get where I need to be on time. So, I'm better off noticing the reaction and assessing what it means in a positive way, instead of cursing the jumping stomach and demand that it go away.

Difficult as it may be to understand, the young people who join gangs do so for a positive reason in their own minds. They want an identity, a sense of belonging and security, a community of people who won't let them down. An outsider might say, "So let them find a better way to get these things." But at that time, the reality for those young people suggests that gang membership seems to be the best and perhaps only path to reach the goal. So, their intent is positive, though their reality is different from ours. A positive motive is hidden behind the actions, no matter how negatively society may view them.

9. Every behavior is useful in some context.

It is within the range of human nature to evaluate conduct and intent within a context. However, if we remove the context and take away the "baggage" it carries, we can reframe the behavior, put it into another context, and we would then be able to call it acceptable. It is wrong to kill someone, for example, but placed in the context of a war and the necessity for survival, killing one's enemy triggers an exception to the rule for many people.

Take time to think about these suppositions as the foundation of communication and your negotiations. They establish a framework within which you can consider other people's behaviors. This is the unique foundation for developing better negotiation techniques, because we shift the focus off our own view of the world and over to an understanding of how others experience life. This is a far more powerful point of view than expecting other people to make any effort to perceive a situation in the way you need—or want—them to experience it. Many people say that their quality of life improves immediately once they begin viewing their interactions with these principles in mind. For me, it has proven to be the path to more success in negotiation and more power in almost all my communications.

In fact, may I encourage you to start practicing this new way of thinking right now. You don't need to wait until you have finished reading this book. Take each principle as it comes and let it influence the way you send and receive information— starting today.

With a foundation to ground you, you are prepared to build the next essential and basic building block of success in negotiation. You can gain a deeper understanding of negotiation by learning how individual people process information. The following chapter explains and explores the importance of comprehension and perception.

CHAPTER TWO

Negotiation Makes Much More Sense — Through Your Eyes

WE'VE ALREADY ESTABLISHED THAT PEOPLE EXPERIENCE events differently, and they talk about their experiences differently, too. The successful negotiator is good at identifying the way thoughts, feelings, attitudes, and opinions manifest in others. In other words, the skillful negotiator has the ability to understand and take the perspective of the other negotiator. Most people are in touch with their own desires and tactics, but think little about how best to control the negotiation *from the perspective of the other negotiator*. Think about the power that underlies this concept. Pursue the concept and you are laying the foundation for success. The good news is that the means of identifying the perspective of the other person exist at a behavioral level. Our mission as a negotiator is to identify the cues that are indicative of what is going on inside the mind of the negotiator.

Arnie has yet to give thought to his boss's perspective. In fact, like most of us at this stage, he doesn't know how to do it. He is still invested in his view that what he wants is logical and justified. But, until he learns to "read" Sandra, he is severely restricting his chances of getting what he wants. That is the central mission in planning for and approaching a negotiation, whether seeking a raise, making a purchase, or managing a relationship.

It isn't always easy to read another person's concerns and attitudes because so much of these things occur below the surface in interaction. We must work at it if we're going to be successful negotiators. Arnie is still hell bent on demanding what he wants and is not considering his boss's individual communication style. He's on the road to failure, or at best, chance success, unless he begins to focus on what is going on with Sandra, the other key person in his negotiation.

CALIBRATION ISN'T JUST FOR ENGINEERS

Let's say that Arnie has learned to identify the emotional state of his boss through increased sensitivity to the behavioral cues she exhibits in their interaction. That's good as far as it goes. But Arnie also has to learn to calibrate to those feelings, that is, match specific verbal and nonverbal responses and behaviors with the internal processes or state that Sandra is experiencing or is in. This is the process of really getting and being in tune with where the other person is at a specific time. You attempt to see the situation as the other sees it; you won't be certain of your accuracy, but you will be closer for the trying. If you don't even try, you never rise to the level of the truly skilled negotiator.

As you calibrate external behaviors with internal states, you will gain insights about the best ways to communicate with other people. Just imagine how much more power Arnie will have when he negotiates his raise if he has taken the time to consider all these factors before he begins. You will learn more about this as we go along—and so will Arnie. We've convinced him to wait a while before he blunders along.

THE COMPETENCE YOU KNOW AND THE COMPETENCE YOU DON'T KNOW

I realize that at this point, you are uncertain about the concept of calibrating to behavior. Not to worry; you will soon understand. This may be a new skill for you and like any new skill, you are currently unaware of what you don't know. Before you do anything for the first time, you are what is called *unconsciously incompetent*. That's a fancy way of saying that you don't yet know what you do not know. Once you're in the situation, you begin to become conscious of your incompetence. You may even say to yourself — or to others, "I don't know what the heck I'm doing. Man, am I out of my element!" As you become aware of new skills you can't perform well, you become *consciously incompetent*, that is you begin to identify what you don't know. Remember the first time you got behind the wheel of a car? You probably thought it was quite easy since you had seen others drive. You quickly became aware of your own incompetence in the task. You needed to study and gain experience if you were to do this new skill well.

Like driving a car, so it is with negotiation and, in this case, calibrating to behavior. Until we actually encounter a negotiation setting and attempt to calibrate to behavior and the mental state of the other person, we are unconsciously incompetent. Once we begin, then we come to understand what we don't know and we can go about learning and practicing the skills we need.

As you practice a new skill, and the skill is learned, you become *consciously competent*, that is, aware of the new skill you are exercising. As the skill becomes mastered, it falls into the realm of *unconscious competence*. When we say that something is second nature, this means that we aren't consciously aware of what we know. If you took driving lessons and now hold a driver's license, you likely drive a car with unconscious competence; you no longer need to think out every step along the way. You have myriad skills, negotiating included, in which you are aware of certain levels of ability and unaware of yet unexplored skills that would help you become a better negotiator. After all, we negotiate every day of our life, so you clearly have a start in the area.

At this stage, you might think of reading other people and matching behaviors and internal emotional states as a stiff or mechanical process. Take solace in knowing that you have done this in other circumstances in a quite natural way. You already have some level of unconscious competence. You also have areas of unconscious incompetence in relation to calibrating and negotiating. You may make false assumptions about people and not be conscious of what you're doing; you just need to learn to be more accurate in your attempt to read people. Understanding what you do and do not know will lead you toward another desired goal, that of becoming an effective negotiator.

CONGRUENCE IS NOT JUST FOR TRIANGLES

Again, our goal is to adopt, and adapt to, the perspective of other people. This means being congruent in your interaction with them. Now, you already know what congruence is because you've experienced it many times—even though you may have called it by a different name. Perhaps you said you were in "sync" with another person when communication was smooth and harmonious. It can also be called "all systems go" in an interaction and it is a goal to work toward. But what does it mean?

A person is in congruence when internal and external strategies and behaviors are in agreement and are working together as a coherent whole. You recognize this as a state of comfort and ease. Your external body language matches your internal mental and emotional state. You also know when you're in a state of incongruence. You're at your Uncle Rick's house but you want to be somewhere else. As you smile at your relatives you're fantasizing about being almost anywhere else at the time. Be honest. You're putting on an act because you don't want to offend good ol' Uncle Rick and everyone else in your family. In fact, if these relatives look for your cues, they would be able to read your discomfort.

Many people are just not in tune with the cues of others because they can't imagine why we would wish to be anywhere but at their home. Do you begin to see how the ability to read others will be helpful when you negotiate? You can begin by reading others' cues in any situation.

The above is a common everyday kind of experience, but in negotiation, incongruence can be a serious impediment to success. If one party is incongruent, then we must work to establish the internal and external harmony. That's where the skill of reading another person becomes increasingly important and why I continue to emphasize its significance.

Let's say that while Arnie is thinking about demanding his big raise, his mind floats to a family event where he has to explain that he can't afford to go on a vacation. Or he sees himself browsing in the clothing store where he was shopping the previous night. He saw that great suit—if only he could afford it! We could say that Arnie in definitely not congruent and is likely exhibiting cues showing that his mind and body are in two different places.

Imagine if Arnie's mind floats to those images while he is actually in the negotiation with Sandra in her office. For most of us, it's a common event to have our minds be in many places at one time, especially when we're under stress or when we are engaged in activities that we don't like. Our outside persona simply doesn't match what's going on internally. A facade of calm in the midst of inner turmoil is an experience to which we can all relate.

To help you better understand the concept, follow along as I break it down for you. There are two types of incongruence that you should recognize and resolve. The first is *simultaneous* incongruence, meaning that the other negotiator (or you) exhibits two (or more) conflicting cues occurring at the same time. For example, Arnie's boss smiles but looks away; or, in response to a question, Arnie says yes, but shakes his head in a manner that indicates "no," or says yes, but with a clear tone of uncertainty in his voice.

Simultaneous incongruence can also be indicated by a person who makes an affirmative statement, but with a rising inflection in the voice. Consciously or unconsciously, this person transmits uncertainty by using the same tone we use when we ask a question. If you are perceptive, you pick up on it. On some level, there is uncertainty. You need to identify it, and calibrate to it if you are to understand the dynamics of the interaction — and control them.

Congruence can also occur as two or more *sequential* conflicting cues, that is one cue is given, but is contradicted by a subsequent (even immediately subsequent) cue. Jimmy, the car salesperson, asks you how you like the shiny new and expensive car. You choke, clear your throat and then tell Jimmy how perfect the car would be for you. Count on Jimmy being adept at reading the sequential incongruence; he learns not to ignore the cues that precede your verbal responses because that is often where he will find the true feeling and meaning.

IT'S ALL ABOUT BUILDING RAPPORT

Understand that this whole notion of identifying incongruence and calibrating to the behavior and mental state of the other negotiator is the foundation of the primary goal in negotiation — building rapport. No matter how large or small the negotiation we're entering into, our goal must first be to establish rapport. Give this some thought and see how it relates to situations in your everyday life.

When you call a customer service representative to discuss a mistake in your shipment, they will often attempt to first establish rapport, at least on some level. In fact, a representative is often formally trained to establish rapport with irate callers. They understand that it's not just the actual spoken words that affect the success of the call and reestablish a good relationship with a currently unhappy customer. We all know when the customer service representative seems to care about our plight and we sure know when they don't. Our reading of that relationship has a great impact on the direction of the conversation and our satisfaction.

You are far more likely to be a "winner" in negotiation if you are aware that establishing rapport is your goal and responsibility. And you'll succeed in developing your negotiating skills if you understand how the important nonverbal cues underlie rapport.

Establishing rapport is similar to a building process that uses many materials. In communication and negotiation, we'll refer to the materials as nonverbal elements: pacing or mirroring behavior, voice, emotions, breathing, posture, and tempo and rhythm. We are the observer of the presentation, intensity, and duration of these behaviors in others. Others are consciously or unconsciously observing us, too. The skillful negotiator will, again, identify and calibrate to it all.

When you begin to notice the way in which rapport is established, you'll notice that a sense of "sameness" is developed. People are more comfortable with people who are like themselves, and conversely may be uncomfortable (in varying degrees) with people who are unlike themselves. This is not to be taken too simplistically because sameness is established in numerous ways. For example, a 22 year old white student may quickly establish sameness with a 62 year Native American professor. Their common interest in ecology, for example, establishes the initial reason for the encounter; their values and demeanor overlap significantly. All the other demographic factors become less important.

We know that rapport emerges between two people who exhibit similarity in behavior and voice. It's simple: People like people who are like themselves. You can work to create similarity by mirroring and matching the behavior of the other person. The next time you are engaged in a face-to-face encounter, consciously match the nonverbal behavior of the other and see what happens. This means that, in a non-parroting and non-mimicking way (because parroting and mimicking are often annoying), you alter your stance, the way your arms are placed on your body, the tilt of your head, the pace of your breathing and of your speech, to match (be in congruence with) that of the other person.

If this sounds artificial to you, realize that you unconsciously do this kind of matching with other people all the time; now you are going to become conscious of this behavior in negotiation settings. When you have a prior existing relationship with the other negotiator, no matter how casual, you will find efforts to match, mirror, and calibrate much easier. However, when you encounter a stranger, you may find the task more difficult. But let's not make this more complicated than it is. A couple of examples will illustrate what I mean here.

Kristie, a friend of mine, drops her laundry off at the same place every two weeks. She and the attendant have a casual but pleasant relationship. The attendant is always warm and asks Kristie about her family. Kristie always responds in kind, and the two of them chat for two or three minutes about their children and the weather and happenings in their neighborhood. One day, shortly after Kristie's father had fallen ill, she was unusually quiet when she went to pick up her laundry, although she was attempting to carry on the conversation as usual. However, the attendant, a very sensitive woman, noticed a change. Without even thinking about it, she mirrored Kristie's body language and tone of voice. A new level of rapport was established and Kristie unconsciously realized it. Within a minute or two, she had told the attendant about what was on her mind, thereby temporarily—and perhaps permanently— deepening the sameness in their relationship. Kristie told me that the only demographic sameness they have on an obvious level is gender, but by mirroring and matching, they connected on a personal level nonetheless.

Another element was added and was probably necessary before Kristie could open up. This element is called "leading," meaning that one person takes charge and follows pacing with leading. First, the attendant sought to establish rapport by (unconsciously) matching body and verbal cues. Then she became a leader in the encounter. Consider the drummer who sets the pace for a marching band. After a few moments, the drummer can increase the pace and intensity and the crowd follows. This is another example of pacing that is followed by leading.

Some months later, Kristie was back at the laundry, but this time she witnessed a very rude woman talking in a nasty tone to the attendant. After the surly customer left, Kristie began to mirror and match the attendant's behavior and set the pace. She noticed that the attendant followed her lead toward a more relaxed state, and soon she became more relaxed and open. The stiffness in the attendant's body and the tight tone of her voice disappeared as Kristie reduced the tension by her mirroring and matching. She did the leading in this case, and by the time she left the laundry, the attendant was, as Kristie put it, "her old self again."

Once again, imagine practicing these skills in many interactions and taking them with you into negotiation settings. For many of us, the majority of our daily encounters are not life and death situations or even events in which we stand to lose or gain sums of money, contracts, jobs, and so on. But the quality of our lives is enriched when we pay attention to the little things. You can practice mirroring and matching in routine encounters to observe how the process works. I urge you to begin noticing how you behave in small, seemingly insignificant encounters. Watch the way others react to you as you mirror and match non-verbal cues. You might be surprised how much you learn from these small illustrations of the process and how much more powerful this makes you when negotiating.

GAINING PERSPECTIVE

As we've seen, rapport is built in a number of different ways, which all work together without our awareness. You help form a relationship in negotiation by building perspective. This means that we evaluate an event from the perspective of others involved and from the perspective of yourself as an observer. We have discussed matching and calibrating to behaviors that occur in interactions. Let's take the concept of rapport building to another level, that of attempting to step inside the frame of mind of the other person.

It's natural for people to remember events by reliving them, because past occurrences remain active in the memory. People may also step "outside" the event in their mind and reflect on the memory from the perspective of observer—sometimes a witness. This is referred to as disassociating from a memory of an event. Try this experiment: Think back to a wonderful experience, perhaps a birthday party or other happy event. If you are like most people, you see only the other people who are with you as you experience what it is like to be at that party or event. You should be able to experience the great feelings once again, and it's really nice, isn't it?

Now, remember that same event, but this time, see yourself at the party. Watch the event in your mind's eye with you attending the event. While a joyous experience, you most likely feel a bit less excitement than if you were actually there in your mind. Generally speaking, we recall pleasant things from the active or first person perspective. We like to relive pleasant experiences again in our mind because they are enjoyable. We may re-experience the intense emotions and we view ourselves as present and aware.

On the other hand, we often recall unpleasant events in a disassociated way, meaning that we place ourselves in our minds as observers of the event. Our emotions are less intense and we may even detach from our feelings. Remember how even the good feelings you had as you remembered back on a pleasant event lessened a bit when you stepped into an observer role in your mind? If you've ever heard a person recall a negative experience of violence in a calm, almost casual and uninvolved way, then disassociation has probably taken place. He or she may be deliberately detaching in order to control emotions and reduce stress. At times though, an observer feels vaguely uncomfortable by the detachment. It's as if we sense incongruence between external behavior and the person's internal state.

Although most people seldom do this, there is another position you can take in your mind that provides significant power in negotiation. Experience what it is like to look at an event through the other person's eyes. It may be the most difficult position to assume in an interaction, but it is also the most valuable. When you achieve this perspective, you gain insight into the other person's values and concerns and the position or stance the person is taking in a negotiation.

Arnie hasn't even given this a thought when he thinks about his raise. All he considers are his own desires and needs. But, he may lose out if he doesn't think about Sandra's concerns, the demands on her, and the reason behind any position she might take.

Try this exercise: Think back to an argument you once had with someone else. First view the interaction as if you are present again (seeing only the other person). Then, step outside and watch the argument as an observer and evaluate the new information this more objective perspective provides. Next, try to take the perspective of the other person; see yourself as that person sees you. Quite interesting, isn't it? Maybe there was another side to that argument. Once again, consider the value of taking all of these perspectives in negotiation, especially the perspective of the other person with whom you are negotiating.

Establishing perspective provides empathy for others and helps to create identification with them as well. The result is a deepened relationship. You have probably experienced this many times in your life. Imagine what life would be like if we never even attempted to get inside another person's head and heart. Those who don't seem to care about other people's feelings are viewed as distant and cold. They may have certain technical negotiating skills, but they don't establish good rapport when they enter the interaction. Just the fact that we have these people pegged as cold and distant indicates that we don't care much for their style. Our goal is a deeper understanding of others and the negotiation process. You are beginning to get the message.

In fact, Arnie's friends perceive him as a great person to be around; he has a knack for friendship. He just needs a better sense about how to apply his engaging personality to a one-on-one negotiation situation. Imagine his growth as a negotiator once he exercises his innate ability to gain perspective in interactions.

Suppose you are ready to make an offer on a house but suddenly the seller backs out. So, you stomp around and mutter under your breath. So much for venting your feelings. You're no further ahead than you were when you started. All you know is that you were ready to buy this home and the seller backs out at the last minute. You wonder, "Hey, what's up with that?" But then you begin to ask questions about the situation. You find out that the seller has a daughter, Melanie, who has her heart set on having her wedding in that house. Unfortunately the wedding is six months away. The parents withdraw their home from the market, although they are sick over having to do it. They were counting on moving to their condo on the ocean. Now you have a much different perspective.

I'm cheating here because I know the outcome of the story, and to be brief, the wedding was held and my student bought the house after all. I'll give myself credit for having facilitated this happy outcome by asking a series of questions over a period of few days. When I first heard that the deal had fallen through, I asked this student of mine, Beau, if he absolutely had to move into the house before June. No, it wasn't that important to him. Would the owner close on the house a day or two after the wedding and agree to move out in 60 days? That would mean that the entire transaction would take about eight months, instead of the usual two or three.

A day later, Beau told me that the negotiations over this house had been reopened and while it was an unusual negotiation, it all worked out smoothly. The contract was signed and the details and dates were negotiated. Beau was able to extend his lease to a short term one, which covered the extra months he needed. All's well that ends well—except that the daughter got divorced a year later. No, no—just kidding.

Beau was operating with unconscious incompetence. He didn't have good negotiating skills and wasn't aware that he didn't have them until he found himself angrily accepting a bad outcome without even exploring the alternatives. As we worked together on his problem, he became conscious of his lack of skills. Because he became interested in learning more he will no doubt become a better negotiator. Now, he gets the point of perspective and exercising new skills. It won't be long before he operates in a state of unconscious competency.

But Arnie is still at the stage where he doesn't know what he doesn't know—he's learning, though. He has only a hint of the role of nonverbal cues—those he's sending and those he's receiving. Perspective is a word Arnie has read in books, but with help he'll see that taking a position in negotiation means much more than setting out the battleground over which to argue. It includes understanding and calibrating to mindset and behavior. Next, Arnie needs a better understanding of language as a component of negotiation, with all its ambiguities and assumptions. Language is a building block in negotiation that can help or hinder us as effective negotiators.

CHAPTER THREE

Watch Your Language

THE BEST NEGOTIATORS AND COMMUNICATORS ARE OFTEN those with the gift to make their point in the form of a story. The story is the easiest and most basic way for others to come to understand your position. Storytelling is a skill you can learn and develop.

You may know that the art of storytelling is the oldest art form on earth, certainly far older than written language. But what makes one storyteller different from another? Culture certainly has much to do with it; there are hundreds of versions of the same myths and fairy tales, each told with a different style. The story is different depending on the age and sex of the storyteller, and religious beliefs and values will influence the way a tale is spun. Sounds a lot like the demographic factors in communication, doesn't it? Do you already see how storytelling becomes an important tool for establishing your position in negotiation? And how individual differences can lead you to modify how a particular story would be told?

Because we live in a scientific world that insists on labeling everything, there is a term that applies to the story-telling model of communication—it's the "meta" model. In simple terms, the meta model is based on the idea that people relate information in story form. As listeners of the story, we add to the information we hear or delete facts or impressions based on past exprience and our interpretation of events. So, your version of events will assuredly be different from mine, even if we've both experienced the same event. The key is to present your position in such a way that the other negotiator can understand and perhaps accept it.

When Arnie tells his best friend Mary about his rotten salary, he tells a story. Or take Andy. He's the new employee in Arnie's office who had been unemployed for six months before getting this job. When Andy tells Mary about the job, he describes the great salary and benefits. Could Arnie and Andy be working in the same place? Sure enough, but with different backgrounds and experiences, they see their situations quite differently. When you talk about the great day you had at the office, you're telling a story. Your partner recounts his or her terrible day, and that's a story too.

The meta model of communication includes a set of patterns that allows us to examine how we generalize, distort, specify, or delete data as we relate information in our stories. We do this so that we can better position ourselves in negotiation by testing the stories of the other negotiator. After all, our view of the world is formed through our first-hand experiences, so we will relate our positions with, by definition, bias.

Arnie's disgust with his salary reflects his experience with his limited information received only from his own milieu. His story would sound ridiculous if he complained about his plight to farmers in Guatemala or factory workers in Estonia or Pattaya. If a millionaire lost a few dollars in a stock market transaction, who should he or she talk to about it? A colleague down the hall, an equally wealthy neighbor, or the clerk in the store where he's buying some shoes? Whose experience would most closely resemble his own? Begin to see the importance of casting your position in story terms that the other negotiator can understand.

Our styles of negotiation reflect the way we process information and experiences, and in turn influence the way we interact with others. We process information in visual, auditory, or kinesthetic (feeling-based) ways. But we may use language to relate our experiences through a story that limits the clarity of the position we wish to express. While all language is ambiguous, we can clear up meaning if we better understand the ways that speech patterns limit us.

WHEN YOU LISTEN TO YOURSELF, WHAT DO YOU HEAR?

Arnie uses what are known as universal qualifiers. He is fond of saying that his boss *never* listens, the office is *always* too cold, *all* his coworkers put in fewer hours at their desks than he does, and *every* day brings the same routine. If you have an Arnie in your life, this probably sounds familiar. "You never spend any time with me," or, "Why do you always contradict me?" The concern is that many universal qualifiers have exceptions to them, but we will miss them unless someone challenges the qualifier. In other words, when challenged, universal qualifiers will admit to exceptions to their "always," "never," or "every" pronouncements. The trouble is, most people don't challenge these folks when they talk—they may not even be listening anymore.

As language develops in a young child, who can't be expected to understand subtlety and exception, we often patiently explain that the universal qualifiers don't apply. When an adult uses these terms, we become defensive and the argument shifts away from the real issue. Perhaps the better response would be, "Is there never a time that your boss listens?" Or, "Are all your days exactly the same?" Seek out the exception when you wish to establish a limitation on the position taken by the other negotiator. The result may be to open up an issue previously perceived to be closed.

Over the next few days, listen to your own language. Do you tend to make these universal statements? What happens when you do? You will find that communication and negotiation generally proceed more smoothly when specific situations are mentioned rather than when you globalize impressions and attitudes.

Some words suggest a lack of choice. "I *can't* do that," and, I *have to* do this," imply that certain things are either absolutely impossible or absolutely necessary. Perhaps you use these limiting words and phrases too. If Tim, the foreman, tells Al, the worker, that a project *must* be finished by Saturday, Al could respond by asking, "What would happen if I'm unable to meet that deadline?" If I tell you that it's *impossible* to reach a particular goal, you could respond to me by asking, "What is it that's preventing you?"

We could say that these "universal" words are just figures of speech and that we all know what we mean. However, we don't always know what others mean, and furthermore, we limit our own possibilities when we use limiting phrases.

Think for just a minute about the times you've declared that you *can't* do something. Why can't you? What stops you? Perhaps you don't actually want to accomplish that particular goal. So, as it turns out, you're limited by desire, not by ability, opportunity, or the means to do a particular thing. Maybe the means aren't obvious and you may not clearly see an opportunity, but you don't look for these elements because, frankly, you don't care enough. These limitations are a concern when your mission is to achieve something through negotiation with others.

Another way we influence thought is by using unspecified nouns—them, they, those, and so forth. This distortion can be insidious in that attitudes are both reflected and formed by these words. If you tell your child that those people are responsible for the litter on the street, your child then absorbs the idea that litter is everyone else's problem. Some children ask the obvious question, "What people do you mean?", forcing adults to come up with some kind of answer, however feeble.

By the time we become adults we are so accustomed to hearing this language that we tend to discount the implications behind it. In negotiation, you will want to clarify the other party's use of unclear nouns to insure what references are being made.

To Arnie, "they" are always getting ahead and he isn't. So, who are "they?" If we ask him, he might be able to be more specific. Unfortunately, no one challenges Arnie and he keeps on making his non-specific statements coupled with his universal qualifiers. Perhaps that will change.

Consider the statement, "Those people complicate deals." But who are "those people," what are the "deals," and why are they "complicating" them? It's true that people tend to talk in verbal shorthand when they're with people they know or with whom they identify in some significant way. (Arnie could tell the Pattayan factory worker about his current plight, but just think about all the details and explanations he'd have to provide!) However, if you use this kind of non-specific speech as a habit, you'll tend to be misunderstood. And in negotiations, this non-specific speech could adversely affect the outcome. You'll see how this works as we move along.

We can add still another language issue when we discuss other nouns and qualifiers. Certain nouns are concrete; dogs, cats, chairs, tables, and computers are specific, concrete nouns. Other nouns are abstract or concept words—happiness, hate, love, truth, and justice are examples of non-specific nouns. When we are communicating and negotiating with others and listening to their stories, we may have trouble understanding what these concepts mean to them. But isn't that a key point when we are formulating a position in response to the other negotiator?

If I tell you that justice must be served in our deal, what does that mean? In order for you to get my meaning, what would help? If you can get me to discuss what justice would be in this case, and what it would take to serve it, we might reach an understanding. When Arnie says that his salary isn't fair, what exactly does fair mean in this context? In order for Arnie to make his point, he's going have to come up with an answer.

These abstract nouns are called *nominalizations*, and they often suggest a limitation of choice and add to globalization of language. If a story teller says, "And the queen never received any recognition from the king," we still don't know much. If we could break into the story, we might ask, "How would the queen like to be recognized?" Then, we might get some answers. "Well," the story teller could say, "the queen is an excellent cook and sings folk songs to entertain the king. Too bad he doesn't compliment her on her talents." Ah, we think, if only the king would wise up the queen wouldn't feel so bad. And we also know that the queen could be more specific about what she wants, and the king has choices about how to respond.

One of the problems between our king and queen involves the king's belief that the queen can read his mind—he thinks he can read hers too. Sometimes he contradicts what she says, albeit in a non-specific way. "The queen doesn't think I'm a jerk," he says. How does he know that? Has he asked her? "The queen knows I enjoy her cooking and singing," he declares in a kingly way. Can he read her mind? How does he know that she knows that he enjoys her talents? The queen in her own vague way emphatically says, "The king should know what recognition is. I shouldn't have to tell him." And so goes the saga of human communication. There are many "kings and queens" all over the world who are engaged in exactly this conflict. No wonder we need fairy tales to help us illustrate our human dilemmas.

Just think how much more smooth our negotiations would be if we admit that we're not clairvoyant and that we need clarification. We may not deal in fairy tales in our everyday life, but we do have situations that arise in negotiations that may appear to be like that of our proverbial king and queen. Consider:

- "Larry would never want to consider that option." Oh? How do we know that? Has Larry specifically said as much? Does never mean never, or just today or this week?"

- "It's not right to do this, it's wrong." Wrong for whom? Why isn't it right? Who is involved in this right/wrong-good/bad judgment?
- "Barry always thinks that his happiness should come first." Does always mean just that, 24 hours a day, 365 days a year? What does Barry mean by happiness? What does the word imply to Barry or to his representative in the negotiation? In this case, does the negotiator mean Barry's desires and wishes? Does he mean Barry's mental state?
- "I know what's best for Raymond." How does the negotiator know this? Is Raymond 50 years old or 50 hours old? In what context is the statement being made?

Perhaps you've already learned that becoming a good negotiator and communicator involves asking many questions of yourself and others. But why do this at all? Well, let's not forget that we communicate because we want something. And since we cannot not communicate when we negotiate, we need to understand the true meaning of the interaction to the extent possible.

SO WHAT DO YOU WANT? WHAT'S THE OUTCOME?

As you can see, hear, or sense in feelings (depending on your preferred communication processing style), negotiation is complex. Sending and receiving is occurring on many levels and involves verbal and nonverbal cues. We're constantly calibrating cues, matching behaviors, and processing language as the interaction proceeds. We assume that there are desired outcomes of each interaction. Whether or not they are conscious desires depends on the negotiation situation and often on the importance of the issue being negotiated.

When you negotiate to have your table changed because cigarette smoke is bothering you, you are conscious of the desired outcome. When you greet the doorman in your building with a pleasant smile and a quick verbal exchange, you may not be conscious of a specific desired outcome. Unconsciously, you may be pleasant because you have formed that habit—it's second nature and falls into the category of unconscious competence. Consciously, you may realize that the doorman is likely to accept your packages and do a few extra things for you because you are gracious and treat him with respect.

You've probably had puzzling experiences in which a person walked away from you unsatisfied with your interaction. You might believe that communication has broken down but you don't know why. This usually occurs when the desired outcome isn't clear. Anne, a friend of mine and a professional speaker, left one of her talks with an uneasy feeling in her stomach. She had given a presentation on women's issues, but the audience's response had been unusually flat. This topic ordinarily brought all kinds of enthusiastic responses from her audiences.

Several days later, she asked the meeting planner about the odd reaction of the group. "Well, I wasn't going to say anything about this," he said, "but you were scheduled to talk about stress management, not women's issues." Anne was stunned, checked her notes about the booking and sure enough, she was wrong. She ended up going back to this group to deliver—for free—her excellent presentation on stress management. In fact, she avoided permanent damage to her reputation by joking about having been under so much stress that she messed up! What if she'd never asked about the cold response she initially received? She'd have gone on thinking that she'd run into a strange audience. She might have avoided that group forever.

What if you're a consultant negotiating with a client over fees, project scope, and deadlines, and the person says, "What I don't want is for this to take too long and cost too much." You now have a classic negotiation dilemma. What is too long and what is too much money? You have a vague impression of what the client doesn't want, but you still don't know what he or she does want.

In situations like this, it's your job to sift through the vague impressions and get to the concrete desires. What is your client's goal? How will he or she know when it's been reached? What's the desired time-frame? Why is that important? Is there anything preventing that from happening? How can these obstacles be removed? Are there other resources needed to reach the goal? Do you begin to see the importance of addressing these questions, both for your clients and yourself?

As you receive answers to your questions, you are processing the information in your style, but you need to understand the way in which the sender is giving the information to you. The verbal and nonverbal cues you receive help you understand the way in which the person is considering the outcome and the process as the negotiation proceeds.

WAYS OF PROCESSING — A CLOSER LOOK

We said before that people generally process information in one of three ways: visual, auditory, or kinesthetic — VAK, for short. These primary modalities are the means by which we make sense of our experiences. However, we also have preference and choice in presenting ourselves and receiving messages from others. In fact, our brains select the most important information, based on our preferred mode of processing.

This is usually an unconscious process, but because we want to learn to both communicate and negotiate more effectively, we'll try to use all the modalities to both understand and send messages. To use only one or two will limit our complete understanding and representation of an experience. And we'll attempt to make what is usually below the level of consciousness known and understood.

Remember too, that we don't process all the information we receive all the time. We select those elements from situations that we believe are important. Let's look at the processing modalities and see how they manifest in everyday language and negotiation.

If I use a visual modality, you'll notice visual word cues, such as:

- Let's *picture* what we want. Is it *clear*?
- *Look* at it from my *viewpoint.*
- What a *bright* idea!
- I hope you can *see* what I mean.

My gestures are probably wide and sweeping upward, and my tone of voice is high and fast when I use these visual words.

If I use an auditory modality, you'll hear me use auditory word cues:

- *Listen* to this, it *rings a bell.*
- I hope you *hear* what I mean.
- *Tell* me what you want.
- Let me *state* my case, it'll *sound* great.

My gestures are less sweeping, and my arms stay closer to my body and face. My tone of voice is musical and rich.

If I use the kinesthetic modality, you'll notice me use word cues that indicate feelings or sensory actions:

- This *touches* me deeply.
- I can't get a *grasp* on this.
- That *blows* me away, *cool.*
- This *feels right* to me.

My gestures are low and close to the body and I may have an open stance, my speaking pace is slow, the tone of my voice, measured.

When we're observing other people, we will notice eye movements to understand if a person is remembering or constructing an experience or information in a visual, auditory, or feeling way. For example, if the person you are talking to moves his or her eyes upward, then the person is processing information in a visual way; if the eyes move to the left or right along the horizon, or down and to the other person's left, then the information is being remembered in an auditory modality. Finally, if the eyes move in a downward direction but to the person's right, then they are processing with their feeling or kinesthetic modality. You can enhance your ability to read other people's cues once you understand these subtle, but real, processing modalities.

Don't get bogged down with these details. Just know that there are a variety of ways to determine how someone is processing information. You can learn and master this information by studying Neurolinguistic Programming at a local institute, or by reading many of the popular books on the topic available in book stores everywhere. (Some of the popular authors in the field include Richard Bandler, John Grinder, Robert Dilts, Jerry Richardson, Anthony Robbins, and Michael Brooks.)

REFRAMING THE CONTEXT

Meaning takes place in a context and can be negotiated by reframing the context, that is, by developing the ability to see a particular situation or position differently than it may otherwise appear. This is an incredibly powerful tool when someone doesn't agree with or understand your position. To reframe, we acknowledge that every behavior is useful in some context. Sometimes we have to reframe in order to understand meaning and context. For example if I tell you that Julie killed Joe, it sounds like murder. So, I add some details: Joe had a gun, the gun was loaded, he was angry at Julie and pointed it at her. Joe started walking toward Julie; he threatened to kill her. So Julie picked up a metal pipe and hit Joe on the head. Joe died. In the courts and in the court of public opinion, Julie killed Joe in self defense. Julie's act is understandable as an act of self protection.

It should be clear that our behaviors and communication gain their meaning only within their context. In order to clarify our position in negotiation we must often change the context so that others understand the meaning. This simply means reframing the concept, information, or impression. Once she realized she'd given the wrong talk, Anne, my professional speaker friend understood exactly why she'd had such a restrained response from the audience.

Remember "chunking up?" That's essentially what we do when we reframe to reach the positive meaning or the underlying value in the behavior. When Julie kills Joe, we chunk up to the concept of self-defense. We reframe the behavior in context. When we negotiate a contract with a client, we chunk up from, "I don't want this take too long," to what the goal of the project is and what the need for speed really means.

When we reframe, we ask ourselves, "What is the intent of the behavior?" Let's say a person with whom we're negotiating says, "You're too slow." The intent is to get this encounter finished. You could say, "Thanks for recognizing my need to be deliberate and thoughtful about this important matter." Slowness, your behavior, is reframed in the context of a higher value, that of careful deliberation.

We can also use some forms of language construction to recreate meaning in another context. The metaphor is the classic example. If we say that our attempts to get clean air in our town is like a fight between David and Goliath, we are presenting meaning in a metaphorical context. Metaphors are powerful tools for triggering an understanding of intent and context. They are useful means for getting someone to understand your position who otherwise does not share your life experiences or view of life.

This particular metaphor works for most people in the Western, Judeo-Christian world. There's a shared meaning in the story, and each person will fit the information that is being compared to the story into his or her own model for the world. For example, some people might associate Goliath with big and powerful; others would add a sinister element. Metaphor is the means to create overlap between two people who otherwise find it difficult to relate to each other.

Every time we tell a "story" we recount the events and our

listeners delete, generalize, or distort the information to fit their available frame of perception. If we see that we're not being understood, we might reframe the material using a metaphor and the receiver reprocesses using that new context. Our king and queen have yet to learn this and both feel unappreciated. Arnie hasn't figured this out either, so he constantly feels misunderstood.

Shallow metaphors are those that are used commonly in business, politics, or religious settings. Their purpose is obvious and in negotiation that means that a change is being demanded or requested. Let's say that a potential client calls Cindy, a public relations consultant. In the course of the conversation, Cindy might say, "Have you heard of Marcia Anderson, the doctor who was featured on "Nightline" last week? She's my client." The message is clear: If you want to be successful, use me. You get much farther by telling people what your clients have said about you, then by attributing credit to yourself.

Deep metaphors are more complex and the message is to be found in the content. Myth, fairy tale, moral tales, and so on, can be understood as a story and can be applied in a symbolic way to other contexts. However, like David and Goliath, this type of metaphor can take the receiver from a nominalization such as justice or courage and put it in a context— a few citizens taking on a "giant" of a company in order to improve their town. Arnie likes this metaphor, because he thinks it perfectly describes his raise—he's going to be little David taking on the big, bad giant, his boss.

CUT THE JARGON PLEASE

No matter who you're negotiating with, you need to adjust your language to fit the context, and that includes deciding whether to use jargon. No one likes to go to a lawyer for help, only to have all the messages related in professional jargon. We aren't impressed. When a doctor does this, we are equally disgusted. Do you have a set of words and phrases that mean something to you, but not to the person with whom you're negotiating or communicating?

It comes as a surprise to many people that professional jargon falls into the category of powerless speech. It actually brings a person's credibility into doubt. Extremely correct and "bookish" grammatical forms also shrink credibility in another person's eyes. Most people do not trust those who use position and vocabulary to impress.

Equally powerless are common and meaningless adjectives — interesting, charming, cute, nice, and so on. These are so overused that it's difficult to reframe context and find meaning. If we hear that another person is interesting, we don't have a clue about what that means—interesting in what way? Using many common words that intensify a message may actually weaken the meaning. He's very interesting; she's so cute; he's too smart. These statements may be understood in certain contexts, depending on the body language and other nonverbal cues that accompany them. However, in most negotiating settings, these will weaken your position, not strengthen it. Similarly, littering your speech with such words and phrases such as "well," "you know," and "I guess," weaken your message, too.

Simply eliminating these weak words and jargon will lead to more powerful speech. Integrating powerful speech with a recognition of how the other negotiator processes information and adapting to that style (using visual words and gestures with a visual person, for example) are important steps in strengthening your negotiation skills. You should be seeing how these skills integrate with your new awareness and ability to experience the negotiation from the perspective of the other negotiator (as discussed in the previous chapter). Next, we continue to build your foundation for effective negotiating with a heightened sense of awareness to nonverbal communication.

CHAPTER FOUR

Body Language — More Important Than You Might Think

YOU'RE TALKING WITH DOTTIE, WHOSE ARMS ARE FOLDED across her body; she's looking at the floor; she moves her upper body away from you when you ask her for help on a project for which you are responsible. With enthusiasm in her voice, she agrees to help you. Why don't you feel good when you walk away from her? Why do you have doubts about her willingness to help? You can't precisely explain your feeling, but you have a sense that she probably isn't going to do the work she has agreed to do, or at least, is not thrilled about doing it. You begin to worry about the deadline that your boss has imposed.

If you've had this experience, you are not alone. We've all engaged in negotiations that on a verbal level seemed to be agreeable enough, but somehow we just weren't confident about what was going on. That disparity between what you hear and what is sensed is generally caused by body language that doesn't match verbal cues. Body language can be simply defined as nonverbal cues; most experts say about 90 percent of our face-to-face interactions are dominated by these nonverbal messages.

Ah, something else to learn. Yes, this is true. But trust me, you already have some experience in this area. In the world of negotiation, the skillful negotiator is sensitive to all of the information that reaches beyond the words. Therein lies the power of skillful deal making.

EMILIO THE CONFIDENT, OR, IS THAT AN AX-MURDERER TRYING TO PICK ME UP?

One of the best situations to understand the power and ambiguity of nonverbal cues in negotiation is in the world of dating. It's one of the few topics I'm sure we all can relate to on some level. And you may see yourself somewhere in the world of Emilio and Leslie. Read on.

Some years ago I read an anecdote about a man named Emilio, who is tall, successful, handsome, and loves to spend money on the women he dates. Seems like a great catch for somebody out there; trouble is, he can't seem to meet many women who will accept dates with him—no wonder he has so much money to spend. What's wrong? Well, it seems that Emilio spends quite a bit of time at singles gatherings, places where he should meet available women. He's always meticulous about his appearance in those settings. But let's look at what Emilio does when he gets there.

It seems that Emilio has made it a point not to stand around with other men, a choice which theoretically should work in his favor. Instead, Emilio tends to stake out a "territory," and he presents himself in a powerful way. There he is, standing with his legs apart, his arms folded across his chest, his shoulders straight and stiff, a glass in his hand, his head held high. That's his relationship negotiating posture.

He scans the room, attempting to catch the eye of an attractive woman. When he does, he holds her gaze in what he thinks is a seductive way, that is, not breaking a smile, but rather attempting a jaunty, challenging look. Emilio believed he was making the most of his rugged good looks.

One evening, Emilio noticed that other men seemed to strike

up conversations with women who were soon laughing and smiling and engaging in the casual small-talk that characterizes these groups. He was still alone. He couldn't figure out why the women were interacting with these other men, who quite frankly, were not nearly as attractive, were more casually dressed in less expensive clothes, and were not blessed with his head of thick hair or his broad shoulders.

Emilio decided to do something bold. After Leslie, a woman whose eye he caught and held for a long gaze, turned quickly away from him, he approached her and began to negotiate for her attention. He said, "Could you tell me why you didn't come closer to me after I gave you a clear signal that I thought you were attractive — I issued a direct invitation. I would have met you half-way."

"Is that what you were doing — attempting to engage me?", Leslie asked as she backed away from him. "Wow, I thought you were scary — you were standing there so stiff and determined that you seemed threatening to me." Poor Emilio had watched too many movies. He thought women would fall at his feet if only he seemed in command, defiantly aloof as he issued his challenge. But rather than appearing like Cary Grant or Clark Gable, he called up images of some unsavory character, like the Boston Strangler. Oh well, Emilio learned the importance of body language, even if he didn't yet know exactly what do to change. We'll see if he figures out the subtle cues he was sending. And remember, the setting that Emilio put himself in involves a form of negotiation. His goal was to meet a woman and have her agree to go out with him.

The women in the group presumably came to the gathering for the same purpose, so the people present were all potential "parties" in the negotiation. The meaning of the interactions becomes more clear because of the context. Emilio's success, as is our own, is dependent on his ability to read the myriad cues being transmitted in the negotiation.

NEGOTIATION IS PARTLY UNCONSCIOUS

For the most part, we send and receive messages, using and evaluating nonverbal cues, in an unconscious way. We judge a person's credibility based as much on our unconscious evaluation of nonverbal actions as on the words he or she speaks. If we could ask the other women in the room with Emilio that evening what it was that turned them off, we would probably get the following answers:

"He seemed full of himself—so arrogant."

"That guy looked like a man who couldn't be trusted—good looking maybe, but threatening."

"He had a fortress around him."

"I don't know, he just didn't look friendly."

"Just his facial expression made me uncomfortable."

Emilio hadn't said a word, mind you. His body language, deliberate as it was, sent messages that were exactly the opposite of what he'd intended. This was not his desired or desirable negotiation position. In other settings, Emilio might know exactly what to do. In fact, perhaps he could teach our friend Arnie how to negotiate a raise. But socially, he was in trouble. And that's the point. We negotiate in so many different situations that we must begin to see the overlap and necessity in our ability to map over our negotiation skills in our professional life with our social and interpersonal environments as well.

We must also understand that while our body language and our reading of others' nonverbal cues are usually unconscious, there are steps we can take to raise these interactions to a conscious level. We can begin by learning the probable meanings of some nonverbal cues.

BEND ME, SHAPE ME, ANYWAY YOU MAKE ME—THEY ALL MATTER

As you read through the following list of common elements of body language, try to think of a time that you noticed these behaviors in others or yourself during a negotiation in either a professional or personal setting. This information will help you as you learn to be an effective negotiator in all settings.

- **The person is sitting on the edge of chair.** This generally suggests interest. If the person was sitting back in the chair and then moves forward, his or her interest is increasing. In the next few days, see if you can notice the settings in which you do this yourself. What has happened to trigger that interest?
- **The person sits back with hands clasped behind the head.** This usually indicates confidence and in some circumstances is also a sign that the person is content. You've no doubt seen this, and it tends to be a body position used more by men than by women.
- **You are negotiating a contract and the other person suddenly leans back in the chair and folds his or her arms.** You can bet that a defensive attitude is being adopted. The words may not match, but watch the body language for more cues.
- **The person crosses his or her legs in the middle of a sentence.** Now you know that competition is in the air — maybe even a readiness to do combat.
- **The person's palm is over the heart or is held up in the "oath position,"** which indicates intent to be honest and sincere.
- **You sit down with a person whose hands are open and in an uplifted position.** This person is probably open to what you are about to say. (Contrast this to what happened to Emilio when he approached Leslie. She turned away and even backed off. She was not open to his words.)
- **The person to whom you are speaking suddenly starts to wring his or her hands and then grips the arm of the chair. Or, some finger tapping begins**. Is this person tense? You bet. Could the person be frustrated with what is going on? That could also be the case.
- **A person starts to adjust eye-glasses and is uncon-**

sciously touching the face. Is this a manifestation of feeling nervous? This may not be the case. The person could be thinking about what you're saying.

- **Why is this person clenching the teeth?** He or she could be angry or anxious.
- **You pick up on the fact that the person is rapidly blinking his or her eyes.** Is the person angry? Excited? Ready to be dishonest in the interaction? It could be any of these things. You can watch all the other cues to determine which it is. Of course, the person could be manifesting all three attitudes.
- **You are talking to a person with whom you have steady direct eye contact.** This person is being forthright with you and is probably personable in most interactions.
- So, here you are making statements that seem reasonable to you. But **the person starts rubbing his or her eyes and they are now covered up.** It could be that the person is tired or distracted and can't listen effectively, or he or she might be resisting what you have to say.
- **You notice that the man is picking at his suit jacket; the woman is picking at her skirt.** Both people appear to be uncomfortable with or disapproving of what is being said.
- **Emilio closed the space between himself and the woman with whom he was talking.** She backed away because his action suggested a threat or a determination to be heard. This is one of the most common ways that people evoke a sense of discomfort in others. You will find that if you are too close to another person, that person will automatically back away. Just as widening the distance too much can create discomfort, closing space can actually arouse subtle — or not so subtle — fear in another person.
- **Tuxedos at the ball park; shorts and a tee shirt at a job interview.** This usually indicates that the person wearing the clothing is not taking the event seriously or doesn't understand the nature of the interaction. (Congruence and context are at

work again.)

Fear not; you don't need a specialized computer program in your brain in order to monitor these second by second and moment by moment shifts in body language during negotiations. (And you're supposed to listen to the words, too?) Rest assured that you can bring these generally unconscious cues to consciousness on a gradual basis, knowing that you have been reacting to them for a lifetime.

The fact is, you do have a specialized computer program in your brain that helps you read body language every day. None of this information is new — except perhaps for the details and the affirmation that you were correct to be confused during some of your encounters and negotiations.

Remember, too, that nonverbal cues are most often ambiguous. For example, the person could be finger-tapping, indicating nervous tension, but the reaction could be about something else unrelated to you or your message. Perhaps the person isn't really "present" in the room with you; the person is actually in the hospital room where a close friend is very ill. This represents internal incongruence. Perhaps the person in the tuxedo is on the way to a wedding and is only stopping by your office to negotiate a few details of the contract you're working out. In other words, no one cue can be taken as definitive. All the cues are part of a larger picture.

CONSIDER THE SOURCE...AND THE SETTING

It's possible that Emilio's challenging stare could produce the results he wants when he's interrogating the suspect in the murder case he's investigating. When he folds his arms across his chest he might be sending the very signal necessary to accomplish his goal. For example, this stance could mean, "I'm in control," when he's talking to his teen-age son who has just come home three hours late.

Let's also remember that if the person you are talking to is rubbing his or her eyes at midnight, after a long night of discussion in a small conference room, the person could be very tired. Cues that indicate distraction may be easily explained in a crowded room, but can be considered significant if you are in a closed, quiet office with only two or three people present.

When Arnie begins to negotiate his raise—finally—he will learn to read these nonverbal cues in their context. We will advise against beginning negotiations at the office Christmas party, for example. "But," Arnie says, "the boss is always in a jovial mood then. Wouldn't she be receptive?" We'll tell Arnie that jolly isn't the same as focused, so he should probably choose a different time or place.

WE'RE ALL ONE-OF-A-KIND...UNLESS WE CAN AVOID IT

Some people have "pet" words and phrases they use again and again; some people pull at their clothes in many settings. Some people have loud voices and others speak more softly. We can call these idiosyncratic cues, and when we are attempting to read these actions, we can watch for their repetition or notice if they appear once and then disappear. If we see that something is a habit, then we may not be in a position to read as accurately what they mean for that particular person. If Arnie's boss frequently plays with her glasses, it may be that she has a habit, but one that doesn't indicate tension or conflict. It could be that she has eye trouble.

As much as we attempt to study communication and how ideas are expressed and received, we must also remember that our thoughts can be stated in a variety of ways. There are many words we can use to say, "This deal has its problems." We could talk in specific terms and say that the contract has clauses that are unacceptable, or we could say that we have trouble with the wording of the cancellation clause, or we could state that we are uneasy with line three of paragraph two. Obviously, the more specific we get, the clearer is our message. Arnie's problem is that he usually says, "Wow, we've got big problems here," even if he has difficulty with only one small detail or two.

An intelligent negotiator will use the tone of voice that matches the words and will choose the words and phrases that send a clear verbal message. A powerful negotiator will also deliver the message with matching nonverbal cues.

LET'S TALK — BUT LET'S NOT SHOUT, OKAY?

Words send one part of a message in negotiation, and the way we say the words complete that message. When Emilio first asked Leslie to tell him why she turned away, he spoke in a loud, commanding voice, causing her to back away from him. But there was also an earnest quality to his tone, which prompted her to take his question seriously. That's why she answered. If his tone had been too full of challenge or had contained even a hint of a threat, then it's almost certain that she would have assumed Emilio was dangerous. She might have quickly moved to become part of a crowd.

Fortunately, Emilio isn't a bad guy. As she answered his question, his face softened and his tone changed as well. He let his shoulders drop a bit as he said, "I didn't mean to scare anyone off." He said this in a slow, steady way, indicating that he was thinking carefully about what was going on. Then, he sighed, thanked the woman for her comment, and left the gathering.

Arnie's boss rushed passed him one day and when Arnie called out to her, she said, "What do you want?", with barely a pause between words. Sandra's rushed and abrupt tone delivered a message that she was busy, or in a hurry, or absorbed in other matters. Whatever the reason, she didn't care to be interrupted.

Let's say that Sandra is a sarcastic type of person. She might say, "So, what do you want now?", with a sneer on her face. And she'd add, "I suppose this is of earth-shaking importance."

Perhaps Arnie is upset with Sandra's tone. He rushes into his office and says to the assembled group, "What a woman." If his voice is a screech, that would send one message. If he sighs and smiles as he says it, it could mean that he actually admires his boss. If he says it in a high-pitched tone and quickly, he could be telling the group that he is angry and ready to blow up.

These are small interactions — but think how often the small interactions set the tone for relationships, take up so much of our day, and often leave lasting impressions of (and on) other people. Again, we both send and receive messages on an ongoing basis. We're always forming and leaving impressions by how fast we talk, the tone we use, and the fluency of our speech—and of course, the actual words we use.

In a crowded room we fall asleep if the speaker talks... s..l..o..w..l..y and in a tone we have to strain to hear. In a small room, we almost go crazy with discomfort if someone is talking so....quicklythatwecan'tmakeoutthewords... and *IN SUCH A LOUD TONE THAT WE WANT TO COVER OUR EARS.*

If speech is peppered with a constant searching for words, then we say, "This person isn't sure of him or herself, this person is bluffing and doesn't know the material, or, this person is weak — at least as a speaker." When the words flow smoothly in an even, appropriate tone and pitch, then we think, "This person is prepared, confident, and is comfortable with me or the audience.

COME CLOSE, GO AWAY

The tone is caring, the pitch is even, the words are appropriate. Then why are we uncomfortable? Maybe it's the tight jaws or the clenched fists. Maybe the other person's head is bobbing up and down. Or, maybe this person is sitting on his or her hands. Any of these nonverbal cues will tell us that the words don't match the body language.

Sometimes a person reveals basic personality characteristics by the kind of gestures he or she habitually uses. Arnie's boss sweeps her hand across her desk to indicate that she is always busy. Her head is perpetually in motion and her jaw is always set and tight. Now we know that she's tense and stubborn. So, if we want to work well with her, we'll keep this in mind.

We will know that we can't jump to conclusions based on the set of her jaw on one day. Nor can we read too much into her busy-busy-busy tone. And we also need to understand that Arnie's boss may have consciously adopted this behavior because she's decided she can be effective if she seems unapproachable. And, as many women in powerful positions point out, the same behavior in a man might be viewed in a positive way. Barbra Streisand says that she's considered difficult when she demands the best from those with whom she works; a male director in the same situation would be considered, not difficult, but dedicated. Same behavior, different gender, means different interpretations and expectations.

We also interpret body gestures from our own context, an important fact to keep in mind when we are trying to read other people. A gesture can mean one thing in one culture and something entirely different in another. For this and other reasons, we can never rely on just one nonverbal cue when we are evaluating the mood or receptivity of a person. Because so much of this communication is unconscious, we are always processing information and our internal "computer" is sorting through the cues and our intuition often gives us a total impression.

As this unconscious process moves into the realm of our conscious thoughts, we will find that our intuitive feelings help us apply some checks and balances as we form impressions. We can determine if the person is tense or if that folded stance is a habit; we can decide if the person's voice is always soft or if he or she is feeling timid and unsure right now; we can evaluate if that shifting glance is caused by the presence of 200 people or is an attempt to avoid a meeting of the minds, starting with our eyes.

WHO DO THEY THINK THEY'RE KIDDING?

Our intuitive evaluation of body language in a negotiation can also help us assess those situations in which we have reason to believe that we're being deceived. Arnie knew that his boss often tried to hide facts from her employees, facts that she believed would discourage them from working harder. Yes, the company's profits were good, but Sandra didn't want her employees to feel too secure about their jobs. Therefore, she withheld information, praise, and optimistic statements, and consciously maintained her abrupt, hurried manner.

Arnie and his colleagues noticed that new employees were surprised that the "old-timers" weren't concerned about Sandra's behavior. Some newer staff members were sure that the company was in big trouble. But the veterans just laughed and said, "She's just bluffing."

In many settings, Sandra's behavior would be called deceptive; she was deliberately down-playing the company's profits and growth; she tried to convince the employees that they better keep working or they'd lose their jobs. Her actions were a study in negative motivation, that is, motivating by fear. It would have worked had not the boss's body language given her away.

One day Arnie noticed that Sandra was telling everyone that profits were skimpy, but she was shifting her feet and her lower body was moving around. At one point the boss coughed as she threatened a downsizing action. The staff listened politely, but they saw the tentative way this information was delivered. For all her bluster and abruptness the boss was not good at deception.

We can't over-conclude here. For example, a slight cough could mean that the person has a sore throat. But the staff knows Sandra and they know when she has a cold and when she uses her signature cough. We could call this a collective conclusion, meaning that the majority of people in the office were able to come up with the same version of the truth—about the boss as well as about the company.

As we watch Arnie become an effective negotiator we will see how much he already knows about his boss, and we will see him learn to use this information as he prepares to interact with her. For now, Arnie will continue to observe and learn. But what about Emilio? I think we can conclude that he'll rethink his super-macho image—and perhaps watch fewer movies. We do know that he left that gathering perplexed. For his sake, we can hope he learns that most people don't want to hob-nob with people who come off like serial killers.

CONTINUE TO INTEGRATE ALL THAT YOU HAVE READ SO far into a congruent whole. In negotiation, you can't isolate the verbal from the nonverbal, or the conscious from the unconscious. Yet, there is no denying that people are people. We need to approach each human being as an individual, with personal attitudes, values, beliefs, and unique approaches to problems. But first, you need a starting point from which to begin. And the most fruitful starting point is the cultural level of communication. The cultural or global level provides the means from which the negotiator can hone in on the individual characteristics of each person.

CHAPTER FIVE

Celebrating Diversity or, What Are You Talking About?

HESTER'S NEWSLETTER IS SELLING LIKE HOT CAKES. NEW subscribers are signing up every month, and every day she gets calls and letters inviting her speak to business groups. So, what is this newsletter about? Well, Hester is a specialist in cross-cultural communication and specializes in helping people develop techniques for doing business in foreign countries. What a skill and talent in a world of global negotiations!

The cross-cultural information Hester presents could not be more timely. An executive, who has never traveled outside of this country, has just been asked to conduct delicate negotiations in South Korea; a small manufacturer is planning to open a plant in Brazil and needs to present proposals describing the nature of the work he's planning to do; the attorney is representing injured workers in Italy. It's a new world and many of us are just realizing it.

Nowadays, much of the interaction between cross-global clients is carried on with fax machines and through satellite conferences. Still, there will be face-to-face contacts too. And for many of us, it can be a daunting task to do well in the negotiating process when we aren't sure what the "rules" are.

By rules, I mean the particular cultural customs that must be understood and worked with effectively. For example, one business woman intended to fly in and fly out so to speak. This was a business trip and to her the negotiations were straight forward. But in Country B, the pace is slower, less frantic, and deals aren't closed until the participants have shared a good meal and the hosts have had a chance to show their foreign guests a few important landmarks they pride. In other words, effective negotiation takes place over a period of days. Our brusque business woman is going to have to change her style. What works in New York City is not going to fly in Country B.

It's no wonder that consultants like Hester are appearing, ready to help us understand the important cultural characteristics that will influence communication and negotiation. Because our country is so ethnically and culturally diverse, we may need this information to conduct effective negotiations within our own borders. I've heard people express confusion about the way a negotiation turned out, only to later learn that cultural customs were operating but were not obvious, and therefore, not discussed.

TRANSLATION GOES ONLY SO FAR

"If we use good translators in negotiations and we're using the same words, then why isn't that enough? Do I really have to look beyond the words?" The answer is an unqualified yes. As we've learned, words are just words. Word choice is important, of course, but what about the meaning behind the words, the body language involved, and all the other nonverbal cues? What about context? Clearly, negotiation is not the same everywhere. How could this possibly be true when we see that, even in our own country, cultural and religious beliefs, values, gender, and socioeconomic differences affect our every interaction? So, while we may need translators, we need much more than an exchange of words to insure an exchange of meaning.

WHAT'S THE MESSAGE?

There is no way we can possibly know how to conduct effective communication with people from every country in the world. However, we can work with some basic questions that can serve as a guidelines. In short, we can be aware of some cultural imperatives that guide negotiation in the minds of those with whom we work. Take time to consider and supply the information sought in the questions asked below. These should be seen as a starting point you can use to think about the issue of cross-cultural negotiation:

• How is negotiation viewed in the culture you're approaching? Is it called negotiation? Is it viewed as an informal or formal process? In our own country, there are still people who finalize details of contracts in a paneled office, but the basic agreement was reached on a golf course. This still puzzles many of us, and women have claimed that negotiations conducted in male-oriented settings shut them out. Some women have taken up golf and fought for memberships in country clubs in order to enter that particular cultural "game." Would that be your strategy, or is there another route to take?

If you're negotiating a contract in Germany or Nigeria, how is this process viewed? Will you be sitting in a restaurant when you iron out details or will you be in a conference room or perhaps an airport lounge?

Maybe you're approaching a negotiation with the idea that it's a win-win situation. However, the culture of the other person dictates that the opposing party must appear to lose. In that culture, there is a win-lose attitude toward negotiation. This information will influence how you present your case and the way you express yourself as you talk. If you don't consider this perspective, you'll never get very far in the negotiation.

• In and out. Let's get this done. Hey, time is money. That's a typical U.S. attitude. We equate time with money and we don't want to "waste" time. However, in many other cultures, time is not viewed so rigidly. Wasting time isn't even a phrase in their vocabulary or a concept in their thinking. They need to take time to get to know the negotiating team and perhaps have a leisurely dinner before business is even mentioned in the conversation. It may take a few days to, as we would say, get down to business. Tom, an attorney friend of mine, says that his trips abroad sometimes seem like vacations because the pace of negotiation in other countries is so much more relaxed and slow.

• How are negotiations carried out? Who speaks first? Are interruptions allowed? When can you consult your advisors? The Japanese, for example, dislike shows of power and react particularly negatively to threats. In our country, people will threaten to sue another person or a company even in casual conversation. But to the Japanese, this is considered very bad form, not to mention a sign of arrogance. Similarly, the loner is not as respected in that culture as it is in ours. Group process is considered more important than individual show-boating. So, where we might respect the person who stands apart from his or her peers when disagreeing with a point, the Japanese negotiators might view this negatively.

• In some cultures, decisions are made after loud arguments, which the participants accept as part of the process. In other cultures, this is considered unnecessary and even distasteful. Brash, aggressive behavior may be viewed as crude and a negative impression is formed.

• Every culture has a definition of honor. In our country, a deal that is sealed with a handshake has traditionally been viewed as one that must be honored. People must be as good as their word. In other cultures, honor has a different meaning and may include the concept of loyalty and not taking advantage of another person. For example, in Japan, it's possible that the word "no" will never be uttered, but the written agreement will look different from what you thought you agreed to verbally.

This isn't deception; it's culture. It's considered impolite to say "no" outright. Honor is preserved by saving others embarrassment and rejection.

- There are appropriate and inappropriate forms that negotiation can take. In some cultures, an intermediary is considered acceptable. In others, it's an insult. Similarly, verbal agreements may be valid in some situations but not appropriate in others. And, in some cultures, much personal information will be disclosed as negotiators become familiar with one another; in other cultures, personal information is irrelevant and will be considered diversionary.

GETTING TO KNOW YOU

Knowledge is power in all aspects of communication and negotiation. For example, one woman noticed that in certain countries, discussions could not proceed until comments about her clothing and appearance were dispensed with at the start of each session. She was negotiating on behalf of her company and was working with a group of middle-age men. These men were stiff and distant until the obligatory compliments were offered. In this case, it was necessary for her to accept the comments graciously or she might have offended them. She had done her homework and knew that these compliments were meant neither to patronize her or to show power. In this country, she might have made some remark indicating that she didn't care to talk about her appearance. And she might have been correct in suspecting that this excessive talk about her jewelry or clothing was a way to disarm her and create an unequal balance of power.

This kind of cultural adjustment occurs in many situations and can be made more effectively if we attempt to understand the customs behind the actions. We may consciously question certain cultural norms we are presented with and then alter our own behavior and reactions accordingly. Of course, we can assume that our hosts or visitors are also studying our culture and will adjust their behavior as well. It's also important to remember that cultural differences are just that; they do not represent better or worse, lower or higher development, or right or wrong.

Too often, people from dominant countries such as ours will assume that they are adjusting to cultural situations as a kind of concession. "I'll go along with this stupid formality," they say, "but I'm not going to like it. When will these people learn the right way to do things?" Translated, of course, the right way means "our" way.

Personal prejudices are difficult to hide; ask any person in this country who is a member of a minority group to tell you what it's like on a day-to-day basis. Alvina is an African-American friend of mine who once told me, "People believe they are hiding their bigotry, but it's impossible. They'd be better off working on their problem rather than attempting to hide it."

Take Alvina's words to heart. If you find that you are making negative assumptions about the cultural traditions of others in a business setting, then examine your own heart for the reasons. Never enter a serious negotiation with a person whose culture you hold in contempt. It will simply not work out well in the long run.

On the other hand, it makes no sense to simply ignore cultural differences and pretend they don't exist. I've heard of situations in which the negotiator simply refused to communicate, which is obviously counter-productive. We are living in a multicultural country and world. We thrive on it, as a matter of fact, and sooner or later we'll be negotiating with people whose outlooks may be different from our own.

The cornerstone of effective cross-cultural communication is respect. We may not completely understand the customs and mores, but we can start out with an attitude of respect. We can also question what we don't understand. Rather than "plowing in" we can proceed with caution until we understand the protocol involved.

In our own country and other countries, we can also focus on our positions and on our desired end rather than on the method being used. In other words, we can pay attention to *what* is right, rather than *who* is right.

It is wise not to make too many assumptions about those with whom you are negotiating. For example, the Japanese are very emotional people, but unlike like others, such as Mediterranean people, they don't show emotion. Where Scandinavians are considered reserved and even stoic, they have feelings just like the more expressive Italians. Stereotypes, yes. While not distinctions to be made with certainty, they are a starting point of understanding.

Perhaps the best rule of thumb to be offered here is to accept your counterparts in negotiations as they present themselves. If they appear to need more time, then it is wise to agree to more time. If some personal information is exchanged, then offer some tid-bits of information about yourself. Closing up and refusing to cross the cultural lines will not help you accomplish your negotiation goals. And remember, this information applies in this country as well as in others. We live in a society that is in the process of reexamining and appreciating what each of our contributing cultures offers. As complex as that task is, consider the sensitive issue of gender.

NEGOTIATIONS AND THE SEXES

Are men and women different when it comes to negotiation? Arnie certainly thinks so. He believes that if Sandra were a man, then he wouldn't even have to negotiate for a raise. After all, he thinks, men are reasonable, they deal with facts, and don't confuse issues by bringing irrelevant issues. (Translated, that means he considers Sandra "emotional.")

When it comes to communication, are we better off discussing differences between individuals and broad cultural norms and simply leave gender out of this? In the ideal world, we could concentrate on negotiating styles unique to individuals, without regard to gender. And, we might be able to talk about the differences in negotiating styles between Scandinavians and the Japanese because the information doesn't threaten our assumptions in any basic way. However, to talk about differences between men and women can be walking on sensitive ground, a briar patch we'd rather avoid.

MARLO AND MIKE MAKE ASSUMPTIONS

When they were assigned to a negotiating team that was preparing to work out the details of a sales agreement for a large corporation, Marlo and Mike found that assumptions tend to be made automatically. A large amount of money was involved and they were responsible for getting the highest possible price for each unit (let's call these units teddybears, just for fun) their company was selling to Playtime Corporation. Naturally, Playtime was trying to get the lowest possible price for each teddybear they bought.

Mike and Marlo had a preliminary meeting to go over the facts as they knew them. Mike began to analyze the negotiating team with whom they'd be dealing, using words like "power," "advantage," "vulnerable areas." Marlo took offense when Mike expressed delight that Playtime's negotiating team included two women.

"That's one vulnerable spot," Mike said.

"Explain yourself," Marlo demanded.

"They'll be the first to give in. We'll overpower them with facts," Mike responded, as if this should be obvious.

"Oh, is that so? Maybe the man on their team is thinking the same thing about me," Marlo replied.

"Ah, yes," Mike said, "but he'll be making a big mistake. You're not like most women. You understand power and know how to take advantage of it."

"Really — and what about their female negotiators? What if they re just like me — and just like you?"

"Then we're in big trouble," Mike said as he laughed. "But I doubt that's what will happen."

"What are most women like, anyway? You sure make some broad generalizations, Mike. Let's deal with facts here and forget this gender stuff. We've got a job to do here, not a battle to win."

"Huh?" Mike isn't sure what Marlo means — he's already rubbing his hands together over the challenge of battle. Marlo is wondering just how they can make this unpleasant part of the business as smooth as possible. For her, the goal is to get the best price possible for half a million teddybears and come out with everyone feeling good.

Marlo and Mike are making quick assumptions and fast judgements, and both are probably somewhat right and somewhat wrong. First, it's not uncommon for men to enjoy negotiations more than women do. Marlo's assumption that this is a less rewarding part of her job—a task to do and be done with—is not atypical. And, some men do discuss negotiating in "battle" terms, or they may substitute sports terms for it.

To "win" a point in a negotiation may seem like "hitting a home run," "scoring a touchdown," or even, "winning one battle in a war." To many women this sounds adolescent at best and they would rather think of a gaining a concession as a means to an end, one step in a tough, but human process. Sports and war analogies reduce a valuable process to a game. In addition, some women dislike these expressions and analogies because they sound aggressive and even violent.

Mike, not unlike some of his colleagues, tends to view the very competent Marlo as somewhat different. They may even subconsciously believe she's "more like us." They see Marlo's business savvy and success in past negotiations as a sign that she's learned the male rules of business and, therefore, isn't like other women. Big mistake. Mike still hasn't, as women often say, "gotten it." He clings to his belief that being male is the norm against which women are judged, and he views his negotiating style as the "real" one. This attitude then leads to the conclusion that women who are good negotiators have learned to be like men.

Marlo, in order to get along in the competitive corporate world, often ignores these assumptions and just keeps quiet about the way she accomplishes her negotiating tasks. Admittedly, she doesn't care much for this aspect of the business—at least not by the name "negotiation." However, when asked about this process in other terms, such as "reaching an agreement," "working out the fine-print of the plan," or "contributing to the bottom- line," she might say, "Oh, I like all that." Well, negotiation by any other name is still negotiation. It's just that Marlo prefers to see this process as one of talking things over, having a give and take session in order to reach an agreement that everyone involved can live with. She's great at compromising in order to reach the ultimate goal of selling lots of teddybears.

To Marlo, this is much like a family or social "let's put our heads together and see what we can do" process. In fact, that's one of her favorite expressions. She thinks that putting heads together is a friendly process, not a face-off with enemies.

Why then, does Mike—and the rest of the "guys" in the office — think Marlo is different, more like them than like other women? Well, first, Marlo has had great success at the teddybear company and she has a degree of power in the group because her "agreement making" has brought in money. Hammering out details seems to be second nature to her, but she doesn't call it by its other name, negotiation. She uses her power to make her way to better positions, but like many women, she doesn't consider power an end in itself or something that makes her feel more successful. Mike and his colleagues see the results, and they admire her for them, but they don't understand her process very well because they haven't paid attention to it.

Mike almost hopes that the people at the other company will think that because they are dealing with a woman, they will have an advantage. (He's thinking this same thing about the other company of course.) In fact, many people believe that female negotiators are at a disadvantage, because it is assumed that the woman will have less power than her male counterparts. However, this position is not completely accurate. For example, women appear to have a stronger preference toward "achieving" than men do.

In this context, achieving means preferring to maintain equality in bargaining and valuing solidarity and harmony. If a person values harmony, then she or he will probably not use war analogies in speech. Adopting a combative attitude would, perhaps, be seen as a failure of the process. When confronted with a combative male negotiator, a woman might perceive that a man she's negotiating with will be uncompromising and will attempt to dominate the interaction.

Marlo has developed a habit of which she's not completely conscious. For example, last month she entered into a two-day negotiation with a company whose male negotiator was quite condescending. Marlo called his attitude patronizing. This man assumed that he'd have the advantage because Marlo was by his definition the weaker party. Meanwhile, she was cordial and professional and held her ground in her usual way. She ended up with exactly what she wanted, and her male "opponent" thought he'd taken advantage of her. Marlo sometimes realizes that she must refrain from pointing out the obvious silliness of this subterfuge, but she knows that change isn't going to come easily. These perceived differences may reinforce a sense of frustration on the part of men and women when they negotiate.

Okay, okay — I hear you. You're a man and you're like Marlo — you're interested in the process; you're a woman and you're like Mike — you love to hit those home runs and win those battles. Well, other studies support your ideas. In fact the research is mixed and when you come down to it, there may not be all that much difference in negotiating styles between men and women, tied strictly to the gender difference itself.

READY, SET, LET GO...OF THE STEREOTYPES

We're in a time of great change in society that affects the workplace in many ways. Most men are accustomed to working with, and often for, women, and rather than mimicking male style, women have brought their own individual styles to the office and factory. But because some people stereotype the sexes they might find themselves making all kinds of false assumptions. They then believe that other people have violated the "rules" when they don't behave like the stereotype dictates.

Understand that stereotypes in and of themselves can provide a useful starting point in a negotiation. If you have never interacted with a particular person and know little about him or her except for cultural information, this can provide a place to start. Once you gain experience with that person, you will quickly see how inaccurate the stereotypes are and you will be able to adjust to the individual style of that person.

Most of us would do well to adjust our behavior to each situation and assess others as individuals. For example, both men and women occasionally use a tentative tone of voice, which can be a mistake in certain settings. Both sexes are equally capable of being assertive and straightforward. But until the proper level of information can be ascertained, consider stereotyped ideas for their positive content, a guide in how to treat someone from another culture with intended respect.

Rather than viewing women as one-dimensional, men would do well to remember that women are known to match their language and style of speech to the situation at hand. In situations in which power is an issue, they use powerful speech. In situations where power issues are absent, women tend to use language less indicative of power. Many men assume that just about every interaction involves some kind of power issue, but to many women this just isn't so.

IT'S DIFFICULT FOR WOMEN TO "WIN"

It sometimes seems that women can't win no matter what they do. Consider California prosecutor, Marcia Clark. From day one of the preliminary hearing in the O.J. Simpson double murder case, public attention focused on Ms. Clark's clothes, hairstyle, personality — even her legs. Not unlike the criticism rendered upon First Lady Hillary Rodham Clinton, this skilled prosecutor was scrutinized. She was accused of being both too strong and not strong enough. She was either too aggressive and cold, or too emotionally involved. In short, she was judged by a different standard — and a fairly vague standard at that. And it all seems to come down to an evaluation of image.

In Ms. Clark's case, the image of what a woman is supposed to be like was put "on trial." And there are plenty of people— men and women — who are ready to serve as judge and jury. In Ms. Rodham-Clinton's case, those who evaluate link her work, appearance, and mannerisms to her husband's success or failure. To put it mildly, this is a odd position to put women in. At best it's confusing, and at worst, it forces many women to attempt to be other than their authentic selves. In a negotiation setting, this can be disheartening to be sure.

THE VERBAL BATTLE OF THE SEXES: WHO TALKS MORE?

Some studies have also produced a few cracks in some other stereotypes about communication style and gender. For example, if we ask both Marlo and Mike to tell us which sex is the most talkative, they both might say that women win that contest. It's true that women are perceived to engage in verbal communication more than men.

However, studies have shown that when men and women communicate with each other, men tend to dominate the conversation in three ways. First, they talk longer during each interchange and they accent their speech with more "fillers," such as "um," and so forth. They also tend to interrupt more frequently.

Men might behave this way in conversations with women because they think they're supposed to. Whether they like it or not, many people expect men to be *proactive* in conversation. Mike is expected to begin bringing up those teddybears early in the encounter. Marlo is expected to be more *reactive*; that is, it is assumed that she will wait until someone else starts talking about the price of teddybears. However, Marlo doesn't fit this pattern and Mike knows it. That's why he thinks that they might have an edge.

The other parties might expect Marlo to be more submissive than she actually is. Of course, Playtime Corporation is probably operating on stereotypical assumptions too; in their defense, that may be a place to start if they make the effort to go further and refine the experience with the individual personal interaction. Still, Marlo is very expressive—people like to listen to her talk, even without the sports expressions.

SO, WHO HAS THE POWER?

Mike's face tends give away what he's feeling; Marlo is able to control her facial expressions. In this way, our two friends conform to some research findings, suggesting that women are better able to control their expressions and maintain eye contact. The latter relays a sense of interest and concern. This can have a power advantage in some settings.

On the other hand, Mike is able to maintain a sense of his personal space with greater ease than Marlo. He can "take up" more space and claim it with authority. Marlo and Mike were once in a small conference room with six people, all of whom, with the exception of Marlo, were men. By the time everyone had finished spreading out their notes, hanging their jackets on chairs, and claiming space for their attaches, most of the space was taken. Marlo's chair barely fit around the table. No one noticed this development, not even Mike.

Marlo had to ask the members of the group to move their chairs around to make room for her. This could be perceived as loss of power, depending on the way Marlo made her request. Although she wasn't fully aware of it on a conscious level, Marlo began to claim space in these settings earlier than she once did, thereby making it more difficult to lose her place around a table. Many women learn to do these small things to offset a perceived loss of power.

Studies also suggest that women tend to be better listeners than men, more tuned into reading between the verbal lines, and are better able to interpret nonverbal signals. As a group, they tend to be more in tune with the underlying components of communication. Researchers conclude that these abilities provide women with a power base, one that can actually be used to control an interaction. Without being sure how he knows this, Mike has correctly perceived that Marlo, by using her skills, is the more powerful negotiator and he hopes that the group from Playtime will be fooled.

WHO TELLS WHAT AND WHEN

Marlo has a wide circle of friends with whom she talks about many personal things. Men often wonder what is so important about the things women discuss with one another. A friend of mine noticed that a group of three or four women in a restaurant always look like they are having a great time. Once, when he was sitting with a male friend, they remarked that women always seem to have so much to talk about. He also noticed that they seem to have a lot of fun while they talk, an observation that puzzled him on the one hand and made him a bit paranoid on the other. He's just sure these women are having all their fun at men's expense. "I always have the feeling that they're making fun of us somehow," he said. (As you can see, there's no way for these women to win. They're either talking about trivia or about men.)

Quite often, when asked about these long conversations, women will say that they talk over everything with their friends — work issues, family triumphs and conflicts, personal issues like weight or clothes, relationships, the causes they're involved in, books they're reading, movies they like, and so on. Is any of this important? Yes and no. Marlo will say that of course it's important because it's the "stuff" of their lives. She'll also say that none of it is earth-shaking — after all, it isn't negotiation, it isn't business, and while the conversations enrich the lives of her and her friends, they aren't making money or "doing deals."

Marlo has learned that her conversation style with her friends is not appropriate for business negotiations. In other words, she doesn't casually disclose personal information to those with whom she's entering a negotiation. When the teddy-bears are discussed with the team from Playtime she won't tell the story of her son's favorite stuffed animal, whose name is Brandymuffin. Not that this is privileged information, mind you. It's just not appropriate to the setting. Disclosing sales to other companies, which compete with Playtime, is privileged information, and Marlo knows not to disclose that either.

Mike is also quite skilled about the "rules" of non-disclosure, and in fact, he once controlled a negotiation because he managed to get the other party to disclose too much information, which weakened the other company's position — at least according to the perceptions at that time. Mike is good at balancing warmth and an easy style with the necessary detached "cool" that is so often necessary in the settings in which he works and communicates.

It's safe to say that both men and women need to guard against unnecessary disclosure and neither sex can be considered as "naturally" better or worse at this skill.

THE FACTS AREN'T ALL IN YET

In recent years, there have been some popular books that have made claims about the inherent differences between men and women, particularly in their communication styles. However, there are others who dispute these claims. For now, it's probably best to consider the fact that the person you are communicating with might see things in a different way and that gender (or culture or religion or race) could have something to do with that person's perceptions. But relying on stereotypes and making bold assumptions could prove disastrous. In general, Mike and Marlo are better off negotiating with a group of individuals. Let's just say that it's safer that way.

No matter who you are negotiating with, or what you are negotiating for, you need to effectively exercise the key skill: being a good listener. It shouldn't surprise you that the ability to listen is more important than the ability to turn a glib phrase; read on to learn how.

CHAPTER SIX

I Missed Your Answer — I Was Too Busy Listening to My Question

GORDON AND CARL HAVE A DIFFICULT TIME COMMUNICATING and negotiating with each other about the simplest things. Gordon says that Carl never listens to him when he offers his ideas about the best way to run their video business. Carl says that Gordon doesn't have many ideas, or, he has a devil of a time talking about those he does have. So, Carl just does what he thinks is right and tells Gordon about it later. Gordon is about ready to explode and the business might implode at any minute.

You may not be surprised to learn that the level of stress you often experience when negotiating and your ability to listen or success in listening are often related. This chapter takes a look at the important skill of listening and the often inhibiting (but truly misunderstood) role of stress.

Now Gordon and Carl find themselves in "business counseling," because they know that if they are going to save their partnership, they must learn to communicate effectively in their negotiations and do so with greater ease. Problems, problems. They aren't unusual problems, and to their credit, Gordon and Carl want to save their business partnership and their long-term personal partnership. So where should they start?

YOU NEVER *LISTEN TO ME*

This is a common complaint in relationships and a concern in negotiations. One person says that the other person is incapable of listening—ever. In this case, Gordon believes his ideas are never heard and in the language of communication, he never gets to tell Carl his "stories." And so, we're presented with two problems here. The first involves Carl's assumption that Gordon *should* know how to express himself on the spot, that minute, when he thinks the decision must be made. Gordon believes in taking his time to mull over the problem.

Because of this, Carl makes assumptions, which leads to the second problem. He thinks he knows what Gordon wants because he interprets and reads between the lines. But, while this is a useful skill, it can also lead to distortion. Making assumptions without understanding personal style (and gender, background, race, and other considerations) can lead to mistakes.

One day, Gordon attempted to tell Carl about his experience with a client, who wanted a demonstration video made for her business. This client had needs that required a new approach and some creative thinking. Gordon spoke with Carl, who adopted a negative attitude toward the project. Why? Well, first he fit the information that Gordon gave him into a familiar framework. They'd worked with similar clients in the past and he considered them hard to please.

So, rather than listening to Gordon and asking questions after he had some information, he interrupted several times and ultimately, said, "No, we don't want to take this on." Carl then abruptly left the room, leaving Gordon standing alone, wondering what happened and why this good business prospect was going to be turned away.

If all had been going well between Carl and Gordon, how would the situation be resolved? First, Carl would have listened to Gordon's "story," the narrative account of his conversation with the client and his impression of what could be done for her. Perhaps Gordon would have mentioned a few special challenges, noting that these would require some creative thinking. In other words, he wouldn't claim to have all the answers that minute.

Carl would have listened carefully, and in his mind (or on paper) noted the questions he would ask when Gordon finished. Unconsciously, when we listen carefully, we are picking up on inconsistency and contradictions. We may also be forming impressions based on what we know about the speaker. For example, Carl knows that Gordon is extremely optimistic, making every project sound blissfully easy. He might form questions based on this knowledge. Instead, he simply rejected the project without careful listening. He assumed he knew what was best, with little on which to base that judgment. After Gordon was through with his narrative explanation, Carl could have then asked his questions.

A QUESTION ISN'T JUST A QUESTION

There are actually many types of questions to be asked when we negotiate, each of which elicits different kinds of information and serves a different purpose. Carl might have used a combination of the these various types of questions as he gathered information to evaluate the position of others.

Open-ended Questions: These are questions that permit answers that can be stated freely without an imposed structure. You've probably heard of the standard journalist's formula: who, what, when, where, why, and how. Questions asked in this way permit listeners to respond in whatever manner they wish. For example, Carl could have asked Gordon for his vision of the project. He could have asked how certain obstacles could be overcome. He could have used one of the old-standby open-ended questions, "Is there anything else you'd like to say or add?"

This type of question is best used at the beginning of a

negotiation and to inquire into new areas within the topic. It's a great tool for gathering information. Unfortunately, Carl didn't know much about open-ended questioning, and the skill of letting someone else speak in a flowing and uninterrupted manner is natural to few of us. Rather, his questions were stated in a negative way that usually left Gordon wondering what the so-called right answer is. "I don't suppose you know how much this will cost?", he'd say.

Close-ended Questions: The answers to these questions are limited to simple yes and no responses, or something that is equally brief. They are best used when the narrative part of the inquiry is over in order to follow up, confirm, or evaluate something said. For example, if Carl had listened to Gordon and asked open-ended questions that required a further explanation of positions and ideas, he might have ended with, "So, given all we know right now, do you want to go ahead and take on this project?" Gordon might have said a simple, "Yes, I do."

There might also have been opportunities within their discussion for close-ended questions, such as those that had a simple factual response. "Did you talk to this client for the first time yesterday afternoon?" "Have you studied all the materials she sent?" Then open-ended questions could follow that would probe impressions about the conversation or materials.

Leading Questions: This type of question suggests its own answer. These questions are asked to confirm information that already seems clear to the asker. If I have assigned a job to a partner, I might say, "You've cleared your calendar so you can attend these meetings?" This question confirms what I'm quite sure of (or clearly expect) already. Carl, as a way to confirm what he thinks is true, could ask Gordon if there are openings in the schedule to handle the new client. Or, he might ask, "The client understands the fee payment schedule?" This question is in a sense, a rhetorical one, because he knows that Gordon always discusses this with prospective clients. He's simply confirming what he is quite sure he knows.

Most us have had experience with this type of question when it suggests a challenge or even veiled anger. Let's say that Carl knows that they will need to hire a sub-contractor to do the new project. Suppose he asked Gordon, "So, Gail's available to do the work?" If we aren't listening in, that could seem like a reasonable question. But tone of voice and known facts are left out. So I'll fill you in. Gordon and Carl both know that Gail is having a baby and won't be available for any work for six months. So, Carl's question was asked in a sarcastic tone and challenged Gordon to come up with another sub-contractor.

A question like this confirms Carl's negativity. It forces Gordon to say, "What are you talking about Carl, we both know Gail isn't available. She's not the only film editor in town."

A more congenial way of asking the question might be, "Since Gail isn't available, is there anyone else we can line up? Do you know of someone off hand?" This gives Gordon a chance to state a plan or confirm that he already has another film editor in mind. Either way, the question is asked and answered for the purpose of continuing the negotiation of the situation, not shutting it down.

LISTEN BY ASKING

Responding to information with a question is one of the best ways to gather information—it also keeps us listening and evaluating what we hear. As a rule, it's best to ask open-ended questions first, which can be followed by close-ended questions to confirm certain conclusions or facts. Leading questions might also be used to confirm unspoken assumptions or facts.

If Carl can ask questions that lead to clear answers, Gordon might be able to then ask Carl about his concerns. For example, what if Gordon said, "Do you have concerns about finding a film editor on such short notice?" Or, he could say, "Other than the deadline, do you have other reservations about taking this on?"

This kind of questioning is new for Gordon. You see, Carl isn't the only "problem" person in this partnership.

Gordon's style is to avoid questions at all cost. He usually phrases his ideas with, "You won't like this, but..." Or, he sometimes says. "You probably won't hear me out so I won't bother to even start..." Gordon needed to learn to affirm Carl's concerns without attacking him. He had to learn to listen to Carl in a way that afforded deeper understanding. They needed to avoid superficial exchanges.

Our proverbial king and queen have the same problem. The king often says, "Would you stop playing the piano now?" The queen is in the habit of saying, "Oh, I suppose there's something else — perhaps — you'd like me to do?" She responds that way because the king seems to make unreasonable demands. He doesn't bother to tell her that important guests from another kingdom have arrived. The king appears to believe that she must drop everything without any explanation and the queen resents his unexplained demands. So, he thinks she's sarcastic, which she is, and she thinks he's insensitive, which he is. Are we surprised? They stopped listening to each other years ago.

If we all learned to listen by asking questions, we'd find that our negotiations would be far smoother. Eventually Carl and Gordon leaned how to do this. They even learned to chart their conversations and see their communication as a script. I taught them how to create a question tree, which illustrated how each "branch" extends the overall information. When questions are off-track or not timed well, they may move the information backwards instead of forward.

For example, either Carl or Gordon could point to a time when a similar project led to loss of money and other problems for the business. When they chart their communication on a tree, they can see when they come to the best point in the conversation to discuss the past. Carl tends to want to do this early, and Gordon would prefer not to do it all. But there is an appropriate time, probably after the new project has been fully explained. They could then compare the new opportunity with situations in the past.

The purpose of the tree is to demonstrate a move toward completeness of communication and information. It also helps to keep communication moving toward fullness and each branch becomes part of a whole, rather than a fragment with no connection to the whole. Think about the most unsatisfying conversations or negotiations you've had in your own experience. I'd bet that information was never fully exchanged or connected, and perhaps, neither you nor the other party asked cogent questions.

If our king and queen had a royal family therapist on hand, they might be able to straighten out their communication, too. The king would learn to tell the queen that guests were arriving and she was needed on the royal balcony. This is a reasonable request to which the queen would likely respond positively. Our queen might learn not to react with sarcasm and simply ask the reasons for his various requests.

LISTENING ISN'T JUST HEARING

Hearing is a physical activity. Sound bounces off the ear drum, and by itself, this is not listening because it takes much more to interpret what the sound means. Listening is the process of applying thoughtful attention to what is being said, how it is said, and the body language that goes along with it. Carl's body language didn't always match his words. Try as he might to maintain a distant or sarcastic tone, Carl genuinely respects and cares for Gordon, so his body language indicates a friendly and warm attitude even when his words are negative.

Many people consider listening a passive activity within a conversation. But this isn't true. We have the term, "active listening," to describe the ability to take in the substance of what is being said and confirm the information. Therefore, follow-up questions will actually add to current information or ideas, rather than confuse them.

Active listening is actually a process of continuous clarification of information. You can try the skill of "back tracking," which is repeating back to the other person what they have said in the way they said it. This is a mirroring process, but not mimicking. When we mirror, the person hears the words come back, and then he or she will either acknowledge the accuracy of the words or offer a clarification of what was heard.

One would expect a repetition of our own words to sound like parroting — or mimicking — but handled in the proper way, the process builds rapport and is warm; the result is clarity and affirmation.

When people aren't listening and processing in negotiation, they often end up in a "war of words." Carl and Gordon both described their experience just that way. But with training, they both became better listeners and most important, learned to listen better to each other. Their lives became more whole both at work and at home.

BARRIERS TO LISTENING

There are a number of potential barriers to good active listening in negotiation. It isn't always a smooth process, but if we recognize the difficulties, we can overcome many of them and improve listening.

Physical impairment: Obviously, if we don't hear well, we can't listen. When people begin to lose hearing acuity, they often appear vacant and unresponsive in a conversation. In most cases, this can be remedied, but when hearing impairment is severe, alternative communication methods must be found. Sign language was an important development in helping a segment of the population both "speak" and "listen." In fact, sign language is our proof that communication isn't comprised of putting a bunch of symbolic sounds together.

Physical distractions: Sounds such as background music, traffic, machinery, and so forth can impede listening. Gordon and Carl must address this kind of distraction if they are going to really listen to each other. Business can be discussed and deals made over dinner, but you'll seldom see people negotiate in a crowded bar where people are dancing. Rather, people choose a quiet restaurant with private tables or booths. In most cases, distractions can be eliminated when all parties are serious about the task at hand.

Disinterest: There are times when neither Carl nor Gordon is interested in an issue the other is trying to raise. Carl doesn't much care about the advertising for the business. That's always been Gordon's "department" and he handles it alone. Gordon doesn't handle the day-to-day accounting details and defers to Carl. Both discovered that they need to schedule time to talk about these details and make sure each approves of the other's work. As long as they maintain their disinterest, neither will listen to the other. We must be sure of our interest in any negotiation in which we are a part

Psychological distractions: A bad day can be enough to halt meaningful negotiation. Everyone occasionally goes through a period of extraordinary stress, which may make the ability to listen significantly diminished. Gordon and Carl have the usual stresses in their lives, but none are impeding communication right now. That's good, because their business counseling requires all their attention. Should this situation change, they can talk about ways to handle the business and necessary communication during an unusual time. Unfortunately, most of us don't do this "checking in," with others and we allow communication to deteriorate. Then we aren't sure what happened—or why.

Mental Argument: Some people are argumentative by nature — Carl came to describe himself that way. Just as Gordon shut down when challenged and walked away feeling "misunderstood," Carl didn't think he'd made his point if arguments didn't result. Arguments seemed more real to him than "mere" conversation. Some self-examination helped both understand that their attitudes and their mind-sets worked against their best interests.

LET'S TAKE A CLOSER LOOK AT THE ROLE OF INTERNAL distraction and mental argument. Together, they highlight a very important human condition — stress. Let's face facts. If you aren't accustomed to negotiating — consciously and with informed purpose, that is — then it's possible (perhaps even probable) that you will be nervous and anxious as you prepare yourself. This is a normal reaction, especially if the outcome is particularly important to you. If you don't care very much you won't be as anxious. In the parlance of the day, we'd describe this as your level of personal investment in any given interaction or issue. The good news is, stress does not have to be debilitating in negotiations.

Let's say you've discovered your dream house, but in order to close the deal you'll need to put together a very complex and creative financing deal. It's possible that you'll be quite anxious as you proceed through the steps because your level of personal investment is high. On the other hand, if you take the attitude that there are many homes available, then you'll likely be more relaxed as you negotiate your financing deal.

LOOK FOR THE MESSAGE BEHIND THE MESSAGE

Being anxious or stressed out, as the saying goes, may be an expected and normal response. Others involved in the negotiating process may feel the same way. If both parties are to a greater or lesser extent emotionally ruffled in some way, negotiations may be impeded. When the parties have a history with each other, as is the case with Carl and Gordon, the difficulties can be even more pronounced. At the very least, the accurate flow of information may be stymied, the atmosphere may become charged, and everyone's composure begins to crumble. This happens in many situations, from exchanges between a detective and a suspect, a teenager and a parent, a boss and an employee (such as Arnie and Sandra), and so forth.

However, if we're aware of certain cues indicating that this is a stressful situation, we can make decisions about continuing the negotiation, delaying it, or exploring the reasons for this anxiety or stress. We do have choices about the way we respond either to our own internal and external cues or to those of others. But remember, any of the manifestations described below can interfere with communication and therefore, with the negotiating process.

- "You won't like this, but....", or "So, now that you've heard what I said, you'll probably go away." In both cases, a negative statement is made at some point in the process of delivering information. The most obvious cues are when this negativity appears at the beginning or at the end of a statement. If you find yourself doing this, examine your behavior carefully and determine if this is a habit you've acquired or if you do this when you are anxious or feeling insecure. Arnie does this a lot, and his friends even tease him about it. However, he doesn't view it as a problem, at least not yet. He thinks he has a particular irreverent style and he's proud to be a bit of a cynic.

Watch for this behavior style in your negotiating partner. Ask yourself why the person is prefacing or ending every exchange with a negative remark. Is the person upset or nervous or insecure? If both parties feel this way, the communication could be very awkward.

- "And this is what I must have to live on, Ms. Boss. I had a difficult childhood, you know." What? You might as well have said, "Did I mention that my dog turned 12 yesterday?" Why does a childhood (or a dog) have relevance in a salary negotiation? When people are tense, they will often include irrelevant information. Sometimes the tension is due to lack of preparedness; at other times the stress indicates the emotional investment involved. But irrelevant information that seems thrown in, so to speak, is a good indication that internal anxiety is going to impede effective communication.

• "Let's talk about the bottom line. Could I see the manual for that software you bought last week?" Now we're in a different realm, that of confusing shifts in the conversation. On the one hand, a clear message is sent—we're going to talk about profit and loss. On the other hand, a side issue is being brought in. Perhaps the subject of profit is too overwhelming at that moment, so you or another person shifts the conversation. You might notice this in yourself or in another person.

• "I just can't remember how many clients we have," or, "I just don't know if it happened last week or the week before." If you're the 3M corporation, then it makes sense not to be able to pin-point a particular number of clients. However, if you're a one-person consulting practice then not remembering the scope of your clientele may seem illogical to others. If a person adopts this attitude with you, you might have suspicions aroused.

If you've agreed to loan a person some money for his or her business and you're negotiating the details, then this lapse could seem significant. You may ask for proof that there is a client base. If your boss can't remember if you've been with the company for five years or just started working there six months ago, there is an emotional conflict going on. Pay attention to these kinds of lapses. They could be significant and cause you to make some decisions about the direction of the negotiations.

• The person can't remember how he or she felt when the roof collapsed on three children. "I was upset," is all that is disclosed. Upset? What about horrified, sickened at the sight, terrified when he or she ran to scrape away the rubble with bare hands? What about the sadness and sense of defeat when it was discovered that one child had been killed and the two other children were badly injured? "If only I'd gotten there sooner," the person says, "I might have been able to save that child. I'll live with this regret the rest of my life." Now we have details, and not just a general sense of being upset.

General statements about feelings often indicate that the person simply isn't identifying what the emotions are or can't face them for some reason. Emotional state, or affect, can provide information about many aspects of the interaction and in some cases will establish or discredit the person's credibility.

- "He must be a real jerk," Mary concludes. Why? Because the price he wants for his house is higher than she wants to pay. In this case, Mary is making a broad generalization about the person in question. The reasons for the price of the house are not separated from the person, and therefore, a quick judgement is made. Mary may have an emotional issue that is getting in the way of negotiations. Similarly, the owner of the house could conclude that anyone who questions his price is nothing more than an idiot. In either case, some kind of emotional response is impeding the exchange of information.

- "But, yes but, no but." One party responds this way to every suggestion on the table. Now we know we have a problem. We've all run into the "yes but" people. Sarah comes to you for help in changing her social life. You offer six suggestions and she has a reason, presented instantly, why each won't work, couldn't possibly work, and is dumb to boot. You can be sure that "yes but" people are resisting any assistance, even if they ask for help.

It's nearly impossible to communicate with a person who protests that every idea is nearly impossible. Another approach will be needed if communication is to continue. Effective negotiation can't be accomplished in an atmosphere in which every idea is immediately put down.

- "Let me explain—again—that you are in danger every time you leave this house." Well, here's Dad again. Explaining and explaining and explaining. This time he's going over car accident statistics in an attempt to explain to 16 year old Jan the reasons he refuses to let her drive the family car. This isn't going to work either because in all these explanations his fear for her safety is lost. Jan will continue to look the other way and in practical terms, she stopped listening to her father as soon as he started his fact-filled lecture. He's soon going to switch from car safety to explaining the chemical changes in the brain when two ounces of alcohol are in the blood. Oh dear, he can't talk about his fear so he's running on and on about technical details. Are there times that you've done this, too?

- "The company, as I've said — repeatedly — is in big trouble." The phone rings "Oh, hello Harry — yes, couldn't be better, profits are way up." This is an obvious example of inconsistency and most people wouldn't be foolish enough to make these contradictory statements back-to-back. However, in many exchanges, there will be inconsistencies or even big gaps in information that is being presented. The question is why these gaps exist or information is inconsistent. It could mean that deliberate attempts are being made to cloud the facts, but it could also indicate that the person is experiencing great stress and anxiety over the situation at hand.

- Ben is shifting around in the chair and won't make eye contact. There are many explanations for this behavior, including fatigue, anxiety, and general stress. It may have everything to do with your communication or nothing to do with it. We'd live in a more harmonious world if the stressed out person simply said, "I can't listen to you right now because I've been up all night with my sick baby. We'll have to postpone this discussion, but please don't take it personally, it has nothing to do with you or our proposed contract." Not everyone will be this open, so we must note certain behaviors and then sort through all the information we have.

STRESSED OUT? CHECK IT OUT

The most skilled negotiators can experience stress that renders them unable to effectively communicate a desired position. Leo noticed that Diane was distracted and was picking at her clothes. She was shuffling papers as she spoke and kept rocking back and forth in her chair. "Is this a bad time for you," Leo asked, with a kind but firm tone in his voice. "If it is, I could come back tomorrow or on Friday to talk about my newsletter." As it turned out, Diane was worrying about a pressing appointment with her child's teacher. She was running late already, but she didn't say anything out of fear that she would appear unprofessional.

Leo noticed Diane's distracted behavior because it was out of character for her. Normally a focused person, the nonverbal cues alerted Leo to a change. As it turned out (as it often does) the timing of the meeting wasn't crucial to Leo. The newsletter that he needed Diane to design could wait another day or two. Diane's stress level dropped just as soon as Leo spoke.

Andy came into the room late, but he noticed that Jimmy was tapping his fingers on the table, his jaw was clenched, and he'd pushed his chair far away from Bobby. Andy knew that something had happened before he arrived and sure enough, the negotiations over a travel contract for the company were not accomplished. Unbeknownst to Andy, Bobby had made an offhand remark about Jimmy's business ethics. Bobby assumed that his company was going to be "ripped off" in whatever deal was made, making Jimmy feel attacked and defensive. Andy learned about the remark after the disastrous negotiations were aborted. But now it was too late. After tempers had cooled, Andy admitted that if he'd been on time for the appointment, Jimmy wouldn't have had to "kill time" with Bobby, who for his part, was hostile from the start.

Bobby carried a lot of baggage into the negotiations. It was his job to negotiate the travel contract and his boss was furious that the former travel agency had delivered such poor service at such high prices. In fact, Andy and Jimmie didn't know that Bobby was in danger of losing his job if he didn't come up with a better deal. Bobby was so threatened that the hostility oozed from him, and he greeted Jimmie with the "rip-off" remark. Meanwhile, Jimmy was angry with Andy for being late, setting the stage for poor communication all around.

When we find ourselves puzzled by the tone an interaction is taking on, don't forget that it might not have much to do with the particulars with which we work.

Use the Stress Monitor form whenever you are preparing for negotiation. Eventually, this information will become second nature to you, but for now, use the chart to remind you of certain signs of stress in yourself or others.

Of course, some stress is inevitable — is natural and expected. For example, if I asked you to negotiate with a person who speaks six languages, but one of them isn't English, you'll probably have an immediate nervous reaction. It will be especially pronounced if you've never done it before. That doesn't mean that you won't do a good job. Why? Because you'll know that you must prepare for the special challenges this negotiation presents.

DID I HEAR YOU CORRECTLY?

As we've said, part of listening is confirming that we heard what the person said and have interpreted the words as intended. This was perhaps the most important lesson in communication and negotiation that Carl and Gordon learned. For a period of several weeks, they practiced confirming that the message they heard was the message that the other intended to send.

Sometimes, people misinterpret this step in active listening. For example, what if Gordon says, "Of course, we can't use Kristie because she's having a baby. We'll have to make other arrangements and I think I can do that."

What if Carl responds, "So, I hear you saying that we can't use Kristie and you think you can make other arrangements." This is simply a parroting response. This would not be an effective use of backtracking. Carl is better off if he said, "You sound a bit concerned about the fact that Kristie isn't available, but you think this problem isn't insurmountable. Do you have an idea?"

Gordon then says, "Yes, I'm concerned, but I know a freelance writer who works with film editors. I'll call him right away and get some recommendations."

Carl responds, "So, you have a plan, a place to start, and you've been thinking about this. As you said, there are other film editors. We've just been spoiled because Kristie gives us priority."

Gordon says, "You're right. I'll be glad when she's back. We really should think about a present for the baby."

Carl nods his head and says, "Let's do that, but not right now. Let's fix this problem first and talk about the present next week."

Gordon agrees when he says, "I can see that you're anxious about this, so I'll get on it right away. I'll keep you posted."

Now we're talking — negotiating — and listening. In this case, the problem at hand seems like a simple enough situation to handle. But, because of past communication problems it was necessary for each party to confirm what they heard the other say. This was exactly the kind of problem that at one time had caused them trouble.

The above exchange also indicates how seldom many of us are willing to convey emotion. They each had to note and express their observation of each other's concerns. Most of the time, people are reluctant to say, "I'm upset, anxious, angry, sad," and so forth. That's why it's important to look for verbal and nonverbal cues and "feed" your perception back to the other person through active listening and backtracking. That's what Gordon and Carl did and their communication was stronger for it. In addition, some competing concerns and emotions were expressed — confidence that the problem could be solved, a sense of loss about Kristie's unavailability, happiness for her, eagerness to get the problem solved, and so forth.

We've seen Gordon and Carl save their partnership because they learned how to listen to each other. It's not too difficult to see how tension in one part of a relationship can extend to other parts of the relationship as well. We should always be aware of the implications of our behavior in the short and long term.

Arnie isn't pleased that he had to learn all this before he could negotiate for his raise, but he will find that the information pays off—if he begins to apply it on a day-to-day basis. While he practices, he can learn some basic premises of negotiation.

In Part II of this book, you'll learn to apply the communication-based skills to the many negotiation situations you find yourself in, over many different kinds of issues. Who knows, our king and queen may just pick up a tip or two as well.

Form #1: Stress Monitor

1. Look for the following signs of stress in yourself or others. Check the box when you find yourself experiencing any of these in a variety of negotiations, regardless of the setting. Then note any details or other comments. These signs may appear during negotiations in both a personal and professional setting. This form is meant to be helpful in recognizing when stress is apparent. It is not meant to make you feel bad about yourself when you experience stress. It's a universal experience, and usually lessens only through experience—and knowledge. Use the form in a positive way.

- Negative comments made at the beginning or the end of the statement.
  ___Yourself ___Others ___Both

Details: ____

- Inclusion of seemingly unrelated or irrelevant ideas.
  ___Yourself ___Others ___Both

Details: ____

- Unclear shifts in conversation.
  ___Yourself ___Others ___Both

Details: ____

- Inability to remember specific details.
  ___Yourself ___Others ___Both

Details: ____

- A memory for only vague or general emotions.
  ___Yourself ___Others ___Both

Details: ____

- Inability to separate behavior from attitude or self-image.
  ___Yourself ___Others ___Both

Details: ____

- Excessively protesting against every inquiry.
  ___Yourself ___Others ___Both

Details: ____

- Explaining every statement.

___Yourself ___Others ___Both

Details: ____

- Gaps or inconsistencies in a person's comments.

___Yourself ___Others ___Both

Details: ____

- Behavioral cues that signal discomfort.

___Yourself ___Others ___Both

Details: ____

Other Notes:

2. Now, take the information and assess what is causing the stress for you. You can't second guess others, but you can examine what it is about the situation that results in your higher than normal stress levels.

A: Internal Causes

- The dispute itself? (i.e., it has an intense emotional component.)

Notes: ______________________________

- You have difficulty with the process. (i.e., you are unsure of your skills or the atmosphere seems stiff.

Notes: ______________________________

- You have difficulty with the other participants. (i.e., you dislike one or more of the other parties or you care so much about the other person that emotions get in the way.)

Notes: ______________________________

B: External Causes

- Competing time demands (i.e., you're due somewhere else in 30 minutes or work is piling up while you take care of a personal negotiation.)

Notes: ______________________________

- Judgments of the other parties are creating a threat to your ego or self-image. (i.e., the other party is better prepared and has control over information in situations you normally dominate.

Notes: ______________________________

- Bias or self-interest is tainting the accuracy of your perception. (i.e. you are invested so deeply in the outcome that you can't hear the other party's information or position.)

Notes: ______________________________

PART II

CHAPTER SEVEN

Win-Win Is Great — But What Does 'Winning' Mean?

CONSIDERING HOW OFTEN WE NEGOTIATE IN BOTH OUR work and personal lives, it's astounding that the skills involved are not emphasized in education. Or, when the skills are taught, they aren't labeled—or connected with—the art of getting the best deal possible. Arnie often wonders why the business courses he took in college never mentioned negotiation, as least as a process that applies to the average person.

One of Arnie's professors, Dr. Leahy, even said that this was an inborn talent and that some people simply have a capacity for it and others don't. Therefore, there was no reason to teach it. Arnie believed that and assumed that he must be one of those unfortunate souls that didn't have this inborn knack.

I believe that we have de-emphasized this skill because most education is theoretical, rather than practical. In other words, we emphasize the philosophy of something and generally stop there. We fail to move from examining concepts to implementing day-to-day applications of what we've learned.

Some people expressed dismay when high schools began to teach practical life skills, such as using a checkbook and filling out job application forms. School, they said, was not the place to teach those skills, that parents or peers should be responsible for these areas of life. Most students differ with the older generation on this and are thankful that they know the nuts and bolts of applying for a job. I hope that this book is doing the same for you—taking the mystery out of negotiating and obtaining the best possible outcome in many life situations.

HOW DO I KNOW IF I'VE FARED WELL AT THE TABLE?

Arnie believes that he should get a 20 percent raise. Anything less would be failure, at least in his own mind. Julie believes that she should be allowed to work at home three days a week; that's her position and she intends to stick to it. Michael has decided that he is entitled to play golf on his vacation and his wife is obligated to come along with him, even though she'd much rather read and relax in a secluded cabin on a lake. Tony and Cathy share an office and they need a bigger space, but so far, their office manager hasn't agreed on a time to discuss the situation.

Each of these challenges represents a fairly ordinary life dilemma, which is not to say that each is easy or can be negotiated carelessly or casually. Each must be handled with skill and finesse if all parties will be satisfied. It's important to remember that defining success in narrow terms can be deceptive.

Let's say that Arnie gets his raise, but his boss, Sandra, is left feeling bullied and intimidated. She approved the raise simply because she had no time to handle the issue and her boss was pressuring her to finish a major project. Two months later, Sandra is told she must cut staff, and because she and Arnie have been at odds, she lets him go. He's laid off and she no longer has to deal with him.

Or, what does Michael win if Jackie grudgingly goes along with him on his golf vacation when she'd rather be somewhere else? What assumptions underlie this steadfast refusal to compromise or work out another vacation plan that would be satisfactory to both of them? And, perhaps most important, why would Michael's victory seem so hollow?

In all these cases, is there one way to accomplish a goal, or are there many ways negotiation skills could be applied? If everyone involved believes this is essentially a negative process, how will they feel about the outcome? What if Tony and Cathy achieve their goal of having a bigger office, but they have to fight and whine to "win?" Unfortunately, many people avoid negotiation settings simply because their attitudes are so negative, and each situation is tainted with stress and anxiety.

DEFINING OUTCOME

Outcome must be defined broadly if we are to correctly evaluate how we fare in negotiations. We have to put the outcome in context and have a sense of being true to ourselves and our ethical standards if we expect to come away with a sense of true accomplishment. Ideally, others should have a sense that negotiating with us is a generally positive experience. Those who might enlist our skills to negotiate on their behalf should believe that we are competent and that our negotiation style is compatible with their values — and the values of all parties involved.

Sometimes people see (or at least play) negotiation as a civilized argument. Arnie believes that characterization is true, and he even has trouble believing that it should be civil. Poor Arnie. He grew up in a family of strong minded, argumentative people. His parents (while generally kind and loving) argued much of the time — they never negotiated. They weren't particularly unhappy; it was just their style. Naturally, Arnie's definition of negotiation means scrapping around until someone gets his or her way.

Michael thought that he shouldn't need to negotiate at all — his wife should simply go along with his wishes and enjoy whatever he enjoys. After all, his seven employees comply with what he wants, why shouldn't his wife and children? Who's the boss here? Many people have this attitude, because they aren't able to communicate effectively in a variety of settings and change their style to match the occasion.

My friend Art is a school teacher who just can't drop the lecturing tone when he's at home with his family. His teaching style, emerging often during conversations at the dinner table, has become a topic of family humor. His lectures get him amused looks and grins of the family, but his demands can often get lost in the moment.

Misconceptions about the process stem from a basic belief that being a good negotiator is synonymous with being a slick, or unethical person. In our culture, negotiation is usually associated with trickery or at least cunning. A wrong move means loss of power, and loss of power is always viewed negatively. Nothing could be further from the truth.

The effective and successful negotiator should never have to cross the boundary and move outside of proper and ethical conduct. In fact, the effective negotiator should be able to detect when others have set out false information. The answer lies in being able to dig out the truth through the negotiator's most powerful tool: the question.

Many people don't realize that most negotiating takes place between people that indeed have ethical standards and a sense of morals, even if they aren't conscious of the role of these concepts in the daily give and take of life. That's the good news, I guess.

ETHICS, VALUES, & MORALS INTACT — NEGOTIATORS ARE PEOPLE TOO

Contrary to popular opinion, everyone who negotiates comes to the table with a set of values, ethical standards, and moral precepts. It might not seem obvious, but it is *always* so.

When Michael expects Jackie to happily play golf with him, he is operating from a set of values that includes underlying assumptions about men and women. He considers himself head of the household; he makes the most money, and therefore, vacation plans should please him. Furthermore, there shouldn't be a need to negotiate because it's his wife's job to go along. He doesn't verbalize his beliefs in precisely this way, and may not be conscious of the extent to which these assumptions operate in his life.

Nowadays, this might sound odd to most people, but Michael is from the so-called "old school." What if we called Michael immoral? He wouldn't take well to this because he is honest about his values and he cares about Jackie. So we need to look deeper.

But, what if Michael promised Jackie a week alone in a cabin on a lake? "You come golfing with me," he'd say, "and in the fall, you can go away alone for a week." That could represent a satisfactory negotiated compromise. But what if Michael had no intention of making good on his offer? What if he deliberately tricked his wife? Come fall, he would find some reason to deny her what she wants. We'd then say that Michael was deceptive and a liar, and perhaps we'd say he was on shaky moral ground. We'd also know that he is an authoritarian man and has the power to give and take away — and we'd one day be able to say he's divorced!

Fortunately, Michael isn't like this, and in fact, has never tricked Jackie. So, she knows that when she talks with him, he's going to be open with her. She may not like what she hears, but she can deal with him and attempt to persuade him that his attitude is antiquated. Jackie does not have to worry about deception. This is the heart of the relationship. These dynamics are not dissimilar to what occurs in every negotiation, for business, personal, or social reasons. It's about relationship, satisfaction, and doing the best we can in the process.

Arnie knows that Sandra is basically an honest person, a fact that softens his attitude toward her when he thinks about his raise. However, he also knows that her communication style is fear-based. She tends to make gloom and doom statements and rarely asks open-ended questions. If he's going to negotiate effectively, then Arnie is going to have to note these characteristics.

We usually can't separate the negotiator from his or her set of values. Most of us trust or distrust people based on a total impression of what we know about them. We might label our impression an evaluation of character. When we say someone has strong character, that usually means that we sense that the person has convictions, high ethical standards, and consistent actions. Now that you understand the power of nonverbal cues from previous chapters, you can expect negotiators to demonstrate this strong character through actions in various settings.

Similarly, if we believe our neighbor, Angie, has weak character, we might cite her lack of consideration for neighbors, her nastiness to the building's maintenance person, her complaint that bill collectors hound her, the racist comments she made when a new person moved into an apartment on her floor, and on and on. How would we feel if we found that Angie was representing the owner of the summer home we'd like to buy? We might be on guard, for sure, and perhaps we'd tell our own real estate broker that we know all about Angie.

It's possible that you haven't considered how your ethical standards and value system fit into a negotiation setting. Remember that you negotiate every day, from what time you'll wake up, to a decision about whether or not you'll go to work, to which outfit you will buy. Your personal values come through in everything you do. Your reputation is on the line every time you interact with others. Don't ever compromise your morals.

Remember that the process of negotiation — what actually happens in an exchange — represents the value systems of those participating. If you believe it is possible to have a win-win outcome, then you bring that value to the table. (Mind you, that may not always happen.) If there are ethical conflicts, you bring your own judgment and standards to the discussion in your attempts to resolve them. Keep your head up in the process, knowing that your success in negotiation is dependent on a series of skills that you can master.

IS THAT A MISREPRESENTATION OR A LIE?

While it's true that you are not required to tell your whole "story" in the early stage of a negotiation, you may have an ethical dilemma if you are asked a direct question. Some people believe that lying is part of the game, so to speak, and it's okay to lie since everyone does it. However, an effective negotiator should not need to lie or deliberately misrepresent information. In fact, I find the fun of negotiation to be an ability to state a position the way I want others to see it and to do so without uttering a single false word.

Keep in mind that you never actually have to lie in a material way. For example, when you watch an advertisement on television and they ask you to call before midnight, do you run to the telephone? Did they tell you that they would not sell you the item after that time, or did you just assume it? And who's fault is the improper conclusion since you can buy that item for weeks and months afterwards? Just look under your bed at all the junk you have purchased this way!

Furthermore, once this lie is exposed, then the negotiator's credibility is greatly diminished. Consider how to negotiate on the up and up, with the basic truth on your side. As you will see, there is a great deal of difference between carefully planning the way in which information will be disclosed and planning to lie. How we phrase our statements is important as well.

THE STRATEGY OF WORDS

If I tell you that you must make up your mind about my job offer by tomorrow at noon, you may get the impression that I'm being a bit inflexible. You have the sense that at one minute after noon tomorrow, your chance to accept this job is over. However, if I say, "I can't guarantee that this job will available after noon tomorrow," I'm implying that the door might still be open. Therefore, I leave the door open for you to offer another statement.

Once, when Arnie had momentarily lost all his reasoning power, he told Sandra that he would never work one minute of overtime ever again. Arnie was actually angry about working overtime when his salary was inadequate. Since he wasn't involved in a salary negotiation, there was no good reason for him to make such a statement. But Arnie thought that Sandra would get the message that he was tired of the lousy money.

The message that Sandra received, however, was that Arnie was stating his intention to be uncooperative. Arnie is revealing his anger, but he's not negotiating. In fact, he's proceeding to make negotiations very difficult.

In many of life's interactions, we don't think that we are planning a strategy or measuring words for a certain effect. Certainly, in many situations, there is no need to measure words or plan strategy. Communicating with others is not always a matter of achieving something. However, when needs and desires are involved, then planning a strategy is wise, and the way we phrase our statements is a big part of that strategy. Keep this in mind as you read more about the myriad factors involved in effective negotiations.

I SHOULD'VE, I COULD'VE....

Odd as it sounds, Barry was upset when he named a price for his services and the client agreed without even a frown. He was sure that he should have asked for more, even though he asked his usual and customary fee and almost always got it. Next time, he thinks, I'm asking for a couple of thousand more and negotiate down.

To some people, Barry's attitude would seem quite silly. But to others, his attitude is logical and sound. After all, if we haven't had some give and take, then the process seems incomplete. Some people just love to put deals together.

The dissatisfaction with an immediately accepted offer is not necessarily related to objective value. Rather, it has to do with the psychology of negotiation. Most people don't want to believe that they have settled on terms that could have been better. Barry believes that his client will now begin to offer less and want more for the fee he is paying. In other words, Barry believes that he's lost a certain edge.

The bottom line is that negotiation is a psychological process. We must experience the "give and take" that accompanies the haggling over price. If someone accepts our offer too quickly, we think we have offered too much. We'd actually feel better paying more for an item if the other person would only fight with us over the price. We need to experience the process. One secret to successful negotiation is to recognize that the "give-and-take" is unavoidable, so don't try to skip it.

Most people in business have had the experience of stating a fee — or being offered a fee — that is well outside the range that is possible for the person making the offer or the request. David, a friend of mine who is a fine arts photographer, makes part of his living photographing family events. A friend called him and asked him what he charged. When he named his standard fee and included an explanation of what was included in that fee, the friend was horrified and said so. "I didn't think an artist could demand that kind of money," she said.

To this woman, an artist, by definition, should starve and she put little value on creative work. Therefore, anything but a token fee of a few dollars just to cover expenses was too much. In this case, negotiations were simply not possible because the gap between client's expectation and the value this artist placed on his work was too vast. They had a Grand Canyon of difference. Kristie, another friend of mine who consults with professional health care practitioners, was asked, "How can a woman charge a fee like that?" The gap between the client's expectation and the consultant's standard fee was also too large to overcome. He assumed that a woman would work for less than her male counterparts. In this case, there was simply no sense in carrying the negotiations further, because an untenable psychological situation had been set up. (Fortunately, Kristie is a successful consultant, good at what she does, and didn't need the work. If she had encountered this man during a dry spell in her business, the dynamics and deal might have been different.)

At other times, misunderstandings merely mean that we need to step back and reevaluate. Perhaps the gap seems wide but we can close it with clarification. Marcia, who offers $100,000 for a house valued at $150,000, calculated her offer based on eliminating from the deal the five acres of land adjacent to the house. Unfortunately, the seller didn't know that and he was insulted by the offer. A few phone calls clarified the offer, and in this case, the seller was happy to proceed with the negotiations. He still had land to sell or build on and Marcia had the house at a price she could afford. In this case, the Grand Canyon became a bubbling brook that could be crossed in one small leap.

ARE YOU, OR ARE YOU NOT, MY ENEMY?

It's difficult to avoid the notion that negotiating is an activity carried out between adversaries, or at least by fierce competitors. However, we may approach the process with a more positive attitude if we think of it as parties coming together with a set of interests and needs. We can't expect a person to come away satisfied with the outcome of negotiations if his or her basic needs and interests are not fulfilled. Therefore, negotiations should proceed with the goal to meet three broad levels of satisfaction.

Basic Needs: In any negotiation we must get our basic

needs satisfied. If we are negotiating work hours with a potential employer we may have a fundamental need to work forty hours a week. That's our minimum requirement. So, if there is a full-time job open, then we have the basis to negotiate. If a part-time job is offered, then we may have an insurmountable gap. However, I recently heard about a situation in which the employer, who wanted to hire a particular person but could only offer him part-time work, called a colleague and found that he too had a part-time job opening. A day of negotiations produced two part-time jobs for a person who had the financial need to work forty hours a week. You might say that the fundamental need was met.

Michael's fundamental need was to play golf on his vacation. He isn't aware of it yet, but all his other needs are secondary. He doesn't know this because he hasn't thought it out. Perhaps in the course of her negotiations Jackie will nudge him to think about needs versus desires.

Arnie hasn't determined his basic needs, a situation that is working against him when he plans his negotiations. He is not unusual, however, because many of us confuse what is essential with what we would like in addition to the basic need. In a sense, this has to do with lack of training, not only in the art of negotiation, but also about a lack of information concerning the various ways we can clarify our values.

Intermediate Wants: Beyond our basic need to work forty hours a week, we may have a desire for (but could live without) health insurance. Our two part-time employers understand this and each offers an additional sum of money so that we can buy our own. Neither is obligated, but both want to hire us and they offer this extra employment incentive so that we don't look further for a full-time job. (It could be argued, that we actually don't need to work forty hours; rather, we have a need for a certain minimal sum of money. Maybe we could find a job that gave us the same money for only 30 hours a week. But that's a different issue.)

Michael wants Jackie with him on his vacation, not necessarily because he wants her company, but because he thinks they're supposed to be together. He's expressing a value here, a desire based on an assumption he's made. Perhaps he'll be happy with another arrangement when it's presented. We don't know yet.

Arnie is interested in making more money. He also wants respect and a sense that the company believes he is valuable. To him, this translates into monetary reward. But, what if Arnie were offered some perks or some equal value trade-offs? Perhaps Sandra will be able to negotiate with Arnie for something other than direct salary increases.

Highest Achievable: We decide that we would like a month of paid vacation, so now that we have these two job offers, we go for more. Each employer could offer two weeks a piece, we say, of paid vacation. Well, we've pushed too far. Part-time employees get five days paid vacation in these firms. We'll get two weeks and that's what we'd be likely to get in one full-time position. One of our potential employers is now getting a bit impatient with us, but we're smart and know when we have a pretty good deal. Most professional negotiators agree that it is in this highest level of negotiation that unfair or unethical tactics are most likely to emerge.

It's important to differentiate the levels and categories of needs and desires when entering a negotiation. It is through this process that we can later evaluate our results. If we decide that we will pay $100,000 for a house, we need to define what our basic needs are for that house. For example, we must have three bedrooms and two bathrooms. We need a fireplace and a front porch. We would like to live in one of four neighborhoods—any one of them will do. These are our basic needs.

Our first job is to communicate our requirements to the real estate broker with whom we work. Perhaps we have some intermediate desires. Three bathrooms would be preferable; a full basement would be a plus, too. Four bedrooms would be even better. A double lot would represent one of our highest achievable goals.

A savvy broker might ask us if we care about a modern kitchen or big windows or a landscaped yard. He or she might determine if these are secondary or intermediate needs or simply have no relevance. Perhaps we're willing to trade off a few things in order to get those features we consider basic.

One available house is almost perfect. But it doesn't have a fireplace and one of the bathrooms is only a half-bath. Do we turn it down? Maybe, maybe not. As it turns out, the price of the house is a bit less than $100,000, and the broker tells us that there is an exterior wall appropriate for installing a fireplace.

We investigate prices of adding fireplaces and converting the half bath into a full-size bathroom. We find that we can take one large bedroom and turn it into two rooms. We can use some of the money that we would have paid for a house to make these alterations. But there won't be quite enough money, so we negotiate with each other to determine if we're willing to wait for the fireplace or the bathroom or whatever.

Next, we attempt to learn if the owner is eager to sell the house. This could influence the size of the offer we make. If we find out that the owner is being transferred out of state and must leave in 30 days, we determine that the asking price is probably quite flexible. Furthermore, the owner has been in the house for only a year, and we learn that the price was considerably lower and virtually no improvements have been made to the property. So, adjusted for inflation, we make a considerably lower offer.

The owners are not happy, but they knew they were asking a high price. They're pleased about getting a buyer so fast and their counter-offer is modest enough to save some face, so to speak. We accept and the paperwork is started. The owner negotiates to take a few things out of the house that were included in the original inventory to compensate for the lower price. Basic needs are being negotiated all around. We get some intermediate needs met, but in this case, the seller doesn't. It isn't exactly win-win, but the seller is able to move knowing that the house is sold.

We've taken advantage of the owner's need to sell, which is not unethical by any means. We could say that the seller had a need for peace of mind, in that he wanted to leave the area free from any burden of that house. The seller also traded off the lower price for more of the inventory of the house, which is also completely ethical.

Obviously, negotiations could have broken down and no one's needs would have been met if everyone involved had simply said, "Oh well, we can't go anywhere here—it's all written in stone."

NEEDS AND WANTS — FIGURE THEM OUT

Before you begin negotiating anything, assess your own needs and wants. How can you determine the best outcome if you haven't established a hierarchy of needs? We always communicate more effectively when we have clear, organized thoughts and ideas about a situation. I believe negotiation breaks down because we haven't clarified these things for ourselves before we begin. It's too easy to believe that we've been taken advantage of when we claim that we need and want everything available. Business, law, family life, and relationships between friends and lovers simply don't work quite that way.

CHAPTER EIGHT

Keys DO Open Doors

OUR NEGOTIATORS HAVE MANY ISSUES TO NEGOTIATE. Arnie is still determined to get his raise. Michael and Jackie must figure out what they're going to do on their vacation. Julie must attempt to win working three days a week in her home office, and Tony and Cathy need to decide how to achieve a new office arrangement, one that will give them more room to work. How well these negotiations turn out for all parties involved depends on many things, including how well the keys to successful negotiation are understood. All the following keys will discussed in full later on, but for now, let's look at them as a whole.

PREPARATION

Arnie rarely thinks about this concept; Michael thinks he doesn't have to prepare to discuss any issue involving his family. The rest of our negotiators have varying degrees of understanding of the importance of preparation. However, let's agree from the outset that the idea of preparing to negotiate is a simple, fundamental key to success—no exceptions, no excuses. When we hear coaches talking about working on fundamentals in baseball or basketball, they are talking about a basic set of skills required to play the game at any level. When we decide to negotiate about an issue in our lives, it makes no sense to be well-schooled in communication skills without understanding preparation. It's fundamental to everything we do.

There is no other factor more important than preparation because it incorporates and integrates so many things. Part of Arnie's preparation is discovering his needs. Well, he says he needs a 20 percent raise. That's his stated need, but what are his others? Does Arnie actually need something else, something that this raise is just but one part? Furthermore, Arnie hasn't determined Sandra's needs or for that matter, the needs of the company.

Preparation may also influence what information we disclose and what we protect—or hold back for some reason. We may also decide how best to communicate our three levels of needs, wants, and achievable goals when we prepare to negotiate. We may spend time preparing facts and figures—especially if we anticipate that the other parties involved will be producing information as well.

What if Arnie has no information about comparable salaries for identical staff positions in his own or other companies? For her part, Jackie could present some information about lake-side cabins that are close to golf courses.

Taking the necessary time to prepare to negotiate has many psychological advantages, too. When we are well-prepared we exude confidence because we feel internally confident. We enter a negotiation knowing the weaknesses and strengths of our positions. Let's face it, we are far more likely to become flustered and lose our composure if we aren't prepared. Doesn't this make sense in a process that is fundamentally a psychological one?

FAMILIARITY

This is closely related to preparation, as are all the factors mentioned here. When we evaluate our hierarchy of needs and desires, we become more familiar with ourselves—our motivations, desires, goals, and plans. We may also become more familiar with the needs and desires of the other parties involved.

In simple terms, we would say that Arnie must become familiar with his own thought processes and the needs that Sandra will certainly state in her part of the negotiation. These would include the issues that could logically be known to Arnie right from the beginning.

ANTICIPATION

In addition to what Arnie can absolutely know and prepare for, there may be other needs and interests that arise. What can he anticipate? In other words, for what should he plan? If Michael were thinking clearly, what issues can he anticipate that Jackie will surely raise? What issues will she raise that might compete with on the one hand, or be similar to, on the other, his interests?

When Tony and Cathy prepare to negotiate for their new office space, what issues should they assume will be raised at some point? They might have become familiar with their office building and be aware of some currently empty spaces, but what if those offices are already earmarked for someone else? How can they anticipate this? They may not be able to cover all the conceivable objections raised, but they can anticipate as many as possible.

Unfortunately, most of us do not anticipate the kinds of things that could happen in negotiations because we have neither prepared ourselves nor become familiar with the potential needs and desires of others involved. When people become surprised by things they could have anticipated, they tend to lose a sense of personal confidence and even a sense of power. This is not power over someone else, but rather the sense that they are personally empowered.

Julie, who wants to work at home three days a week, would

be foolish to just ask for this provision in her working agreement without preparing herself. If she said, "Hey, Joe, I'd like to work three days a week from home," she would lose a sense of her personal power if Joe responded, "What? Are you nuts—nobody does that in this company." Joe might even think she's joking. If she didn't plan her proposal carefully, all the while anticipating possible objections, she would end up feeling a loss of self-respect and perhaps even be worried that her position in the company was seriously weakened.

You might be thinking about situations in which you felt shot down, so to speak, and now you feel bad about it because you hadn't done your homework. Well, you can change this from now on—at least once you finish reading this book. You're mastering a skill that you probably were never taught in the first place. You're preparing to replace a lack of confidence with a sense of personal empowerment and new-found strength.

EVALUATION

This is a key that many people overlook. But evaluation of options, possible challenges, and so forth, is part of choosing your position and planning your strategy. An element of evaluation involves considering the personalities of the other parties. We already know, for example, that Arnie's boss, Sandra, is prone to making negative statements about the condition of the company. She operates from fear much of the time. We know this, but does Arnie?

Arnie may have the facts; he might even characterize Sandra as a negative person, but has he evaluated this information in preparation for his negotiation? Probably not yet. You see, Arnie just files away these things as facts, but he hasn't done much with his impressions or even with those things he knows to be true. He hasn't compared them with other things he knows about Sandra—what he perceives as her basic honesty, for example.

Therefore, he doesn't know what techniques to use when talking with Sandra, nor does he know how to use these facts to plan his strategy. However, he's going to learn. If he doesn't, he'll spend his life moaning and groaning over his fate. Unfortunately, that's what many of us do. Fortunately, we can change. We can learn to evaluate information and use our conclusions to shape our negotiating tasks.

CONTROL

When we prepare and become familiar with the issues involved, anticipate needs and desires of all parties, evaluate the information we gather, and so forth, then we are more likely to be able to control elements in the process. If Michael tells Jackie that they are going to a particular golf resort and that's that, she might, if she's prepared, tell him that the cabin on the lake she would like to go to is a mere three miles from that resort. In a sense, Michael has lost some control because he is not prepared to receive this information. He is left with little but his usual response, that all this other information doesn't matter.

But Jackie could proceed to another stage in the negotiation from there. In a sense, she has control of the negotiation, because she has control of the information. Michael has nothing but his posturing from which to operate.

Let's say that we know that Julie has had a job offer that will allow her to work at home. If Julie's boss just laughs off her request and doesn't take it seriously, then she might choose to disclose this information. Determining when to disclose this fact is part of Julie's strategy in controlling certain aspects of the negotiating process.

Having control doesn't mean that we have the right to lie or deceive another party. It simply means that the work we've done to prepare helps us maintain our position and not be shocked or thrown off track by unanticipated questions, facts, positions, and so on.

UNDERSTANDING

Arnie might decide to reevaluate his position about a 20 percent raise. He could make this decision based on understanding the limitations he learns about when he educates himself. Perhaps one limitation is the financial state of the company. Another could be a recent incident that made Arnie look bad with a customer.

Or, there might be logical boundaries involved. A worker at a fast-food chain will earn a salary within a certain range. A person who attempts to get a salary that is twice the amount of the highest salary in that range is not understanding boundaries. On the other hand, what if we didn't explore boundaries at all? What if we made assumptions that simply don't hold up against the facts as we later learn them to be? If Cathy and Tony hadn't explored the possible office space that is or could be made available, they might have assumed that there was none available. They could have imagined boundaries and limitations that weren't actually there.

COMMUNICATION

We emphasize communication skills because we know that all the preparation in the world won't help us if we can't communicate our plan, a strategy, the facts as we know them, or our needs and wants. Poor communication is the single most prevalent problem plaguing negotiators. An inability to meaningfully express needs, desires, and positions may stand in the way of establishing rapport. Poor communication may cause all other parties some discomfort, perhaps enough discomfort to halt negotiations.

What if Michael decided to try the so-called silent treatment? Jackie states her needs and he walks out of the room, not because he is angry, but because he refuses to communicate? What if Julie sent a memo to her boss, which stated that as of mid-year, she was working at home three days a week.

Obviously, this is a poor way to start a negotiation. In fact, she is not even offering to negotiate and is communicating very poorly. Arnie's original idea to just storm into Sandra's office and demand more money falls into this same category. It's not that the expectations are off base; it's in the "how to do it" area that we place our criticism.

Not all faulty communication is this obvious. Sometimes, poor communication skills are manifested in more subtle ways. Rigid, hostile body language coupled with soft, friendly speech is inconsistent and may leave parties confused. Interrupting others while they're talking is another indication that the ability to communicate is weak at best. And remember, people can interrupt without being outwardly aggressive or brash, further confusing the situation.

If a person begins a negotiation session by mentioning irrelevant details about another party's family or religion, we would say that things have started off on the wrong foot, or with bad vibrations, or with a cloud hanging over it—depending on how you like to express yourself. Take your choice.

PREPARATION MOVES: FROM HERE TO THERE AND BEYOND

You have a fact here and an impression there and some vague information that you are trying to clarify. So, you have begun your preparation. You call your assistant to clarify some data and you sit down with a notebook and a pencil in a coffee shop to make notes and think about what your goals are in this situation. Later, you list some questions that must be answered before you can pin down two or three facts that are needed to complete one piece of your plan.

What you are doing here is engaging in the progressive nature of planning and preparation. You state what you do know, you clarify what you don't know, you begin to frame your own list of needs and interests. This process could apply to many situations, from buying a house to negotiating for a raise to dividing up the housework at home. What if you and I lived together and I came up with a list of household chores that I thought you should do. Imagine as well that I hadn't asked you about this distribution of chores, nor had I noted what chores you seem to do energetically and without griping.

If I left a note for you on the kitchen table stating that I had completed the division of chores, you would be understandably resentful, even if you ultimately agreed with the substance of the division. The problem, once again, lies in how the matter was handled.

Progressive preparation might involve some observations on my part. I would note that you appear to like the yard work and you also like to cook. I notice too, that you wait until the last minute to do the laundry. I can deal with the laundry and I'd sure like it if I didn't have to buy groceries or cook. You don't even see dust but I'm always cleaning, watering the plants, and straightening up. So far, I've done some preparation about possible division of the chores, based on my observations and some of my needs or interests. However, I still have some work to do.

When and where will I approach you about my ideas? Will I wake you from a deep sleep in the middle of the night? Or, will I leave a note for you and suggest one or two possible times we can talk? If you say yes to a particular time, can I state clearly what my goal is? How will I react if you tell me you'd like a little time to think about the issue before we talk? Am I prepared for you to take this position? In fact, do I perhaps plan for that possibility and ask questions about the amount of time you'll need?

Well, you're leaving town for four days and can't even consider this issue until you get home. I know that, but I'm leaving town just about the time you get back. We set up a time to talk in about 10 days. Makes sense. We've established a time and now we decide that we'll go to the cafe down the street and talk about our chores there. We haven't seen each other very much lately and it would be good to go out and have a meal together.

You'll bring your list of needs and interests and perhaps even a sample plan for the division of the chores. We'll compare our notes and see what we can create. (If we weren't getting along very well, it might be a bad idea to go to this cafe. We could be setting ourselves up for a public argument.)

I've included a form for you to use as you prepare to negotiate, giving you a visual image of the progressive preparation pattern. Use it to plan an upcoming occasion for negotiation. Use it, even if it seems a bit formal to you, to record your process. Believe me, it's not frivolous. You will learn important elements in the process when using the form for even a small issue. Then, when a major negotiation is going to take place, you'll have some experience in negotiating.

There are many tools that can help us in our planning and defining our positions. Remember, we're trying to bring together our levels of need and the practical steps we need to take to prepare to negotiate.

YOU'RE NOT IN THIS ALONE

Arnie, Julie, Michael, and Tony and Cathy must become aware of the needs of the other parties involved. Why are they spending time doing that right now? Well, most of us "get on a roll," so to speak, when we begin to think about what we want and how we're going to get it. Let's say that through brainstorming, Arnie determines that he wants a raise, plus a new office, and two additional weeks of paid vacation. Arnie, being Arnie, becomes fixated on these items and begins to think of them as goals.

What if no one in Arnie's company has a private office except for Sandra and the two owners? The other 30 people share office space with at least four other people. And Arnie's company offers all employees who have worked for them more five years

25 days of paid vacation. Arnie has now determined that he wants 35 days. So, he begins to think that if he doesn't get these things, then all is lost and he's been defeated.

You might be thinking that Arnie hasn't looked at the facts before he begins formulating his own goals. You'd be right. He's not looking at anything but those things he's been day-dreaming about. The other party involved, in this case, Sandra, has goals, restrictions, needs, interests, and so forth. If Arnie doesn't spend some time considering the other party, then he's entering the negotiation process with a weak position, not a strong one.

When you consider the other party in your preparation, you are not necessarily cutting down your options. Rather, you are recognizing that you are part of a give and take process. The other party has his or her own set of objectives too. While you don't want to limit yourself too early in the process, neither do you want to form goals that are not within possible parameters.

SENDING YOUR BRAIN OUT TO STORM

Brainstorming is an old technique that works in many settings. You can, for example, use it when you're trying to solve a problem that has been lurking about in your life. The problem could involve only you or it could affect others as well. The technique is often used by people meeting in groups who are trying to come up with ideas to improve a situation or establish direction.

A company might initiate a brainstorming session to come up with ideas for a new marketing plan. An organization could brainstorm to come up with fundraising ideas or techniques to recruit new members. You and your life partner could brainstorm to discover the decor you want in your new home.

The key to effective brainstorming is to keep the flow of ideas coming — you don't want to eliminate anything out of hand, no matter how ridiculous it sounds. This is very important. My friend Brian, a master in marketing, likes to point out his favorite part of brainstorming, which is the tendency to stimulate creativity, thoughts, and impulsive ideas. That's the point. But this creative thinking can be shut down in a hurry if someone says, "No, no, that's silly (or stupid, out in left field, or impossible)."

Let's say that Arnie is describing his ideal job, a process that has nothing to do with his current job. He sits down to brainstorm and comes up with a long list of items that would be part of his dream job. Included on that list are the 35 days of vacation and a private office. That's fine. We won't tell Arnie he can't have those things. We won't judge or critique or in any way shoot down those items that were written down on his brainstorming list. In fact, Arnie would probably benefit from this kind of exercise — as we all would. Brainstorming is a valuable tool to expand our mental horizons and ultimately, expand our view of what is possible for us to have or accomplish.

Maybe, just maybe, when Arnie begins to negotiate for a raise, he'll be able to get some of the other things he'd like that ended up on his list — access to an employee membership at a health club down the street, for example. (Others in the company do have that employee perk, so we know that the company won't have to create something new just for him. This is part of the preparation.) The point is that Arnie will be negotiating with a real person in an actual company; he's not negotiating with an ideal.

This distinction is important because we know that Arnie and our other friends may use brainstorming in many settings, and their purpose is to produce information that can later be analyzed and shaped. Therefore, the context is important. Ideas will be generated about the situation before them, not about an irrelevant set of circumstances or problems

THE CABIN ON THE GOLF COURSE

Let's say that Michael and Jackie decide to figure out what to do about the problems they are having over their vacation plans.

Michael has agreed to engage in a brainstorming session, which is a big step for him because he had previously been so obstinate. Now he realizes that he can't dictate the plans. Jackie is not agreeing to the golf resort option — at least not for her. Before they begin, Jackie describes the process of brainstorming and explains the ground rules.

First, the question is posed. In their case, the question is: How can we plan a two week vacation which will satisfy both of us? Second, any and all ideas generated are recorded (yes, written down, because each item is important and should be remembered). Third, no idea is eliminated during this stage of the process. Fourth, no idea is laughed at, ridiculed, or judged as it's put on the table. Fifth, these ideas don't have to be practical or feasible; they are simply ideas and thoughts and the parties don't have to offer proof of their viability.

Michael and Jackie were both somewhat familiar with this process, having used it in work settings. However, they had never used it at home, and Michael wasn't pleased that their conflict had reached this point. Still, he agreed to the ground rules. During their session they came up with the following ideas:

1. They would go to the resort that Michael chose, which had a swimming pool for Jackie.
2. They would go to a cabin on a lake that was close to a public golf course.
3. Jackie would rent a cabin and stay there by herself for two weeks.
4. Michael would go to the resort by himself.
5. Jackie would rent a cabin for herself and visit Michael at the resort on the three weekends involved. She'd stay by herself at the cabin during the week.
6. They would buy a cabin near a golf course and settle the whole issue forever.
7. Michael would stay with Jackie during the week and go by

himself to the golf resort on the weekends.

8. They would stay home and Michael would play golf at the club near their house and Jackie would relax at home.

Without too much difficulty, they eliminated option eight. They put it aside, however, as a reasonable plan if, for some unforeseen reason in the future, they didn't have the money to go away. But this year, they had discretionary income and didn't need to use that option. They also eliminated option six because they didn't have enough money to actually buy a cabin, or even time to look for such an arrangement for this year. However, they did hold it out as a possible solution for the future.

Jackie was strongly against option one, because it effectively kept her from getting the solitude she wanted. Besides, it put them back to the proverbial square one. They'd exercised that option for years! Michael didn't want to wile away his days at a cabin, wishing he were at a golf course, so option two was eliminated. Options three and four were acceptable to Jackie, although she didn't really want to be away from Michael for that long. Michael didn't favor those options either because he didn't like the idea of separate vacations. It went against his idea of what a married couple's vacation should be.

They were left with options two, five, and seven. Each sensed a deadlock. Michael wondered if Jackie would agree to the weekend visits, and Jackie correctly assumed that Michael would hate the idea of playing golf only on weekends. Knowing this, she agreed to drop option seven. She didn't want Michael to be miserable just to make her happy, and a glum, restless companion would ruin her solitude anyway. Now they were down to options two and five.

Michael and Jackie had come a long way. While option two was the best — they both agreed on that—they weren't sure they had time to find a suitable place that would satisfy them both. Michael was happy in a cabin if he could drive to a golf course every day and have lunch with new golfing friends. Jackie would have the solitude she craved during the day and Michael's company in the evening. Option five was their second choice, mostly because it would likely involve long drives back and forth for Jackie and taking two cars on their vacation.

Because of brainstorming and honest discussion, Michael and Jackie have narrowed their task to locating the best place available that is acceptable to both of them. Before brainstorming they were deadlocked in a power struggle. Sometimes brainstorming can actually lead to consensus and actual negotiation time is minimized. Do you see the application of the process in your own life?

TONY AND CATHY USE THEIR HEADS

Tony and Cathy want new office space and they are prepared to negotiate for it. When they brainstorm they are discovering the possible ways to solve a problem and get what they need. When they brainstormed with each other, they came up with the following list:

1. Relocate to an available space two floors below the main office.
2. Exchange offices with a person across the hall. That person works alone and could manage fine with a smaller space.
3. Knock out a wall in their current office, which would allow them to expand into the supply room.
4. Ask the company to relocate the whole operation to a larger suite of offices. They've noticed that almost everyone is crowded into space that has become inadequate. Tony and Cathy will volunteer to serve on the working group conducting the search.
5. Move some of their file cabinets and storage boxes to a couple of closets in other offices; they will then have room to spread themselves out in their current space.
6. Look for jobs in different companies, effectively breaking

up their current working partnership.

7. Look for jobs in a different company that will hire them as a team.
8. Quit their jobs and start a business of their own.

As we said, nothing is too ridiculous to mention in a brainstorming session. Cathy and Tony eliminated option six because neither one wanted to go through the process of changing direction and they enjoyed working as a team. Besides, they liked the company for which they were already working. Interestingly enough, option eight was retained — not for the moment, but as a viable idea for future reference. In fact, each had wondered at times if their partnership wouldn't be enhanced in a small firm of their own. They'd just never said this out loud to each other or to anyone else. And, once on the table, it was never put aside.

Tony and Cathy had a short term problem though, and that was what to do about their office situation *now*. In their case, they decided to take a close look at options one through five, but after their discussion about starting their own company, they decided not to put option four on the table. That left them with some solutions that involved small, relatively quick solutions to the dilemma at hand.

Their task now was to determine the best options to take to the negotiating table. Remember, they are not the decision-makers. They could put in a request for a joint meeting with the office manager or one of the owners, but in making this request, they would need to prepare. They fully expected that a request for a new office would be met with, "What? You must be joking," response. So, instead they were preparing a list of options, which included a hierarchy of value to them.

Defining their situation in current terms, they preferred option one. There was a large space available in the building and it was only two floors below the current corporate offices. This was ideal in that they did much of their work alone and generally worked on site. However, they knew that this would involve extra expense for the company. But they also noted that others in the office were complaining about lack of space, too. If they proposed moving their space, others might follow along. So, while that was their first choice, they decided on a hierarchy of preferences with other options following.

Option two was their next favorite option, but that involved displacing another person. Tony and Cathy thought that this person didn't need such a big space, but that was their opinion, and one not necessarily shared by others, particularly their co-worker who would have to move. Still, their current office has a window and other desirable features, and the bigger office –doesn't. They decided to check this option with the affected person before they put it on the negotiating agenda.

Option three would do — but that involved a major construction project. They would have to meet that possible objection in their negotiation session with the office manager. They would need to determine potential costs and the office building's regulations.

Their least favorite option was moving their files and storing material in various closets in other offices. This solution might not sit well with those in the other offices, but everyone knows that Cathy and Tony are more crowded than anyone else in the company. It isn't unreasonable to expect some cooperation. Tony and Cathy are in the process of preparing to negotiate. They've done some preliminary work and they've also kept other parties in mind. What if they were to simply ask for the office space of their co-worker? They would probably find themselves in a situation fraught with conflict. Instead, they are carefully planning their strategy—and it's possible that a new business might come out of their brainstorming.

JULIE CONFRONTS BIG OBSTACLES

Julie has always liked to work alone and with today's office technology, she knows how easy it would be to do much of her work from a home office. Julie knows that many companies are instituting these work-at-home programs, referred to as telecommuting. But, her challenge is to convince her boss that she has a viable plan. Her brainstorming involves thinking of all the ways in which her plan benefits the company, while being workable.

Her list looks like this:

1. She is better able to concentrate when working alone.
2. Her productivity will increase because she is free of unnecessary interruptions.
3. Her office phone and fax can be forwarded to her home office, thereby lessening the secretary's work load.
4. Clients can reach her directly, without going through the company's switchboard.
5. Telecommuting programs have been mandated by the city and state as part of energy conservation and to take pressure off the highway system. The company would move toward compliance with this mandate.
6. Her two days in the office, consulting with coworkers and handling certain in-office issues, will be more productive because her other work will be handled at home.
7. She can offer to consider her work-at-home plan as experimental and up for a review every three months. That way, neither she nor the company is locked into a plan.

In Julie's case, her brainstorming will not involve a hierarchy. Rather, it represents information that Julie will use in her session. In a sense, she's brainstorming in anticipation of objections that are bound to be raised.

ARNIE MAKES A START

Arnie has a lot of work to do. Brainstorming is a new process for Arnie, one that feels odd to him. He's used to thinking about what he wants and being resentful when he doesn't get it. Now, he has to think about a bigger picture. His initial list looks like this:

1. Document his salary history over the years he's been with the company.
2. Document salaries of comparable positions in other companies.
3. Prepare of list of his accomplishments with the company, paying special attention to his expanding role in new projects.
4. List recent responsibilities that have been added to his work load and have expanded his job description.
5. That reminds him that he needs to review the job description on file and compare it to what he actually does every day.
6. Document his role in increasing profits for the company. He knows that he has saved at least three accounts, because of his experience combined with his ability to get along with clients.
7. Find out how many employees are given memberships to a health club down the street and determine if at his level, he qualifies for such a benefit.
8. Decide the range of salary increase that will be acceptable to him. In order to do this, he must complete his documentation.
9. Begin to think about what Sandra is likely to say about raises and other company policies that affect him.

Arnie, like our other friends, has made a start. As you can see, Arnie is just beginning to think about the obvious. Before he learned something about the process of negotiation, he would have just walked into Sandra's office and demanded a raise. But now he realizes that he must prepare. He must gather information, think about his positions, and go from there. He may be a neophyte, but he's learning. Arnie will eventually move on to a different stage of brainstorming, one that will involve determining his goals and objectives.

BRAINSTORMING LEADS TO PROGRESS

Interesting things can happen when we brainstorm and begin evaluating our goals and objectives. Remember that Michael and Jackie were simply trying to solve a problem between them, one that could have led to long-term resentments. In fact, those resentments had already built up. Jackie was sick and tired of being dragged along to golf resorts just because Michael liked them. Michael, although on an intellectual level he knew better, was upset that Jackie would actually refuse to go along with his plan. Cathy and Tony needed more office space. It was that simple and it was the reason for their brainstorming session.

In both cases, the brainstorming process opened up new paths, new ways to view a dilemma. Each idea was evaluated later for feasibility and in some cases, set aside for further consideration. Other ideas were eliminated and time wasn't spent on further evaluation. We also watched as our friends were able to determine some initial challenges that faced them as they moved through the process.

Tony and Cathy couldn't demand their coworker's office; Michael and Jackie couldn't afford to purchase a piece of property that would solve their conflict. Arnie realized that he had much work to do before he would get his raise; Julie knew that she was breaking new ground and objections would surely fly. However, each could explore these other options before going ahead with other choices.

AN EYE ON THE PRIZE

It's important to remember that both the brainstorming process and determining the best options are done with a goal in mind. Arnie has a stated goal of getting a raise. Actually Arnie's goal is to get better compensation. That compensation could take forms other than cash in his pocket. Until he sat down and did some thinking and brainstorming he wasn't aware of the flexibility of the concept of compensation.

Tony and Cathy present an interesting example of how goals can be expanded. In the weeks that followed their brainstorming session, the two colleagues and friends discussed their primary goal of expanded office space. But they found that the idea of starting their own new business kept creeping into the discussion. One evening they stayed late at the office to look at the feasibility of their idea.

"Don't we have to separate these two issues?," Cathy asked. "Yes, we do keep mixing up the two ideas when we talk," Tony agreed. They decided to discuss the possibility of starting their own business, independent of the their current space needs. That involved some brainstorming, first to determine if they really wanted to do it, second to evaluate the feasibility, and third to figure out the steps they would need to take if in fact, they decided to do more exploring. In their case, it turned out to be an exciting process.

Let me explain what I mean by exciting. When we are creatively brainstorming we usually feel energized and alive. We are generating ideas and involving all our mental capacities. Later, when we begin to go through the ideas and explore them, we may feel emotionally flat about some and enthusiastic about others. These responses are important. Tony and Cathy both felt a surge of energy when they came up with the idea, which seemed absurd at first, to start their own firm. The ideas for converting office space each brought its own emotional response. They liked the idea of moving their office to a different floor. That sounded great. But then, they became reluctant to bring it up because of the other idea—the actual possibility that they would leave the company in the near future. Hence, their after-hours meeting.

Tony suggested that they first examine setting up their own company. What were the advantages and disadvantages? Their brainstorming looked something like this:

1. They worked well together and enjoyed each other's

company besides.

2. They trusted each other.
3. They had complementary skills and talents.
4. They had job security and good salaries in their current positions.
5. Businesses often failed and what made them think they would be different?
6. They both worked hard, were creative, and loved what they did for a living.
7. They didn't know how much money they'd need to strike out on their own.
8. They could initially work out of their home, which would save some start-up costs.
9. Working for themselves would involve a lot of self-discipline.
10. How would they market their business?
11. How long would it take to do the necessary research?
12. They liked the company they worked for.
13. Would they miss their coworkers?

As you can see, Tony and Cathy came up with both statements and questions. They had to think about the feasibility of their idea and do some research and planning if they were going to move ahead. Tony suggested that they take three months to study the idea, which would involve thinking about start-up costs, coming up with a viable mission statement for a new business, and so forth.

Both would do some self-evaluation to determine if they had the discipline to work on their own. This would mean setting their own deadlines, marketing their services, and in short, wearing all the hats that small business owners by necessity must don. They also had to be honest about their own financial status at this time. This discussion was moving their already close relationship to a different level.

Cathy agreed with the three month period to think and study, but she also had an excited feeling in her solar plexus. "I just can't imagine that we will say no to this idea," she said. "I agree," Tony said, "but we can't decide this all today and we need to solve the other problem about which we started this conversation."

The two friends decided that the space issue was still on the table. Even if they left the company a year from now, they still needed the new space. But they were approaching this from an entirely different stand-point. They had two potential goals, and while one was long-term and one was immediate, they approached them as concurrent though separate.

Arnie didn't have this concern. His goal was better compensation. Julie's goal was working at home part of the work week. Michael and Jackie wanted to take a mutually satisfying vacation. In all cases, the brainstorming they did enabled them to come up with goals and objectives that were clear and within each goal, options appeared. Their task was to review their options and evaluate them. Each option could be placed on a continuum. On the form at the end of this chapter, we can see how the options appear when actually pictured this way.

The visual continuum also helps you spot illogical or completely untenable options, those that have no relationship to the stated goal. For example, Tony and Cathy's option to start a business wasn't going to be used in any way during their negotiations over office space. They weren't going to threaten to leave if their office space problem wasn't solved. Instead, they took that idea off the table and put it, figuratively speaking, on an entirely different table. Yes, it influenced their position, but it no longer confused them as they prepared to negotiate.

CREATE AND CALCULATE

A process of evaluating and establishing goals then leads to creating a position. The position is then presented at the negotiating table. If a family has evaluated what they want and need in a new house, they are in the process of establishing a position they then take to a real estate agent. This gives the agent information on which to act, which in turn simplifies the entire process from beginning to end.

If you're negotiating with your teenager over telephone rules, your goal might be to keep the phone free for your own use during certain hours. A secondary goal might be to lessen the conflict in your home. You might also recognize that the hours spent on the phone are undermining your adolescent's performance at school. Your goal becomes complex in a sense, because you have a number of different issues, some involving your own well-being, some involving the well-being of your child. Your position, the actual bargaining position you take, will have to cover all these areas. Because you are the parent, you may determine that some points are less "negotiable" than others.

In a similar way, Tony and Cathy would be foolish if they didn't put their negotiating points on a continuum, in order to have a range of acceptable solutions. A range of acceptable solutions then makes it possible to have what we call integrative potential (excuse the jargon). In short, integrative potential is the extent to which the parties can reach an agreement to each of their satisfactions. All our negotiators should have the expectation that they can reach a satisfactory solution.

Reality is also part of integrative potential. For example, if Arnie stuck to his demand for 35 days of paid vacation, then he is putting himself in a situation where negotiations can break down easily—and fast. What if you insisted that your teenager never use the telephone at all? What if Tony and Cathy determined that they had only one acceptable option, that of taking over the space belonging to another person? What if Julie decided that if she couldn't work at home three full days a week, then she'd be defeated? Perhaps these positions aren't realistic, and may need modification in order to have the expectation that a satisfactory agreement can result.

WHAT MORE DO YOU WANT?

Let's say that Tony and Cathy decide on three acceptable alternative plans to solve their space problem. However, they still like the idea of moving to an empty, larger office. Should they keep that on the table after all? Perhaps they eliminated it too fast. Perhaps they should offer it as an opening, optimal position. Sure, it's more than they would actually find acceptable, but they aren't sure that they will start their own company, and even if they do, that space could be used for new employees.

So, when all is said and done, they determine to use this idea as an opening position. Who knows? They could find that it is a very acceptable position to their supervisors. Let's just say that it isn't outside the range of reality.

Arnie's 35 days of vacation is also outside the range of reality, but his health club membership probably isn't. Once he determines how many employees have this perk, he'll be in a better position to decide if this should be a negotiable item on his agenda.

Julie is introducing an innovative program in her company, so she can't be as sure what the reaction to her proposal is going to be. In Julie's case, however, she has decided to put her ideas in the form of a written proposal. In fact, she might find that all her negotiations are done through written material. Through the process of thinking out a position, she can determine just what she should ask for. Some of the items might be more than she would find merely acceptable; some items might be closer to her personal "bottom line." The point is, in forming a position, she takes all these possibilities into consideration.

WHAT ABOUT THE OTHER SIDE?

We're back to considering the other side, the other party or parties with whom you negotiate. As you can see, the process of determining a position involves evaluating your own desires and needs as well as placing them within a context. That context includes consideration of the other people involved.

In Michael and Jackie's case, brainstorming and negotiations couldn't begin until Michael decided that there was another party's needs to take into account, namely his wife's desires. Arnie had to learn the same lesson and when Julie first thought about her goals, she wasn't considering the needs of the company. That's changed however, and now these people are able to move back and forth between their needs and evaluation of the other's needs.

In no case are our negotiators entering this thought process blindly. In fact, they are well aware of many characteristics of each person with whom they will be dealing. Arnie knows all about Sandra's negotiation style; Michael knows about his wife's needs. Tony and Cathy are aware of their company's rapid growth and they are friendly with the office manager. They also know the person whose office they'd like to have as their own. Julie is not very familiar with the decision-maker in her company, but she does know what the overall concerns are.

Each person is coming closer to a plan, a careful negotiation outline — except, of course, for Michael. Once he opened his mind he and Jackie were able to solve their initial problem easily. Sure, they may need to negotiate further when they come up with their actual options, which are the possible places that are available that meet both their needs for a pleasant vacation. Our other negotiators, however, have many different positions and choices. Which they choose will be at least partially determined by the needs of the other parties involved.

A SERIOUS LOOK

Take a look at the form at the end of this chapter. It will help you (as it helps our negotiators) keep a clear focus on the needs you must consider and the available options. These needs may be financial and can be shown in black and white figures. On the other hand, the needs may be less specific and not as easy to define, such as the impact on others in the company for which Cathy and Tony work. Their success might lie in the way in which they handle that potential to have an impact on others. Perhaps the other worker will respond negatively to being asked if he would vacate an office by Friday, but may respond positively if he's told he's being switched to an office that has a big window and more attractive furniture.

In the end, we must understand that our needs in negotiation can't be met if others' needs are not met too. It's that simple. That's why we take the time to carefully consider the other parties to our negotiation. While we can't guarantee that everyone will win, we increase the chances of a satisfactory outcome if we take the time to consider the other people who have a stake in the outcome. It's another important element in preparation and we can't underestimate its importance.

Once prepared and with options considered, we get closer to actually beginning the negotiation. We still don't know, however, just how the negotiations will proceed. For example, will we write down our requests? Will we have a face-to-face meeting? Will we invite the parties to our office? Will we go to someone else's space? These kinds of issues are addressed in the next chapter. I imagine you are beginning to get a sense that just walking into a negotiation and proceeding isn't the best or smartest course of action to take. Good thought.

No one said success would be easy—but it is worth the effort.

Form #2: Preparation Tracking Sheet

THIS FORM CAN HELP YOU IN NUMEROUS SITUATIONS. Consider it a tool that enables you to determine what you want and translate your desires into a viable, negotiable position. You can use the brainstorming process in a variety of settings, and you will see that it helps you clarify what you need and want and what you consider an acceptable outcome. You can also track your progress as you prepare to negotiate and use the checklist to remind yourself about the details you need to consider.

1. Determine your needs and desires. What are your specific objectives in this situation?

Notes: ______________________________

____

____

2. What are the goals that drive the specific needs you identify? In other words, consider the answer to the question, "What is important to me about what I want from this negotiation?" The answers to that question will suggest the goals that drive you.

Notes: ______________________________

____

____

3. Translate your goals and needs into a position that you will take to the negotiating table.

Notes: ______________________________

____

____

4. As best you can, consider the needs and desires of the other party or parties.

Notes: ____

____

____

5. As far as you can determine, what is important to the other side? What drives them to go after what they seek?

Notes: ____

____

____

6. Brainstorm for possible outcomes. Just list them, but don't evaluate them at this point. Note any solution or outcome that comes to mind. No idea is off base. List them all.

   a. ____
   b. ____
   c. ____
   d. ____
   e. ____
   f. ____
   g. ____
   h. ____
   i. ____
   j. ____

7. Now evaluate the ideas you generated. How practical is each one? What obstacles exist? What are the benefits?

   a. ____
   b. ____
   c. ____
   d. ____
   e. ____

f. ____
g. ____
h. ____
i. ____
j. ____

Notes and details: ______________________________________
____

9. Now, determine how each factor effects you, the other party, or others who may not be directly involved in the negotiation but may be affected by the outcome.

Effect on me   Other party   Indirect effects:

a. ____
____
b. ____
____
c. ____
____
d. ____
____
e. ____
____
f. ____
____
g. ____
____
h. ____
____
i. ____
____
j. ____

10. What steps do you need to take now to prepare for the negotiation? This could include: gathering information, checking facts, doing a comparison and contrast analysis of choices, consider the ramifications of achieved objectives and goals, determining time, place, and mode of negotiation. Use the following as a general guideline.

    a. information needed to proceed.

    ____

    ____

    ____

    b. facts that support your position or that could be in dispute.

    ____

    ____

    ____

    c. the most important features of your position.

    ____

    ____

    ____

    d. points of potential weakness in your position.

    ____

    ____

    ____

    e. the optimal timetable — when would you like the issue resolved? What factors can you control within this time frame? What external factors effect or dictate timing?

    ____

    ____

    ____

f. the optimal place—where would you like the negotiation to be held, if you have a choice.

____

____

____

g. if you are "hosting" the negotiation, what must you do to prepare? How comfortable (or uncomfortable) do you wish the participants to be?

____

____

____

h. written communication as a tool of the negotiation.

advantages: ______________________________

____

disadvantages: ____________________________

____

i. telephone communication as a tool of the negotiation.

advantages: ______________________________

____

disadvantages: ____________________________

____

j. face-to-face communication as a tool of negotiation.

advantages: ______________________________

____

disadvantages: ____________________________

____

k. tasks to accomplish and projected dates for completion.

1. task______________________________ date________
2. task______________________________ date________
3. task______________________________ date________
4. task______________________________ date________
5. task______________________________ date________
6. task______________________________ date________
7. task______________________________ date________
8. task______________________________ date________
9. task______________________________ date________
10. task______________________________ date________

Notes and details: ____

____

Anything else you need or choose to consider as you prepare.

____

____

____

____

____

____

____

____

____

____

____

____

____

____

CHAPTER NINE

Timing and Turf

BY NOW IT IS CLEAR JUST HOW IMPORTANT IT IS TO PLAN carefully for a negotiation prior to entering into it. Let's say that Tony and Cathy dashed off a note to the office manager that said: "We'd like to talk with you about moving to Fred's office, because we need more room and his office is bigger. If you'd rather move us both to a new suite of offices, we'd approve of the relocation provided we get a bigger space." Kind of abrupt, wouldn't you say? The building manager is likely to respond negatively. Tony and Cathy would be on weak ground and may not ever get past this point in the negotiation.

The ground is weak because they aren't offering the other party any support for their position — or any room to create one— and their personal attitude could be construed as thoughtless and demanding. Fortunately, Tony and Cathy have a good sense about effective communication and wouldn't write abrupt notes about their problem and their idea for a good solution. But, what would constitute a sound plan? How should they approach this negotiation?

WHAT TIME IS THE RIGHT TIME?

There are many things to consider when we decide to open up negotiations. First, is there a deadline involved? Remember the scenario where a group of roommates are dealing with the question about how they will split up the chores? We know that some very bad times could be chosen, occasions that would almost insure that negotiations would proceed poorly, if at all. We don't approach our roommate when he or she is working on a report that is due the next day. Nor would we try to negotiate in the midst of a party with our neighbors or when we've taken the "red eye" flight back home from a grueling business trip. (I can personally attest to that one). No, we'd wait until we could be in a relaxed atmosphere with few distractions.

Arnie must consider this when he approaches Sandra; Julie must consider timing when she talks with her boss, Joe, who isn't known to be an open person anyway; you want to consider timing when you talk to your teenager about the use of the family phone. Remember too, that we can be caught off guard. What if Sandra calls Arnie on the intercom and says, "Come into my office right now. I want to talk to you about your salary?" What if Arnie hasn't finished planning his strategy? As we've seen, Arnie is not a quick study.

On the other hand, unbeknownst to Arnie, Sandra could have received approval for a very large raise. Therefore, a delay might work against Arnie. However, this is not the way change proceeds in this company, and it isn't likely Arnie will be surprised in this way.

Decisions about timing can be more complex than they first appear. For example, some people have rather even, level personalities, meaning that unless something truly dramatic happens to them, they are likely to be about the same in the afternoon as they are when they first walk through the office door. Other people become known for their shifting moods. "I never even talk to my wife, Karen, before breakfast," one man says. In response, his wife says, "By 9:00 in the evening Greg's brain is dead, so I never bring up anything important late at night."

In certain situations, we know that we are on adversarial ground. Julie's boss, Joe, has a gruff demeanor and she never knows exactly where she stands with him. She can't count on his being open to her ideas at any particular time. Therefore, she might want to consider carefully the way in which she approaches him. Cathy and Tony are on good terms with their very busy office manager, who tends to be up on most details. So, they know that careful planning is essential, but they won't be able to take up too much time to get the request across. They will probably choose a combination of approaches, each with its own strategy concerning timing.

SHALL I PUT IT IN WRITING?

Sometimes we tend to think that negotiating through the written word is more tedious and perhaps too distant or removed from interaction. While time consuming, writing as a form — or mechanism — of negotiation has many advantages. Perhaps, in these days of e-mail, where people on the same floor of an office send messages back and forth all day, we will see a revival of this form. There are numerous advantages to written negotiations and some of our friends may choose to make use of this mechanism.

1. It's easier to avoid misunderstandings when the words are carefully chosen within a well thought out structure. If Tony and Cathy, for example, put their proposal in writing, and carefully time its delivery, they will avoid any misunderstanding about what it is they want and why they want it. They can then ask for a mutually satisfactory time to get together and discuss the ideas. Or, because the office manager is busy, she could dictate a written response and they could go from there.

Some people find that using the written word can be helpful in certain situations in which there is a chance that the communication could get emotionally volatile—negotiating with a teenager, for example. Julie might find that sending a written proposal would avoid the easy dismissal that her boss is likely to do with a wave of his hand — "not now," "it's impossible," "we've never done this before," and so on. It's fair to say that personality issues have less chance to interfere when we negotiate in writing.

2. A written proposal containing negotiating points allows the recipient time to review the details, check on some facts, explore ideas, and perhaps get advice from other colleagues. He or she can note questions and evaluate the areas in which there is some room to be flexible. Tony and Cathy might trigger a check on the availability of space in the building. Or, they might want to speak to the owners of their companies about any number of solutions. Julie's boss is likely to be less annoyed by a piece of paper than by a verbal exchange, in part because he'll have a chance to think about the situation and the proposal.

3. In many situations, there will be an oral—verbal— negotiating session, and doing the preliminary work in writing does not preclude this. In fact, it may take less time to reach an agreement when the written material has been presented first. Arnie could easily prepare a list of his concerns and proposals, present them to Sandra, and then simply leave it alone until she has a chance to get back to him, either in writing or in person. This is true for all our friends, although in some cases, the negotiations could be done almost entirely in writing.

In Tony and Cathy's case, the response could come back with a couple of alternate plans or a list of reasons why certain ideas won't work. Perhaps the office on the other floor has just been leased, or a new employee is going to be sharing the larger office that their colleague now has all to himself. Tony and Cathy could then respond again in writing and finally, a face-to-face meeting could result to iron out the details.

4. The ideas can be expressed and issues dealt with in the absence of interruptions and other distractions. Both the writer and the receiver can produce and consider a proposal without having the call waiting signal come through or without the other person jumping in with new ideas. Julie knows that her boss

loves to claim that he is due in a meeting in 30 seconds and the sound of the ringing phone makes him feel important.

There are a few disadvantages to conducting negotiations in writing that you should consider before you determine which mechanism is the correct one for any given situation.

1. A proposal can be carefully considered and the details can be studied. Therefore, a response can be carefully planned and it may be that spontaneous back and forth exchanges are lost. A person could get a better deal, so to speak, when concessions are made on the spur of the moment.

2. Written negotiations can be slow, sometimes far slower than telephone or face-to-face sessions. Delays can be detrimental if timeliness is very important. Your teenager's telephone habits may be getting serious — too serious to spend weeks or even days straightening out. (On the other hand, an initial written approach might avoid histrionics.)

3. Your time, and that of the other party, is going to be taxed in written negotiations. Cathy and Tony have spent considerable time planning and putting their proposal into writing. Still, it's important that they do this because there are a number of options and the company needs time to react. The request will trigger time to track down other facts and thinking about a counter-proposal. Arnie is taking more time than he ever imagined to create his proposal.

If you determine that negotiating in writing is the best option, then realize that you must take whatever time is required to do it right.

You might find that written negotiations — at least initially — are advantageous. Weigh the advantages and disadvantages and see if this mechanism is right for the situation at hand. You may reject it if time is important or if you believe that you'll be better off with another form. But don't eliminate it until you've considered it carefully.

One of the most common mechanisms is the telephone.

Even with fax and e-mail, the telephone, which allows person to person conversations, is often still preferable.

THE TELEPHONE—PERSONAL OR IMPERSONAL?

When you think about it, most negotiations end up taking place on the telephone. We state an offer on a house over the phone and the real estate broker presents it to the owner in another phone call. Then it's accepted or rejected over the phone and the information is conveyed to us that way. Sure, written materials are ultimately involved. This is true in almost all negotiations. The written material follows in order to clarify positions and to establish a record not based on disputes involving memory and so forth.

Telephone conversations are more personal than written communication and less personal than face-to-face encounters. Remember that nonverbal cues, such as eye contact, facial expressions, body language, and so forth, are not among the information available to you. In certain situations, the telephone affords a degree of comfort and a sense of control not present in face-to-face contact.

Do you remember what it was like to make a telephone call to set up your first job interview? You were probably young and neither confident nor experienced, and face-to-face communication with a person who is perceived as more powerful was intimidating. A frown or crossed arms could easily be seen as disapproval. The telephone avoids this distraction.

For some people, the telephone breaks down certain inhibitions and more information can be gleaned. You might find that others use this tactic too. For example, questions that might not be considered appropriate when posed face-to-face could be "slipped" in over the phone. Arnie might find himself talking to Sandra about how badly he was treated on his previous job, something that he wouldn't do during a face-to-face conversation, nor should he, because it weakens Arnie's position. But on the phone, his guard is down and he finds himself going into all kinds of irrelevant information.

Julie will probably find that telephone negotiating is not a good idea in her case. First, her boss is abrupt on the phone, even more brusk than in a face-to-face encounter. As many of us discover, people who lack certain social and verbal skills in person-to-person conversations tend to lack them even more during phone conversations. Their lack of verbal skills becomes even more pronounced when nonverbal cues are not there to act as a check and balance system. That's why people blow up on the telephone when they wouldn't behave that way in person.

Even in the absence of outright rudeness, negotiations can be terminated very quickly over the phone. The other party can plead that another important matter must be handled right away and quickly end the conversation.

On balance, telephone negotiations have the following important advantages:

1. As with written negotiations, nonverbal cues are minimal. While these cues can be helpful, they can also be distracting. People who attempt to control situations with their body language will not be able to do this. We all know people who seem to take up more space in the room than their physical bodies warrant. It's psychological space that they're taking up, and over the phone they simply can't dominate in the same way.

Keep one point in mind. Because we process information visually (as well as in auditory and feeling-based ways), we will fill in the image of the person with whom we are negotiating in our mind, even if the interaction takes place over the telephone. (To illustrate this point, think about a time you have talked on the telephone with a blind date before you ever met that person. Didn't you create an image in your mind of a very attractive desirable person, only to be incredibly disappointed upon meeting face-to-face? Same concept here. By the way, the other person on the blind date went through the same process!)

The power of our visual images means that if you find the voice on the telephone and the image you visualize intimidating, then just do some work in your mind to change the image! It is all in your mind anyway, so make some shifts in the way the other person appears in your mind's eye in order to insure that he or she is not anyone to fear. When you meet that person, you can do the necessary modifications, but there's no need to feel ill at ease any sooner than necessary.

2. Vocal cues can be discerned more easily over the phone. For example, you may be able to note deception when a person is talking. Having only a voice to go on allows you to focus on the verbal exchange, and conflicting body language is not an issue. When Arnie calls Sandra she says she is very busy. But he senses this isn't true. She's simply taking advantage of the anonymity afforded by the telephone to get away from him. However, he's listening carefully and detects this excuse. On the other hand, Tony and Cathy's office manager states clearly and without hesitation that she's just leaving for a meeting with the owners. Her voice has no hint of hesitation nor any tone of putting them off. She promises to get back to them later.

3. Phone conversations eliminate many competing cues. During phone calls, you can listen for tone of voice and inflection, and you can also pay attention to the words and their meaning. This is important when you decide that you need more time to consider a proposal. You listen to what is being said and simply state your need to think about the matter.

4. You can keep your notes handy and consult them often when talking on the phone. If you were to do this face-to-face you would be leaving the impression that you don't know the facts and you also might disclose a document that you choose, for your own reasons, to protect. Last year's sales figures might be used to justify salary cuts for everyone in your department. However, you have a document that shows that sales were actually up, but discounts were offered that lowered the profit. You

may or may not want to disclose this, but you have the document to refer to without the other party being aware of it.

5. For many people, telephone conversations are far less stressful than face-to-face meetings. There is less opportunity for small talk and for discussions to move to irrelevancies such as inquiries about family, sports, or the weather. You can get business done quickly and make progress in matters without expending the time to get everyone together.

6. It's easier for you to say "no" on the phone than it is in person — it's easier for the other person too, so this may or may not be an advantage. If you find yourself agreeing to do things that you really don't want to do, then it might be easier to practice saying a firm no on the telephone.

A friend of mine, Judy, was able to say no to loaning money to her brother — for the tenth time that year — because she restricted their contact to phone conversations. She practiced this assertive stand without having to be in her brother's presence. This can work the other way, of course, so you want to consider how easy it is for the other party to say no to you.

7. If you initiate the call, you control the flow of information and the other party may not have all the facts at his or her disposal. If you find yourself on the receiving end of a call in which an opinion or some information is requested, then you can gain advantage by asking for more time. In essence, you can then regain control. This advantage can be neutralized if a call is prearranged and it is determined who will call whom.

The telephone call also has some disadvantages. Weigh these negative aspects of phone negotiations against your needs at this particular time.

1. Phone conversations generally tend to be shorter than face-to-face meetings. In fact, you may find yourself agreeing to something without all the facts, simply because you haven't had time to explore all your options or possible positions. You might even find yourself distracted by other papers or the computer

while the person on the telephone thinks they have your undivided attention.

2. While it is sometimes advantageous to have only verbal cues to consider, it can be detrimental in determining the credibility of the other party. For example, a person called a friend of mine who is a business consultant. Over the phone this person sounded reasonable and credible. Introductory issues were explored, fees were discussed, and an appointment was set up. In person, however, this potential client was not at all credible and in fact, did not have a business nor money to pay the consultant. His demeanor was flat and distracted, behaviors that couldn't be determined over the phone. Many business people can't adequately "qualify" a buyer or client over the phone. Nonverbal cues are often very important here.

3. Neither person has much control over the duration of a phone conversation. Sandra can cut Arnie off, but Arnie can get busy very quickly, too, and would then need to interrupt the call. Unless time and duration have been established before the call, the ability to control the conversation is diminished. You can hang up if you feel the need to do so, and that can be good, but remember, the other party can do this too.

4. Your advantage as caller can quickly deteriorate if the other person can control the in-coming calls. Julie's boss could put her off for a long time if he had the secretary say he was too busy to talk or is unavailable for any reason. The call then has to be rescheduled.

I recently heard about a situation in which a professional constantly used the excuse that he was doing a radio interview and couldn't be disturbed, or had people waiting to see him outside his office, and on and on. While it was true that this person had recently received a great deal of publicity, he began to use these excuses any time he didn't feel like talking to a caller!

Eventually, my friend had to resort to fax communication that requested acknowledgement and required certain actions.

She was even forced to use subtle threats, that is saying she would take a particular action unless she heard from him by a specified time. He missed the deadline, she took the action, and a frantic call resulted. Using requests for written confirmation of rushed phone calls can help avoid misunderstandings later on.

In many cases, a combination of written and telephone negotiations will settle most issues on the table. Julie found that her negotiations went smoothly with her boss when she put everything in writing first. In fact, e-mail and faxes ended up being her most important tools. Ultimately, however, she and all our other friends still needed to meet face-to-face with those with whom they are negotiating.

YOUR PLACE OR MINE

Arnie knows that eventually he and Sandra will engage in face-to-face negotiations. Tony and Cathy, while able to do most of their negotiating in writing and over the phone, will probably seal the deal in the presence of the office manager and perhaps with others who may be affected by any decision made.

The location of negotiations may or may not be critical, but it's safe to say that in most situations it can be a part of establishing position, enhancing the comfort (or discomfort) for the negotiating parties, and affecting the atmosphere in countless ways. For example, it could be advantageous for Tony and Cathy to carry out their negotiations with the office manager and/or others involved in their office—the office that is too small and is the reason for the negotiating session in the first place. Being in that tiny space might bring home the point they are making. If they're moving file cabinets around just to find places for others to sit down, they make their case in a powerful but nonverbal way.

In this case, it is clear that Cathy and Tony's office is not a neutral location. In fact, it could be considered a "loaded" location. But what constitutes neutrality? If you are negotiating with your teenage son in his room, then you are in his territory. He probably feels more confident and powerful in this location. If you negotiate in your space, it is likely that you have the advantage in terms of power. But you may have too much perceived power.

The kitchen or family room, on the other hand, could be neutral places. You spend time in these locations where "turf" is shared; you both are comfortable there and have shared meaningful time in the past. (If these are sites of constant arguing, then the locations would probably not be good even they could be considered neutral. Both you and your son have unpleasant memories and associations with these places.)

Generally speaking, a mutually agreed upon restaurant or hotel conference room, or some other rented meeting room, could be considered neutral locations (so long as you or the other party are not a regular patron at that location). Simply defined, a neutral location is one in which neither negotiator has unbalanced access to staff or is afforded special privileges.

If I take a client to a restaurant where I am well known and have ready access to people who will quickly respond to my needs, then this is not a neutral location. If I agree to go to a hotel that has business services my client frequently uses, then this isn't a neutral location either. If two roommates go to a local cafe to talk over the division of labor in their household, then that could be considered a neutral location if they are both equally familiar with it and the staff know both of them. A conference room in Arnie's office could also be considered a neutral location in that both he and his boss have access to it. It may also have other advantages, which we'll learn about later.

Our society has set up the ultimate in a neutral location. The courtroom, paid for by all of us, is a place owned by the society collectively. In theory, it is considered a neutral place where both sides have access to the court's services and resources. In this country, we don't hold trials in the prosecuting attorney's conference room or in the defendant's home or office. Nor do we hide the proceedings. We do this to insure that neutrality in all important details is preserved. This isn't accidental; we developed this policy intentionally. This neutrality may be true for the parties in a case, but probably not so for the lawyers and judges who live professionally in that space.

One of the advantages of a televised trial is that we who are paying for the justice system get to see it in action. This has never been more apparent than in the O.J. Simpson trial. The whole world saw our justice system in action (or disarray, depending on your perspective). Yes it's slow; it's tedious, but for the most part, it's neutral. Every challenge to that neutrality is taken seriously, including a symbolic lapel pin worn by prosecutor, Marcia Clark. Great pains were taken to find a jury who would listen to the evidence. Having covered the case for NBC News as well as observing the jury selection process from inside the courtroom, it was clear just how difficult the task was for all involved. But the call for a defendant's right to a fair trial was demanded loud and clear; it may never go away.

Now, it is true that in our day-to-day lives we won't always negotiate in a neutral location, and the place we agree to can be important to the ultimate outcome. Let's start with the advantages of negotiating in your own space, which could include your home, your office, or some other place where you are known and have access to services you might need.

1. If you negotiate in your office, you have access to documents, records, and your supervisors and assistants. If certain materials are needed, then you can call for them and avoid delays. The other party does not have this advantage. Negotiating in your home offers this same edge.

2. You have more control over the atmosphere if you are in familiar surroundings. The room is arranged to your specifications, and if it's uncomfortable, that will have an effect on the proceedings. One might assume that a comfortable environment

will always be best. However, as we've said, for Cathy and Tony, negotiating in their cramped uncomfortable setting could work to their advantage. This illustrates how important it is to plan the details of a negotiation.

3. If we control the environment, we can arrange to be periodically called away. We can plan interruptions, which can offer needed breaks, particularly if tensions are running high or we need a few minutes to consider information that's been presented.

4. There's always a psychological advantage to being at "home." Sometimes this is literally true, especially these days when home offices are common. But even if our office is far from our home, it is still likely a place where we are comfortable and relaxed.

5. We usually save time and money when we negotiate in our environment, while the other party must expend travel time and incur any expense that traveling entails.

These are important advantages, but don't make your decision about location too quickly. There are also advantages to negotiating in the other party's environment. These must be considered and weighed as we choose the best location in which to negotiate the particular deal. We don't have a "one location fits all" option. Some possible advantages of the other party's location are:

1. There are fewer distractions and you are free to concentrate on the task at hand. Sure, you can be available by phone or through your pager, but you can instruct your office to hold other matters until you return. Your ability to focus solely on the matters in front in you signals your readiness to negotiate.

2. You have the ability to control or protect information. While it is unethical to intentionally withhold important information, you are not obligated to help another party who may not have prepared as well as you did.

3. In certain situations, you can request that the other party

get information or speak with a supervisor or manager to clarify a point or get permission to concede particular points. This adds an element of control that could be important. Julie might use it in her negotiations with her boss, Joe. The information about company policies are available—he made the policies, so presumably he has easy access to all documentation. To plead ignorance about policies or to refuse to comply with Julie's request would appear to be an uncooperative stance and reflects an attitude tinged with belligerence.

4. The person who is "hosting" a negotiation may take on the obligation of opening the session. He or she may put the opening position on the table and unintentionally disclose important information, and perhaps more information than is wise. Remember, information is power.

KEEPING IT NEUTRAL

If you and other parties decide that a neutral location is best, then be sure it has certain important features. (These will vary depending on the negotiating task at hand. Consider these as general guidelines.)

Make sure that your setting is private enough to insure that no one can hear your negotiations. You may or may not want a telephone available so that either of you can get information or clearance for decisions. You should agree whether personal beepers and cell phones will be left outside the room so there can be no interruptions. The space must be available for a sufficient period of time. If you're negotiating in a restaurant, then be sure that you have enough time to complete your task before it closes. The same applies if you're using a conference room in a hotel or your kitchen or living room.

You also want to have extra supplies at hand. You don't want to have to borrow a note pad or a pen because you forgot to bring your own. Obviously if you're in your own office or home this isn't a problem, but if you are on neutral ground, then you will not have immediate access to various supplies.

Finally, if possible, be sure that you won't have disturbances in this neutral territory. If you're negotiating with your life partner, then I wouldn't start right before dinner, or if you have children, when all four will be crashing through the door all at once. The same noises that can be pleasant in one setting can thwart our ability to concentrate in another.

HOW DO WE FEEL IN HERE?

Imagine that you are negotiating a contract with an important client. This agreement could mean 25 percent of next year's income. Your client arrives at your home office, a bit frazzled after a long drive—but it was her choice to come to you. You actually preferred to meet in a conference room you often rent in a building downtown. You conceded, however, because your home office was closer to her home and your negotiating session was going to be the last appointment of her day. But, when she arrives, she asks where the restroom is and she sure could use a cup of coffee.

If you've prepared, you've checked the bathroom and have the coffee pot ready to go. If you're unprepared, your toddler's tricycle is blocking the door and you used the last of the coffee this morning. Which situation do think will leave the best impression and enable the important session to begin?

If you are the host in the negotiation, then it is your responsibility to insure the comfort of all parties. This can be important in all settings, and even if a neutral setting has been agreed upon, both parties will want basic amenities. Most people want adequate lighting, nearby restrooms, a chance for quick breaks, and if the session is expected to take more than a few minutes, some light refreshments.

The placement of the parties will also establish a tone and may signal an attempt to establish power. A stern parent (or a negotiator who acts or performs in a parent-type role) might demand that the child sit down, while he or she remains standing. Or, in the case of Arnie and Sandra, she, as boss, may sit behind her desk, clearly in the superior position. On the other hand, you and your roommate will sit opposite each other at a table or a booth, where equality of position is clearly established. Cathy and Tony might do well to sit on their desks and offer the remaining chairs to the rest of the group—assuming that they are the hosting parties.

In general, a competitive negotiator will position him or herself at the head of a table if possible. This suggests leadership and by implication, establishes control over the pace of the discussion. Cooperative negotiators will prefer an oval or circular arrangement, or perhaps an "L" shape, which equalizes the parties.

There are some negotiators, such as Julie's boss, who will not necessarily care much about the other party's comfort, and therefore, will pay little attention to these details. In other situations, the parties will need to work with the facilities at hand. For example, if you're negotiating in your work environment, you will create an atmosphere in a familiar setting, without altering the basic setting.

Remember that the location decision is important in many different kinds of negotiations, from those between you and family or friends to decisions having to do with business deals or working conditions.

Once you've established location, the next issue is timing. This is an area where you may have more decision-making power than you realize.

THE BEST OF TIMES; THE WORST OF TIMES

When we first met Arnie, he was getting ready to barge into Sandra's office and demand a raise. He now understands that he had a lot to learn about negotiations, but he was eager to learn. So, we've managed to slow him down. He has learned to prepare, meaning that he's gathered facts, considered what he wants, and has begun to establish a range of positions. We've taught him to pay attention to his communication skills and to the way others communicate.

He's become a better observer of people and he's also learned to identify his own needs and consider them when he determines what is possible in his current job. He is considering how much negotiating he can accomplish in writing or over the phone and what portion will need to be done in person. We've even taught him a little about location, but now he needs to learn about timing.

All of our negotiators must consider timing as they plan their negotiating strategy. Indeed, careful preparation can go for naught if the timing is bad. Julie has a tough job ahead of her. With her boss, any time is a bad time, so she will need to be particularly careful. While Michael and Jackie have presumably solved their vacation destination problem, they will still need to negotiate about the range of choices they agreed to consider. Tony and Cathy will need to consider timing as well, because the office manager has a busy schedule and is always on the verge of full-blown burnout. They also need to solve their problem quickly because they each have new accounts requiring attention fairly quickly.

Timing involves the scheduling of the negotiating session and the amount of time available to both parties. It also involves the stage of development of the issue or desired goal. Michael was forced into a negotiation because Jackie forced the issue. It was time to actually make the arrangements and Jackie had effectively said, "I'm not doing this — you'll have to go to that golf resort alone." As sometimes happens in personal relationships, Michael didn't listen until the situation had reached a breaking point. They were negotiating in a final stage of development — their problem had become serious and threatened their relationship.

I recently heard about a couple who were going through a divorce. The woman was moving ahead and seemed in charge of her life and was eager to finish the negotiations over child custody and their common property. Her husband, on the other hand, was walking around in a state of shock. He'd taken to calling their mutual friends late at night and on weekends. Over and over he'd say, "Out of the blue — it was just out of the blue. One day everything was fine and the next day, boom, she wants a divorce."

After listening to this refrain for weeks, one friend finally said, "Hey, your wife has been telling you for years that you had problems, that she didn't like certain things that were going on, and that she wanted to see a marriage counselor. You kept denying that anything was wrong — you said it was her problem. So, you didn't listen, and now you claim to be shocked. Get real."

Michael and Jackie were in a similar position. These vacation problems weren't new, but fortunately, Michael finally decided to take Jackie's discontent seriously. Unfortunately, many of us ignore our partners or children, but we wouldn't dream of adopting this attitude at work or even with our friends. The moral of the story is: We need to listen to others when they tell us there's a problem. If we don't, we might find ourselves with an even bigger problem down the road.

Similarly, Arnie has let his problem go for too long. He has been brooding about his salary for over two years. Until now, all he's done is brood. In order for Arnie to accomplish his goal, he will have to put himself on a schedule in order to prepare. Then, he'll be ready to negotiate. In a sense, any negotiation would have come at a bad time for Arnie because he didn't know what he was doing.

Time can also be used as a tactic, and not always a positive one. A competitive negotiator might attempt to schedule a session with a firm time-frame, which then serves as a pressure tactic. The other party could say, however, "Well, I have plenty of time," which then backfires on the person applying the pressure. Another session may be scheduled and the person who wanted to rush is forced to come back and reenter the negotiation anyway.

MISHAPS AND BLUNDERS

If we don't pay attention to timing, we will invariably suffer the consequences. If Arnie charges into Sandra's office without a prearranged appointment, his chances for success are fairly low. He might want to consider such things as the best day of the week and time of day, Sandra's general mood, the demands of the company, and so forth. The fact is, Sandra can be reached; negotiating salaries is one of her jobs. She has made time for it with other employees, so she can do this for Arnie.

Cathy and Tony have a similar problem because the office manager is so busy. That's why they put so much time into their preparation stage. They sent a memo asking for an appointment to discuss an issue that had come up. They specified a particular amount of time that they'd need for this initial meeting. They had their notes ready and they knew what they were going to propose. They were also aware that the manager would need time to consider the written proposal they were presenting. For them, this was a first step.

Julie wrote a detailed proposal and sent it to her boss with a note requesting a meeting to discuss it. She followed this with a phone call, because she knew if she didn't take that step, then she wouldn't get any farther. Joe used avoidance as a tactic, and she had to counter that with her own perseverance. While his voice mail often picked up his messages, he eventually did return these calls because he had to maintain some contact with his staff.

There are difficult people in this world, and Joe is one of them. Because Julie knows this, she can plan her strategy with his personality in mind. This is realistic. Too many people use the same approach with every person, and usually end up wondering why their reasoned, polite strategy fails miserably—at least some of the time.

Julie asked Joe to respond to her proposal, and after two calls requesting a return call, she received an e-mail message, which offered a ten-minute appointment in two weeks. She sent him a message asking for a written response to her proposal prior to the appointment. Joe sent a terse, negative memo, which came a week later.

Julie prepared herself to answer his major objections during their short meeting, leaving him with a document that answered some of his questions. She continued to maintain a positive attitude, in part because she knew that a local statute mandates telecommuting. This knowledge added strength to her position. She also outlined a public relations strategy the company could use to call attention to their newly instituted work-at-home program. She was using persistence and facts to help her stay focused on the desired outcome.

MAKING THE CALENDAR AND THE CLOCK WORK FOR YOU

To the extent she could, Julie made the calendar and the clock work for her. While she wanted to begin working in her home office immediately, she recognized that if pushed too hard or too fast, she'd would lessen her chances to win. Because she was aware of Joe's general demeanor, she worked around him, rather than wishing he'd be different. She did this for every step, including her timing. She essentially cut off reasons for him to find excuses not to see her.

When we are negotiating with people we know well or work with, we have the advantage of being able to analyze their personalities and their habitual responses to certain kinds of situations. We also know what their responsibilities are and can respect what their challenges might be. Therefore, we'll plan our timetable with these factors in mind. This doesn't mean that we ignore our own needs, but it does mean that we know the needs of the other party.

When we don't know the other parties, we may have to work a bit harder to find out how timing affects them. What are their needs and how do these needs either complement our own or conflict with them? What do we detect during phone conversations? Is this a person who stays on track or does he or she interject irrelevant information into the conversation? Do we detect a straightforward tone, and do the words match the tone of voice? Are our telephone calls returned promptly? These are a few factors that can help us as we work with a timetable. The key is to pay attention to these factors rather than proceeding to negotiate on auto-pilot. In many situations, we'll simply ask direct questions and we'll answer directly as well. We'll negotiate the best time to meet face-to-face or talk on the telephone based on stated needs and availability by all parties.

Timing is just one element in negotiation, but it is an important one that is usually considered in every step we take. In certain situations, it is handled easily and without great consideration. But there are times when it must be near the top of the list of factors that can affect outcome.

Sometimes, such things as location and timing are affected by authority and power. We may be in the supervisory position or we may be negotiating with a person whose level of power is greater than our own. So, it makes sense to learn as much as we can about status and power, a crucial variable in the psychology of negotiation.

CHAPTER TEN

The Play of Power or, Are You a Legend in Your Own Mind?

ARNIE MAY ULTIMATELY BE FORCED TO GO ALONG WITH Sandra's timetable and he may find himself presenting his position in the location of Sandra's choice. Why? Simply put, she has more power. Arnie may have more education, but she has more power because she has a position with higher status. She's the boss. Whenever we're in a situation in which the other party has authority over us, then that person has more power and by implication higher status.

Sometimes, we're the party who has greater power and status and we can then assume that we have greater control. Sometimes this can be confusing. For example, if you're a customer in a department store and the service is poor, it might not be apparent that you have any power. You may often feel as if you're at the mercy of the clerks, but, keep the faith, you have the power edge. You can refuse to shop at this store. You can write or call the manager and make a formal complaint. (Maybe more of us should exercise our power more often than we do.) Don't lose sight of your own power.

One of the reasons economic boycotts can work is that this is a practical use of power — the power to withhold our money. When consumers are continuously treated badly, this is a clear demonstration that we aren't using the power we have available to us. Rather than feeling like victims, we can behave as if we hold the power position and exercise it.

We may also have more power if we're the boss in negotiating situations with employees. Julie's boss has more apparent power than she does, but she has been an outstanding employee, which gives her more power than a person who performs poorly. Cathy and Tony may have more power than would be apparent because the company has recently won an important contract based on the high quality of the work this team produces every day. This company— if it's smart—doesn't want to lose them. (If it sometimes seems that people act against their best interests and do things to alienate people they value and need, you're right. This is nothing new in human history. Let's face it, we sometimes use positions of authority unwisely.)

DO I HAVE STATUS OR DO I HAVE POWER?

Sometimes two people could be perceived as being equal in power but unequal in status. Theoretically, a doctor and a patient are equals. In fact, the patient is often the person with the power advantage, in that the patient can seek medical services elsewhere if he or she is dissatisfied with the care. This is true in a lawyer-client relationship as well. However, in many cases, the patient or client will perceive the doctor or lawyer as having higher status.

People in these professions have often been accorded a higher degree of respect in our society than that given to others in different occupations. In fact, many of us internalize the idea that certain people have more education or money and therefore have higher status and following from that, more power.

We've done this in many situations in our culture. For example, until recently, men, just because they are born male, were assumed to have an edge of power over women. In subtle and not-so-subtle ways, males have assumed they are the gender with the higher status. We see this among races as well. There are still some white people who consider themselves superior to those of other races. Therefore, they believe they have higher status and more power. Acting that way doesn't make it so. But, responding to another with the belief that they have more power does make it so.

Women have sometimes internalized this attitude themselves and have afforded men deferential treatment, because they may not believe they have any other choice. A friend of mine told a story about her mother-in-law, who continued to wait on her husband and sons, going so far as to fix them special meals during football games. Why? Because, according to this mother and wife, the men are "entitled" to this treatment, simply because they're male. Live it and it is so.

This dynamic of skewed power and status was certainly present in Michael and Jackie's relationship. For years she'd gone along with his wishes because she didn't think she had other choices. When that changed, Michael believed that his authority in the family was undermined. Fortunately, they were able to resolve this issue and equalize their status. In a sense, Jackie assumed her equal place in the family and Michael, who hadn't thought about this issue very much before, acknowledged it. They avoided a power struggle because of their ability to shift positions and change attitudes.

Despite our proclamations about being a "classless" society, we all know that this simply isn't true. Remember the adage, "money is power," and discussions of "old money," and the "new rich." One day we might be spared the endless banter about the relative status of prep schools and universities, but that hasn't happened yet. So, we must have the factors in our mind as we plan to negotiate.

We talk about status symbols in our society and some people may look upon driving a certain kind of car or living in a particular locale as increasing their status. Today, certain watches, clothes, credit cards, and even pens may be perceived as status symbols. While most of us can laugh this off, there may be situations in which the perception of higher status does in fact lead to a perception of increased power.

The way we treat one another based on assumptions about intelligence, money, power, and so forth is important to keep in mind when we prepare to negotiate. Some years ago, a teacher was assigned to a class comprised, she was told, of gifted students — all well above average in intelligence. She treated each of these students as if they were special and would achieve at high levels. And, living up to expectations, they all performed at above average levels in all academic work. As it turned out, these students were actually considered average and were not expected to perform at advanced levels. This was simply an experiment and the students were chosen randomly. Imagine treating all children as if they are gifted; we'd find that they all do indeed have capabilities we can't yet measure accurately. Live it and it can be so.

(Remember that the reverse situation is also true. If a child is told over and over that he or she is dumb or stupid or slow, then that child will often perform in accordance with low expectations.) So consider the strategic effect of mindset.

Have you ever been in a group whose individual identities were not known? For example, organizers of a men's weekend or gathering may make it a point to withhold information about the occupations of the participants. They do this because if some men are CEOs or doctors or judges, for example, the other men might unconsciously change their behavior towards them. In our society, we are defined by what we do for a living and the organizers wanted to avoid those subtle shifts in power. Each man related to the others as an individual and the occupational baggage was left behind.

Many if not most people assume that a defendant with money and fame automatically has a power edge. And this is probably true. It doesn't mean that justice won't be served, but it does mean that the best legal services are available to him or her. Many people believe we saw this operate in the O.J. Simpson trial. Some lawyers have argued that the wealthiest people can't buy justice, but they can get the best chance at what our system has to offer. With equal resources and study, could the prosecution have been a better match for the defense? Absolutely.

These are just a few examples of the way in which status and perceived power may influence our interactions, even on a social basis, or in a setting where power positions are irrelevant. And let's remember that perceptions often influence behavior and outcome.

IS THIS REAL POWER, OR AM I IMAGINING IT?

Julie's boss has power in that he has the right not to reach an agreement with her. Joe could keep putting her off and ultimately refuse to engage in negotiations. That might not be wise or prudent—after all, she could get tired of it and begin looking for another job. Still, he could exercise that option. We could say that the ability not to reach agreements, not to enter into negotiations, and not have to answer for this avoidance is true power.

In a sense, Julie's boss, Joe, is indifferent to the outcome, making her task more difficult. He doesn't believe he has any stake in this, so he has the power. This can change, and it's Julie's job to influence him, but she is aware that the power balance rests with him. On the other hand, Julie is confident and has great faith in her ability to overcome these difficulties. She may acknowledge his capacity not to negotiate or to keep putting her off, but she is confident about her personal power and knows she is good at what she does and is a valued employee.

WHAT DO WE MEAN BY POWER ANYWAY?

Like most broad concepts, there isn't just one way power manifests. It means different things in different settings. When you prepare to negotiate, consider the kind of power you and the other parties hold.

1. LEGITIMATE: This is the power that a person has because of position or title. Your family doctor earned his or her degree, your child's teacher is recognized by your state to be competent, a lawyer passes the bar, and so forth. This kind of power is equivalent to being an authority in a particular field. Sandra is the boss, so she has legitimate power—or authority. Cathy and Tony's boss has legitimate power as well, but this team also has power because of their status in the company.

2. REFERENT OR INHERENT: This is power that we perceive the person has earned in some way, often by conduct or demeanor. Nelson Mandela is a person who exemplifies this kind of power. We know about his past and his achievements, accomplished despite great odds against him, and therefore, were we to meet him, we'd probably perceive him as possessing greater power than ourselves. Most people treat him with great respect, the kind usually associated with a hero.

In our society, a highly skilled performer or athlete may be perceived as more powerful than the average person. This power is given to a "super star" because of the status that has been attained. Sometimes, we become disillusioned when those perceived to have this inherent power are really not that different from us. This involves perception, which may or may not be associated with the relative value of the achievements.

Many people are troubled because we seem to attach the status of hero or heroine to people whose achievements are confined to show business or athletics. In doing so, we send a message to children (and to ourselves) that celebrity is the same as heroism, that being famous is the same as being heroic. We won't solve that issue in this book, but it's something to consider when we think about who has power and why. Sometimes we assign power where it doesn't belong. We may do this in our own negotiations, too.

3. COMPENSATORY: This is the power to reward, usually using underlying or designated power. A parent has compensatory power in that he or she can reward a child based on the designated power position. Teachers also have this kind of power, as do supervisors or bosses.

4. COERCIVE: This is the flip side of compensatory power. A parent can use his or her power position to withhold privileges from a child. If you take away your teenager's ability to use your car on the weekends, then you are exercising this power. Actually, the existence of this possibility is used as a point of power in other areas. Clean your room and you can use the car; fail to do your homework and you can't use the car.

In the extreme, there are countries that are ruled by coercive power. We call these "police states" because the population is controlled by coercion, that is the threat of violence and even death in the face of disobedience (often called "disloyalty" or being a "traitor"). Unfortunately, there are countless examples of coercive power throughout history.

5. EXPERT: We respect certain people and invest them with a degree of power just because they have special knowledge or expertise. We honor scientists and may even hold them in awe because we know that they have knowledge that seems to be beyond us. We use expert witnesses in trials because they possess information not known to the average person. Therefore, these witnesses have a degree of power that we give to them just because of their expertise. This carries over to the doctor-patient relationship, which is why patients may not exercise their own power in the relationship.

You may be thinking about the various types of power listed here and can come up with situations in which you had power and may not have realized it. Sometimes parents feel powerless, bosses sense that they've lost power, patients believe themselves to be at the mercy of the night nurse. Or, we may believe that we have more power than the situation warrants. We believe we should be able to force our children to comply—and they manipulate us by simply refusing. Since we won't carry out dire threats, we wonder how it is that we could have lost power.

Arnie likes to think he has power, but in fact, Sandra can make the final decision. If Cathy and Tony were to elevate their sense of power, they could make moves that would alienate co-workers and their bosses, which would not necessarily be wise. In a sense, their real power comes from their perceived value and their expertise, not because they have been designated as the people with the most power. This will influence their own negotiating style.

HOW MUCH POWER DO WE—AND THEY—HAVE?

So, we know Sandra has legitimate power, but will she be good at using it? We don't know yet. Arnie has to think about this. And when he considers this factor, he studies her communication style and the ease with which she negotiates other issues. Take overtime, for example. Arnie's department was denied overtime, and Sandra used her supervisors as a shield — "they" wouldn't allow it. No one actually spoke to any of these "higher-ups." From Sandra's point of view, she handled that negotiation rather skillfully.

Julie's boss may have designated power and the ability to compensate—and coerce. However, he's a very poor communicator and hence, Julie has doubts about his ability to skillfully negotiate with her if she ever gets to that point. Sometimes one spouse is afraid of negotiating with the other because he or she appears to be so much better at it—and therefore has more power. Perhaps it's just the ability to think and speak more quickly that intimidates the other person. Or it could be the self perception of having more inherent power.

Certain status influences perceptions. A clergy person, for example, may exercise perceived inherent power during a negotiating session about an issue involving a congregation. He or she may assume a veto power, depending of course on the power that is traditional for that position. A congregation, in many cases, has the ultimate power to hire and fire, so the balance may shift considerably. Families in which there is a belief in the "head of the household" concept give credence to inherent power. In many cases, an assumption of power combined with good communication skills and good negotiating skills can result in a strong negotiating position.

If Julie had to argue her case with Joe's secretary, then we could say that she's spending time negotiating with a person who has no power to influence the outcome. The secretary does not have the ability to create a solution. She may have the ability and the power to set up negotiations, but she can't guarantee the outcome.

Cathy and Tony are in a good position because their office manager has a history of creating solutions that will accommodate the interests of everyone involved. She understands the issues and is known to be a good listener. She has considerable power because of her abilities. This office manager also has a commitment to the process and the ability to keep the sessions on track. Julie's boss doesn't demonstrate the ability to compromise or to think creatively about solutions. By necessity, these ideas will come from Julie.

Consider the concept of power—too many of us don't. We either accept too readily that others have superior power or we don't realize that they perceive themselves as having more power than makes sense in the situation.

Begin now to think about situations in which you've invested others with undeserved or unearned power. In one family, an adult sister, Maureen, becomes angry over little things and attempts to control others with the mere threat of her disapproval. For years, this family has tip-toed around her in fear of her outbursts. She has a great deal of power. But why? So what if Maureen threw a tantrum over a trifling matter? What would happen if others simply ignored her—essentially demonstrating an unwillingness to enter into the game? They might find that her power extends only as far as *they perceive* it.

Perhaps you've done this with your partner or the clerk in the store or even your boss. Or, you may not have realized just how much power a particular person has in relation to you. You are too casual in your attitude and enter into a negotiation unprepared for the other party's facts, figures, positions, and solutions. You may look to your past and examine what you might have done differently if you had known then what you know now.

Have you ever been in a situation in which the perceived power of the other person didn't match the behavior? Or, perhaps you thought a person didn't have much power, but as the interaction went on, you realized that you miscalculated—this person had copious information and a way of presenting ideas that increased credibility immediately.

Check out the Power Analysis Form at the end of the chapter. It is designed to help you recognize and evaluate the power and type of power you bring to and face in a negotiation.

WHY SHOULD I BELIEVE YOU?

There once was a woman who claimed that she had seen an accused murderer near the crime scene on the night of the murder. How wonderful! That should bolster the prosecution's case. That perception lasted about 10 minutes. Why? As it turned out, this woman had claimed to be a witness in any number of cases — in fact, she took money from a tabloid television program to tell her story. Oh well, no one will believe her, the prosecution concluded. They had doubts about her themselves. This actually happened in the O.J. Simpson trial, and it happens in cases that are low-profile too. Witnesses are eliminated because they just aren't credible.

A father told his son that it was wrong to steal. For years this admonition worked. One night, when the boy was about 16, he overheard his father talking with a business partner. They were figuring out a way to hide some income so they wouldn't have to pay taxes on it. It was clear that their scheme was illegal, and they were, in effect, stealing. So much for the father's credibility.

You are overweight and feel very bad about it. You know that these extra 75 pounds are damaging to your health. When you go to your doctor with your problem, she waves her hand. "Don't worry," she says, "a few extra pounds won't hurt you." You know this simply isn't true. Besides, you are carrying around more than a few extra pounds. It does seem odd that this doctor is obese herself. Perhaps she's in denial, and that's why she makes these claims. You begin to doubt her ability to treat any problem you have.

The minister is now a prominent television personality. Oh how he can talk about family values and the sinful nature of much of American life. He gathered millions of followers around him and they were quite a powerful force. The dollars rolled in as fast as snowflakes in a blizzard. What a ministry he built — it was legendary! Too bad he got caught with that prostitute one afternoon. At first he tried to deny it and claimed that God's enemies were behind these lies. But there was that videotape — oh well, another fallen hero.

We are all familiar with situations in which a person's credibility is called into question. Sometimes this is obvious, as in the cases cited above, but the credibility question is often more subtle. Credentials can be defined as the specific skills, education, and experience, among other things, needed to hold a particular position or practice a profession. In many situations having proper credentials is very important. We don't go to a plastic surgeon who has not gone to medical school and who can't demonstrate specific abilities.

If you're hiring a marketing consultant for your firm, you will ask for references and some evidence that the person whom you hire is competent. That's the reason for resumes and sometimes we even use other people to screen applicants for us, and we have confidence that the head hunter or employment service we use is competent. This is demonstrated by reputation and provable facts.

IT'S NOT ALWAYS SO EASY

Credibility is not always an easy concept to define. Conduct and attitude as well as hard facts will certainly contribute to our sense that a negotiator is credible, meaning believable and able to inspire confidence. Behavior doesn't always match credentials, which then puts our confidence in question. When a convicted criminal is put on the witness stand — for either side — his or her credibility is always in question. But, let's say that this person can demonstrate that his or her statements are backed up by facts. Confidence is then starting to be built.

We build our credibility over a lifetime in many different ways. In day-to-day interactions credibility involves reliability; if we're reliable we are consistent and we do what we say we're going to do. However, most of can demonstrate credibility in some areas and not in others. We can't pretend to be what we aren't, at least for very long.

Because this is such an important issue, as well as a difficult one to define, let's look at some key components of credibility.

Competence: The real estate agent has sold many large estates, and has usually found buyers who are qualified and willing to pay a fair price. You are interviewing her and she tells a few stories about some tough negotiating she's done in the past. She can back her words up with a demonstrable sales record. So, you know this agent is credible.

The housing contractor you are using has proven his credibility by showing you a book he's written and the portfolio of articles he's published about solar heating. He's on the cutting edge, so to speak, and his knowledge of new building concepts and technologies is second to none. That consultant you're hiring to train your computer staff recently gave seminars for three companies, in which she introduced an innovative software package. Sounds credible to me.

Sandra has held her position for many years and the company has continued to grow under her leadership. Arnie may not like some of Sandra's decisions, but he has to give credit where credit is due. She is credible when she talks about profit and loss issues.

Julie's boss seems to know very little about anything other than his narrow job. Joe didn't even know what telecommuting was, nor was he aware of the city's policy to offer tax breaks to those companies instituting work-at-home programs. He loses credibility because he doesn't keep up with his field. Similarly, a professional in any field will lose credibility if the client knows more about recent developments and research in the professional field.

Character: Sandra is honest, if a bit secretive; Michael is basically a decent guy, if a bit thoughtless sometimes; Julie is trustworthy, even if she seems a bit stubborn now and then. All these personality and character issues affect how we view credibility. If, for example, Julie was known to lie about her productivity, she wouldn't be a good candidate to work at home. Sandra may not reveal as much as her employees would like, but she doesn't tell outright lies either. If Jackie thought that her husband was a jerk, then she wouldn't expect him to listen to her vacation proposals. Yes, he gets a bit self-centered and his ideas are old-fashioned, but he doesn't want his wife to be unhappy.

These are people who have what is known as "good character." They do what they say they're going to do and if they find themselves unable to carry out a promise or a commitment, they don't try to cover up for themselves by lying. They are willing to take responsibility for what happens in their lives and they take responsibility for their mistakes, especially those that affect other people.

If your doctor is always late for appointments and never apologizes, his or her opinions in other areas may be doubted too. A parent who lies a lot is not considered a credible role model; a politician who claims to respect women and then harasses them in private loses credibility because of character issues.

Sociability: While a back-slapping good time Charlie may not appeal to us, a cold fish who doesn't exhibit any ability to casually interact with us doesn't inspire a sense of confidence either. When we refer to sociability we are talking about that person's capacity to be liked by others. We don't have to be our real estate agent's best friend, but we want to like him or her.

Julie's boss loses credibility because he has no social skills at all. Everyone who works for Joe wonders if he has any friends—and no wonder three wives have left him. Sandra has many allies in the office because she's friendly, if a bit guarded and brusk at times.

Arnie is a likeable guy and his friends sometimes tease him about being such a complainer. In his case, the merits of his positions are lessened by his constant negative banter. Arnie's credibility would rise if he chose his "battles" more carefully. He's a thoughtful guy, so this can be accomplished.

Tony and Cathy are respected and liked by their co-workers. In fact, if they decide to start their own company, many people will miss them. Their office manager is well-liked, too, so three sociable, competent people will be negotiating.

There are negotiators who will deliberately project a kind of rough, no nonsense image. They don't care if they are liked—after all, their client's interests are at stake and they feel no need to get along with others during this process. This may work on occasion, but if they use this stern demeanor to make the process unpleasant, they may lose some ground in the end. Part of credibility involves fairness and those who are unwilling or unable to interact with others lose credibility.

Composure: What if Julie begins to negotiate with Joe and when he says no to an element of her proposal, she responds by screaming and calling him names? Her credibility as a professional would take a nose dive. If the minster who is caught with the prostitute responds by waving his arms around and talking about the press as Satan's messengers, the viewers tend to laugh him off as a buffoon and a hypocrite.

If Tony and Cathy begin to tap their feet and nervously wring their hands, the office manager is likely to wonder why these two people are so upset. After all, they're just having a meeting. In other words, their behavior isn't matching the setting. They have lost their composure, which we can define as a personal demeanor in keeping with the situation.

When a person is composed, that is, behaving in a way that matches the situation, then knowledge and competence are implied. There is an impression that the person has prepared well and is easy with the process. Keep this in mind if you are choosing someone to negotiate for you in certain situations. If you are an actor and your agent stutters and stammers every time he negotiates your fee for a job, then realize that his credibility is probably in question. You may not be getting the representation you deserve—and are paying for.

Dynamism: Most of us like dynamic people, in that we sense an enthusiasm about the task at hand and a self-confidence that can put others at ease. We sometimes speak of this as "presence." This quality works in favor of Tony and Cathy. Around the office, they are sometimes known as the "dynamic duo." This is one reason they can even contemplate going out on their own; they have personalities that exude credibility and when asked to "prove" their competence, they can. This is a dynamic combination.

Julie is also a dynamic person, which could act in her favor. If she prepares well, has information ready to counter her boss's negative responses, and can keep her composure, she might prevail because she has strong presence.

Stature and presence can be undermined if inexperience is exposed by other negotiators. If Julie tells her boss that she's never negotiated anything, then she's losing an element of dynamism and presence; if Sandra opens a negotiating session by telling Arnie that he should leave the details to her, she may be trying to gain control by presence. Arnie may challenge this statement or he may slump further down in his chair. If he does the latter, he's giving up any chance to show that he can be dynamic and confident too.

Clothing and personal behaviors can add to or detract from a negotiator's presence. When George Bush sat in his golf cart and spoke to the press about his order to send troops to Saudi Arabia, some citizens thought he was being too casual about such a serious matter. The fact that he was on vacation only served to reinforce this image. He had to work to regain a sense of seriousness and dignity when he later spoke about this issue and attempted to gain the confidence of the public.

Similarly, when Bush called his two opponents "bozos" (in relation to foreign policy) during his re-election campaign, many Americans thought he was behaving inappropriately and foolishly. (This thoughtless name-calling was particularly damaging because Al Gore was both a Vietnam veteran and supporter of Bush's foreign policy.)

President Clinton has his own problems with credibility, mainly because of some personal issues and the appearance that he changes his positions a lot. Some people even criticize his willingness to be seen jogging on the streets of Washington. Somehow, that doesn't fit the image many have of the high office. On the other hand, people say that Al Gore is too stiff and he's even made jokes about this himself in order to counter that image.

(If it sounds like it's difficult for a politician to win no matter what he or she does, you're right. We like our presidents to be accessible but not too casual, likeable but tough, and dignified without being stick figures. Now that we see them so often and in so many settings, there is no mystery surrounding them and this balancing act can be nearly impossible.)

Let's say that Julie's boss decides to let her work at home two days a week. But, before he gives the final okay, he wants to see her office set-up and he agrees to stop by to evaluate it on a Saturday morning on the way to the gym. We know that Julie is smart, so she'll make every effort to present her home office well. Will she answer her door wearing a bathrobe or jeans? Probably not. She'll wear casual clothes, just below the level of professional office garb. Her husband will take their teenage daughter to the mall and they'll stash the clutter in the hall closet. The isolated office will be in "ready-to-go" condition.

What if the fax machine was in the kitchen and the cat was sleeping on top of the computer? (Of course, those of us who have home offices know that the cat is likely to do just that.) Julie will shoo her cat, Shadow, away at the last minute and close the office door so the critter can't get back in. The office will speak loudly for itself and so will Julie. Sure, Joe can show up in cut-offs and sneakers, but he's got the power here. Julie has to project dynamism and competence — a powerful combination.

I've seen people who should be credible, but aren't. They are generally people who either believe that they already have so much power that they don't have to worry about mere appearance and projected image. Or they may believe that all this image business is silly, outdated, and beneath them. They want to play the game, so speak, by different rules. Trouble is, the other parties don't know this, nor do they know the new rules.

Understand that you can't isolate the components of credibility. Each of the pieces are important to the overall picture. If you play competence to the exclusion of everything else, you may be seen as competent, but not very likable; that makes negotiation difficult. If you play character to the maximum and to the exclusion of competence, people will like you, but feel bad as they give the job to someone else who was less likable but clearly up to the task at hand. I separate the pieces of credibility to help you understand the concept, but keep in mind that it takes all the pieces to produce the most positive perceptions of your credibility.

Image, appearance, and presence will vary widely from locale to locale. Let's say you are a small-town veterinarian, and you are going to negotiate with your landlord for more space for your office. The landlord is a lawyer who knows you well and the two of you attend the same church. You are both equally liked in the community and you have about the same social status. You finish with your last "patient" of the morning, throw on your jacket, and head across the street to your landlord's office.

You expect to find him with his shirt sleeves rolled up and his feet on the desk. Instead, he is in his "court" suit and has an associate with him, a man who is unknown to you. This stranger is wearing expensive clothes and every hair is in place. There you are in your sturdy boots and denim jacket—you're going to a nearby farm when this meeting is over.

Somehow, all this doesn't fit and you begin to wonder if you're being tricked in some way. Remember, you didn't know about this "city slicker" associate. You thought you were dealing with a friend and you were doing what you've done for years — negotiate space, rent, lease provisions, and so forth. Because your landlord didn't tell you about his new absentee partner in property arrangements, he has lost credibility in your eyes.

You now shift your thinking. You're not going to agree to anything today. That's your first thought. You'll study the proposals and go from there. When you return a week later, you dress a bit differently and you bring your personal attorney with you.

While this is changing somewhat, people from urban areas are more likely to want to move more quickly and keep the process going. They also tend to take deadlines more seriously and credibility is often determined by the way in which the other party will meets those deadlines.

In smaller cities and towns, a more casual attitude may prevail, and as a negotiator you may have to adjust your expectations. Similarly, a negotiator from a city who is in a rural setting may hear a person react to an idea or a proposal with a statement like, "We don't do it that way here."

Preparation is the key to overcoming some of these obstacles and establishing — and evaluating — credibility. That's why our vet was smart to delay action. His preparations had been in response to what he perceived as a normal or usual situation. Elements changed and so did he. When he returned with his own attorney, he was making a credibility statement.

TAKING STOCK

It can't be emphasized enough just how important credibility is when entering negotiations. Saying one thing and doing another detracts from credibility. Claiming you have a skill you don't have does the same thing. By the same token, clearly laying out your skills, accomplishments, and abilities adds to credibility, and when you back up statements with information, you add to it again. Remember, you can't isolate the pieces of credibility, they all work together.

Use the Credibility Assessment Form to measure your credibility and that of others. Look at your own strengths and weaknesses and weigh them against these qualities in others. You will always want to think about these issues as part of your preparation. You'll find that it pays off richly in rewards. At the very least, you'll be more relaxed and confident because you are informed and prepared. And you could find that you gain advantage because you've done this important work of evaluating credibility.

IS THERE SAFETY IN NUMBERS?

Most of our negotiating friends will act as their own negotiator and will plan their strategies alone. Tony and Cathy are the obvious exceptions and other conditions could appear, which would change the atmosphere. What if Joe, Julie's boss, brought in the corporate attorneys? Wouldn't this change the conditions under which the negotiation would proceed? There's no doubt that the dynamic of the negotiation changes when each side presents itself as a team, rather than as individuals.

GOING IT ALONE

If you are negotiating with one other person, the atmosphere will take on defined characteristics. As you practice negotiating you'll notice the following elements:

1. You'll be directing all questions and statements to one person and that person is in the same position as you. Sandra will talk to Arnie and he will respond to her statements and questions without anyone around to consult. Julie is probably going to be in the same position, and because of Joe's abrasive personality, she will have to work hard to maintain her positions—and her composure.

2. The responsibility for the terms rests with you. Whatever is said and the manner in which your positions are stated become your sole responsibility. The same is true of the other party. If Sandra agrees to a particular term, she must take responsibility for it. If she must get clearance from her boss, then she'll make the agreement on a provisional basis. However, she is still responsible for everything she says and does.

3. If you negotiate with one person there is no chance for internal disagreement during the process itself. But, let's say Tony and Cathy begin to have a conflict between them. What might happen? The office manager could take advantage of their disagreement. If Joe has his corporate attorney with him but they haven't had extensive conversations about the work-at-home program, then they could begin arguing about various details. This could work to Julie's advantage, or it could delay progress. Julie has to maintain her credibility and offer her clear positions regardless of what Joe and the other party do.

4. When you enter a negotiation alone, you will be required to make decisions on your own. Of course, in certain situations,

there will be delays because the other party will need to seek outside authorization for certain provisions. That one party is the sole representative of whatever entity for which he or she is negotiating. There is no chance to correct mistakes or contradict what is put on the table.

5. Negotiating alone provides a degree of control not present when in a group. There is also a certain status associated with going it alone. The status holds, however, only if the negotiator can perform well alone and doesn't have a serious personality clash with the other party.

In many of our day-to-day negotiations, we are alone. Much of the mundane negotiating we do is with our co-workers or family members or the store manager. If we operate a business, we may negotiate alone, but with more than one other party. However, when it is appropriate to be part of a group, we'll need to watch the dynamics and iron out any possible difficulties ahead of time. But this is the good news. You are already realizing that the topics being discussed in this book and illustrated through the important negotiations in the characters' lives are the same factors you need to consider in each and every negotiation you experience. From whether to get out of bed and go to work or to take a personal day, or to drive to work or take public transportation, you go through the same processes and need to consider many of the same issues. What is improved for you now is your awareness of the entire process in your own life.

THREE'S A CROWD?

Tony and Cathy are an equal team. Because of their personal friendship, sparked by the chemistry between them as a working team, they don't have an established hierarchy. In some settings Cathy is the dominant person; in others, that role falls to Tony. However, some teams are not formed on a completely equal footing. For example, the owner of a company brings his top assistant to help negotiate a long-term contract with a temporary employment service. The owner is still the owner, and the assistant does not have the same status or degree of power. Still, the owner has turned over the preparation to the assistant, and therefore, will rely on the information he provided. When it comes to the final provisions of the agreement, however, the owner has the power.

What would happen if the assistant began to contradict the owner in the final phase of a delicate negotiation? Well, the owner could wield power and instruct the assistant to "butt out." That would probably work to correct the situation at that moment, but it would taint the negotiations because the roles became confused. Later, the assistant could be reprimanded or even suffer the loss of his job because he sparked an embarrassing situation.

On a more personal level, what would happen if Jackie invited their children into the vacation negotiations. Michael is then put on the defensive, because Jackie has primed her children to be on her side. It is likely that they would not reach an amicable solution, because Michael would have lost face. He might even resent being made to appear as an unreasonable bully and his feelings might be hurt as well. As it turned out, Michael and Jackie did the right thing; they kept their problems to themselves and worked it out alone.

I've witnessed any number of negotiations where one team member is in charge of the majority of the preparation work. Meanwhile, everyone is too busy to look over the plan and review the positions. When they are actually in the session, the person with the most power is unfortunately ill prepared and begins to say things that can't be backed up with the facts. Oh dear. The other party can then take advantage of the situation—and astute negotiators usually do.

On the other hand, these situations can fall easily into confusion, making an outcome nearly impossible. The moral of the story is, if you're going to be part of a negotiating team, make sure the strategy is clear to everyone. If one person in the group has more power, then that person will control the flow of information and the responses to the offers.

There are some advantages of a team approach, which include:

1. The opportunity to have the back-up of technically knowledgeable people in certain key situations. You are negotiating with a contractor and you bring along your brother who happens to be an architect. You have the power, but there is a person who can ask relevant questions and probe more deeply into quotes and material costs than you can by yourself. Or, a manager brings the chief engineer to a sales conference because she can explain the technical advantages of a particular approach to solving a problem. The presence of that third party as a source of information can be a powerful tool.

2. If I'm weak in figuring out costs, I can defer to my negotiating partner who is strong on the financial picture of our proposal. We see this deference happen in trials. One attorney knows all about DNA evidence; another is familiar with top expert witnesses on sexual abuse. These attorneys defer to each other when handling these witnesses. Having team members with various areas of expertise can be valuable and in some cases even a bit intimidating to the other parties.

3. Sometimes a group can come up with a much better answer than one person operating alone. Brainstorming, for example, is a dynamic process that a group can engage in to bring forth the most creative solutions possible. Sure, we can and often do brainstorm alone. But, get a group together and the process can take off.

We tend to be individualistic in our culture, but this is beginning to change as we adopt a team approach to management and production. I've recently read any number of articles about team learning and cooperative teaching, both of which point to a growing trend to ease competition and emphasize cooperation. These trends will carry over into almost every area of life.

THIS ROOM IS FULL OF PEOPLE — WHAT ARE THEY DOING?

Some situations require that many people be involved in determining an outcome. We call these "multiple person negotiations." The baseball owners have a team; the players have a team. Individuals from the owners' group may be able to find some areas of agreement with members of the players' team. This can be complex, but depending on the personal characteristics of the people involved, they may have the power to bring about important areas of agreement. In a sense, these owners and players have formed a coalition around certain points, thereby moving the negotiations ahead. Sometimes these coalitions can cause the power brokers to call off the session and regroup. What happens has to do with who holds ultimate power and the ability — or inability — of other parties to compromise.

Cooperative negotiators may actually freeze out the competitive negotiators because they are operating from a different place internally, meaning that it is within their style to come to agreement without undo rancor. On the other hand, the competitive negotiator might rely on his or her power to refuse and everyone is back to the proverbial square one.

You can't anticipate the dynamic of every negotiation, but you can attempt to understand the possible scenarios that could unfold in a variety of situations. Eventually, one day, your preparation will be over and the actual negotiation will begin. Now, all this hard work and the analysis you've learned to engage in will pay off. No one understands this better than our group of friends. Let's take a closer look at the styles we and others bring into negotiation.

Form #3: Negotiation Power Assessment

USE THIS FORM TO EVALUATE POWER, BOTH YOUR OWN and that afforded others. This is an important part of your preparation.

1. Checklist of perceived and actual power:
   - Does it come from a legitimate source, such as position or title?
   - Is it earned?
   - Is it compensatory? Do you or the other party have the power and ability to reward?
   - Is it coercive power? Do you or the other party have the power and ability to punish?
   - Does the power come from expertise?

   A. List the possible sources of your power.

   ____
   ____
   ____
   ____
   ____

   B. List the possible sources of the other party's (or parties) power.

   ____
   ____
   ____
   ____
   ____

2. How much power do you or the other party bring to the negotiation? How actively do you or the other party use the power? Use the checklist below to evaluate this issue.

- How knowledgeable and skillful are you or the other party when it comes to negotiation?
- How effective are your communication skills? What about the other party?
- Who has control of the facts? Are you well-prepared? Is the other person likely to be equally well-prepared?
- How credible are you? Is there anything standing in the way of appearing credible? What about the other person?
- Can you create equitable solutions? Do you have that ability? Have you done this in the past? What about the others involved?
- Can you argue the merits of your position? Do you expect that the other parties can argue the merits of their position?
- Have you evaluated the proposals? Are you competent in this area? What expectations do you have of the others involved?
- Are you committed to the process? How much does the outcome of this negotiation mean to you? What about the others involved? Is the outcome critical to their well-being (financial, emotional, and/or personal), too?
- How dependent are you or others on reaching a solution?

A. Important factors for you in this negotiation.

____

____

____

B. Important factors for others.

____

____

____

Form#4: Evaluating Negotiator Credibility

EACH OF THE FOLLOWING ARE COMPONENTS OF CREDIBILITY. Evaluate each for yourself and the other participants.

1. Appearance
   - Overall physical appearance
   - Voice
   - Appropriate attire

2. Competence
   - Background
   - Credentials
   - Experience

3. Character
   - Trustworthiness
   - Follow-through
   - Image of fairness

4. Composure
   - Appearance of being in control
   - Appearance of being prepared
   - Knowledge of the issues
   - Comfortable or at ease with the process

5. Personal Dynamism
   - A sense of personal presence
   - Ability to communicate
   - Ability to hold attention and impress others
   - Ability to control the process

PART III

CHAPTER ELEVEN

Is That Your Style, Or Just a Tactic You're Using?

OUR FRIENDS ARE READY TO GET DOWN TO BUSINESS. They have done extensive homework on the issues, as the politicians like to say. And following the political analogy, they are ready to debate the issues with their colleagues. And, of course, they're trying to get the best deal possible for themselves. At this point, negotiation becomes a matter of style.

If it seems easier to negotiate with our clan members over which cave we were going to claim for our family, we're partially right and partially wrong. We deal with technological and intellectual sophistication these days, which make our negotiations more complex, and there are simply more things to negotiate. Taking Maslow's hierarchy of needs as a model, we could say that today, we enter negotiations over ideas and things that meet many of the higher needs — the need for personal fulfillment, greater material comfort, and so forth.

The needs our forebears negotiated over were more basic—food and shelter from the elements. However, no matter what the objective of the negotiation, there were strong and weak negotiators way back when, just as there are now. There were domineering types, and we all know what it's like to deal with them, and there were the soft-spoken negotiators, too, who probably could be tenacious nonetheless. Our ancestors no doubt had to deal with jerks once in a while, and there were people who thought that their wishes should be granted—without even having to ask for it.

Most of these folks of the past were probably much like we are today, which means that some things don't change very much. Even the cavepeople probably had the same basic styles we find today, and each type, when well-prepared, analyzed and decided upon tactics as well.

STYLE AND TACTICS — WHAT'S THE DIFFERENCE?

Every negotiator has a style, determined by personality and training. As we've said, style can be identified by paying attention to the negotiator's behavior. We might say that we all have a natural disposition and it will determine our style. Cathy and Tony are confident but not particularly competitive. Julie is determined but prefers to cooperate. Julie's boss, Joe, is a competitive type, and because Michael is a competitive negotiator at work, he thinks that style is just fine at home, too. Jackie doesn't agree. Arnie likes to think he's competitive, but actually he's not. Bluster is not the same as being a competitive negotiator. Once he becomes more knowledgeable he will probably be a solid cooperative negotiator.

Tactics, however, are not the same as style. But certainly, the person's style will influence the kind of tactics decided upon during the preparation phase. We can think of tactics as our toolbox of techniques and strategies. When Cathy and Tony make decisions about where and at what time they prefer to negotiate they are determining their tactics. When they decide which of their options they will present first, they are also dealing with tactics. These decisions don't change their style, but style will be one factor in choosing tactics.

Tony and Cathy, competent as they are, have a strategy. They have decided that they prefer an office on another floor, one that will provide them with all the room they need for now. (Remember, they still have the possibility of their own business looming in the future. This has influenced their choices and the hierarchy of positions they have adopted.) They would be almost as pleased if they were able to move into the co-worker's office across the hall.

They consider this their fall-back position, because it would be a workable solution and not unduly disruptive to the company. Part of their strategy will be the timetable used for presenting that solution. Deciding between themselves at what point they will present their position during negotiations is part of the tactics they'll use to implement their strategy.

When Jackie decided to present another vacation plan — one she would implement alone if necessary — she was working out her strategy and her tactic was to talk with Michael about this when they were alone and not likely to be interrupted. She didn't rush into his office and break into a phone call, nor did she bring it up when they were entertaining guests in their home. Those decisions that revolve around timing and place were part of her strategy to open up a discussion about the way decisions are made in their family. The vacation was her first issue and part of her strategy was to allow enough time to change Michael's usual plan, and her tactics were represented in the way she sparked the negotiation.

Remember, Michael didn't think that he was going to be negotiating. It came as something of a surprise to him that there was an issue at hand. To his credit, he handled it well, especially when he realized that Jackie was serious—the fact that Jackie presented this as such a crucial issue was part of her tactics, based on how strongly she felt about the vacation plan.

IF YOU'RE A COMPETITOR, WHY ARE YOU SO EASY TO GET ALONG WITH?

Remember that the two major negotiation styles are essentially presented on a continuum. At one end is the prototype of the competitive negotiator; at the other end the prototype of the cooperative negotiator is represented. Most people adopt styles somewhere in between the two extremes, and many of us are able to shift back in forth in that broad middle ground, becoming more or less competitive in some settings and more or less cooperative in others. It is also possible that a competitive negotiator, such as Joe, can employ tactics compatible with a cooperative style. This can confuse the other party and is sometimes part of an effective strategy.

Why would Joe do such a thing? Well, even the most difficult person will change tactics in attempt to win something. Let's say that Joe has no intention of granting Julie's request, or at least he will use all manner of tactics to delay a decision. However, he's a smart manager, and he knows that Julie is a valued employee and in fact, he values her too much to completely alienate her. Why she might even look for another job! He can't have that happen. So, he might employ some cooperative tactics in the hopes that he can keep her content with the possibility that "he's working on it." Julie is also smart, and she could counter his, "I'm doing the best I can on this," by suggesting some time limits on the decision.

While it isn't safe to assume that a particular negotiation style will result in a particular set of tactics, there are some generalizations we can discuss. For example, a competitive negotiator could use extreme impatience, threats, or anger. Arnie used these tactics from time to time, even though he didn't have a particularly well-thought-out strategy. It's just part of his style. In his case, these tactics are a sign of weakness and incompetence.

Joe uses these tactics too, but they are an integral part of his competitive use of power. In other words, he employs threats because he can. Nowadays, this style has fallen out of favor in many settings, and the competitive negotiator may avoid using anger as a tactic because it can reflect badly on him or her in other situations.

A competitive negotiator might ask for information before it would be strategically advantageous to release it. Sometimes the request could be viewed as an attempt to manipulate or control. However, a cooperative negotiator could be asking for information because he or she is genuinely attempting to meet the other party's needs. On the other hand, it could be a manipulative attempt to appear cooperative when it is really an attempt to gain the upper hand — a cooperative appearance with competitive motives.

Let's say that Michael demands information about possible destinations for their vacation. He makes that demand knowing that Jackie wouldn't have had time to gather all the details. If he puts a deadline on it, for example, he could be trying to manipulate her because he knows she can't meet this demand. He is hoping to say, "Oh well, it's too late to change the plan now. Maybe next year, dear." There are situations in which this tactic will be used in an effort to win at any cost. This would be an example of extreme competitive style.

Cathy and Tony, on the other hand, will withhold all their ideas in their initial casual discussions of their problem with the building manager. They control the information because they are the ones who gathered it. This team will not ask for a meeting to discuss their problems until they have their strategy planned. They know the manager is not an ogre who likes to thwart people, but they also know that if their proposed solutions are known too far in advance, she will have time to find reasons why none will work — human nature can be like that sometimes. Therefore, timing the disclosure of information is of prime importance.

Traditional negotiation theory holds that a negotiator's style could be determined by observing behavior and tactics. Sure, this is true in many cases, but the reality is often far more complex as professionals become better trained in negotiation skills. For example, if Joe were being trained today, he might attempt to appear like a cooperative negotiator, but at strategically planned moments, the underlying competitive style would emerge. Thus, he's a competitor in cooperator's clothing. The reverse can happen as well.

Many women are raised to be cooperative negotiators. They may believe that this is the morally superior style, or on the other hand, that it is behavior that signals weakness. However, these women may find themselves in a competitive work environment and learn that they must sometimes adopt the competitor's tactics in order to move forward. They sometimes do this because it is necessary but they still don't like it; others believe they have actually learned the more effective way and are stronger people for it.

As we've said, there is more involved here than just a decision to adopt a particular style. Body language, choice of words, and even the way we dress can all subtly influence how we actually manifest our negotiation styles. And most of us will fall into one category or another and most of the time our tactics will reflect this style. The key here is to be aware of what is natural for you and to be sensitive to the style of the others with whom you negotiate.

IT'S A MATTER OF BEING A WINNER

It's important to point out that competitive negotiators aren't an anomaly in our society, and in fact, this is a style we have both admired and fostered. It can sometimes appear that these are the "bad guys" of the negotiation world, but this isn't necessarily the case, especially when you take the long view.

Competition is prized in our culture, and we even teach young children the value of competition. Remember, a sense of competition is always present throughout each negotiation; we always want to do the best we can for ourselves.

From the first moment they enter school, children are placed in a virtual pool of competition. They compete for grades, achievements, honors, awards, and class rank. Students compete on the playground and in the classroom — hey, it's the American way, the creed by which we live. One of the most complimentary remarks that can be made about an athlete is that he or she is a *great* or *fierce* competitor. In short, it's not about being good or bad, it is about being effective or ineffective.

One of the byproducts of competition is the concept of winning and losing. The negotiator who has a competitive style views the process as an adversarial one, which means that there always must be a winner and loser. The competitor is not particularly interested in the other party's needs, because that person is the opponent and if he or she loses, then that's way the process works.

When Michael Jordan assesses a team of opponents, he evaluates individual skills and the team's playing style. But, he also focuses on the team's psychological stability and emotional profile. Could this or that player be rattled and weakened? If that team falls behind, how do they react? Do they pull together and fight back or do they tend to lose confidence? Virtually all top athletes become astute at this kind of psychological assessment.

Competitive negotiators in other settings do the same thing. They assess the progress based on the emotional issues involved in the bargaining. The most effective competitive negotiator will watch for loss of confidence or weakened position. This competitive person may have a friendly, even casual demeanor, but he or she still believes that the outcome is a win-lose situation.

To a competitor, every opponent is an adversary. One reason that sports analogies often carry over into other areas of life, most especially the business world, is that the true competitive type adopts an attitude that the other party is an adversary. Some people find it odd that athletes can be so adversarial on the court or field and the next day play golf together and invite the other team's members over for a friendly backyard barbecue. Similarly, many people watch the courtroom behavior of lawyers and find it difficult to believe that these adversaries may actually like and respect each and often see one another socially.

Some people are very good at competing alone, and when achievement is based on individual performance, these individuals will excel. But put these loners on a team, where winning depends on working together, and they may not shine so brightly. Competitive negotiators who are part of a team must learn to compete together or they will end up in opposition to each other. A well-coordinated team is indeed a formidable opponent.

The most competitive baseball team, for example, prefers never to concede even one run. The shut-out is the ideal and every game is played with that goal in mind. The competitive negotiator also will fight not to concede anything. Sure, it doesn't always go that way, but that team will then play the cards that are dealt and do what is necessary not to concede another run.

The most competitive negotiator starts with a similar premise. When he or she uses cooperative tactics, this is usually done to cover up the reality of the goal, which is to win every point. A concession might be something that was not very important anyway — although that is rarely disclosed. Remember, there's no good or bad here; it's about being effective and ineffective.

Many people use words such as tough, dominating, and aggressive to describe the highly competitive negotiator. It's no accident that these are also the words used to describe our most high-achieving athletes — and attorneys and CEOs. And it's important not to make moral judgements about the competitive negotiator, even though he or she is not always be particularly well-liked. This isn't a matter of good versus bad, right versus wrong. It's smarter, for our purposes here, to evaluate the negotiator based on effectiveness. Because, after all, there are both effective and ineffective competitive negotiators.

There are times when a person can appear to be all these things — tough, dominating, and aggressive, and still be enormously admired by his or her peers. This admiration is usually the result of knowing that the person has basic integrity and is fair. He or she also usually has good social and communication skills and is, therefore, not personally abrasive or even offensive. These are usually the most effective competitive negotiators.

Those people who are impatient, always annoyed, and look like they're ready to explode are usually not effective negotiators, no matter how intimidating their bluster can be. One reason they aren't effective is that their egos get in the way. Again, imagine how ineffective athletes are when they appear to be nothing more than big egos that care little about others on their team. The ineffective competitive negotiators tend to be short on ethical standards, just as they are short on social skills.

Julie's boss, Joe, represents a competitive negotiator who can often far less effective than he might be were he to have reasonable social skills or high ethical standards. But Joe doesn't really care about that. He believes he can manipulate Julie and essentially shut her up, and his superiors, who might even like her idea, will be none the wiser. He intends to rely on bluff and anger as a way to brush her off. But because he doesn't want to lose her, he might just dangle something — a possibility that he'll okay her request — to keep her waiting. Julie, however, is on to Joe, so we'll see what might happen.

If you know you will be up against an effective competitive negotiator, then you should take extra care to be well prepared. Any weakness on your part—and remember that you will, for the time being, be an adversary — will surely be taken advantage of.

He or she will not look at this as an ethical issue, but rather one where greater competence leads to a natural conclusion. An effective competitive negotiator might consider it a lucky break that you didn't have your act together. This is not considered related to the issues of good and bad or right or wrong; it's simply a matter of advantage and disadvantage, and ultimately, being effective or ineffective.

Competitiveness is an innate quality, and most of us have it to one degree or another. In a person who has a strong dose of it, this quality drives the person and may dominate all relationships, both private and business-related. The competitive negotiator doesn't like to lose a game of tennis either and may need to believe that he or she "wins" more in personal interactions.

One of the reasons Arnie is so uneasy with negotiations is that his mother was an extremely competitive and influential person, who projected the importance of doing well and doing right onto her son. If Arnie received an A in biology he would soon ask himself why it wasn't an A+, and if he could get an A in that class, then why couldn't he get one in history as well. Unconsciously, Arnie turned off to the whole process. He simply stopped trying to please others, because there was literally no way to win.

There is always a greater possibility that negotiations will break down when one or more competitive negotiators are involved in the process. If you are buying a house from a person who won't give an inch either on price or on terms, then you know the feeling of having to either give in to everything or simply give up. If you ask that the washer and dryer be included in the price, what will you think when the person says, "You must be crazy to think I'd give you that," or, "What do want that for?" (You can bet real estate brokers don't like this kind of client either.)

Some extremely competitive types will believe they are losers if they concede any point; they'll risk the outcome and wait for a weak negotiator to show up. On the other hand, those who have to win everything all the time, can end up with nothing, so there are ways to bring these stiff competitors around. After all, the person does ultimately want to sell the house. If you're confronted with a hostile statement in any negotiating setting, it's best to bring good sense and rationality back to the process. Your strength will be your ability to resist the bait to get into an exchange of sarcastic remarks.

COOPERATIVE NEGOTIATORS WANT TO WIN, TOO

Many people believe that cooperation is the happy road to resolution, and they place a high value on commitment to a process. Cooperative negotiators would usually say that they believe in a win-win situation. They see the process as essentially fair and it's most certainly not a game. The athletic analogy doesn't work here, because of the clear need not to have a one-up, one-down outcome. Much as we in this country love to talk badly about our politicians, legislation is often a process of cooperative negotiation. In fact, when it's not, it's often unsuccessful. Legislators are often superb cooperative negotiators because they know that's how to get things done. However, they may then turn into fierce competitors at election time, where there is inevitably a clear winner and clear loser.

In general, cooperative negotiators rely on communication to uncover the interests, values, and attitudes that are shared by all the parties involved. The common ground is then used as a basis for the inevitable give and take. The very cooperative negotiator will consider the best process one in which a mutual exploration of the issue results in a satisfactory resolution. Mediators, whose job it is to bring parties together to reach a mutually agreed upon solution to a problem, are probably the best example of cooperative negotiators. They start with a mindset that working together has great value in and of itself.

There is a reality in negotiation that even cooperative negotiators can't deny. When there are two or more people advocating different positions, there is going to be a natural tension between two conflicting motivations. There will always be the competitive drive present, which leads to the desire to maximize the gains and rewards. But there is also the countering desire to reach a decision that is fair to all involved. The competitive negotiator focuses on the first motivation, and often could care less about the second. The cooperative negotiator will have to find a way to reconcile both objectives.

Cooperative negotiation should not necessarily be considered the better approach, because it is simply one route to a destination. In addition, not all cooperative negotiators are equally skilled and they can do things that sabotage the process, too. Cooperative negotiators can be either effective or ineffective and a cooperative spirit doesn't guarantee success.

Cooperative negotiators want to win, just as their competitive counterparts do. However, they care about the process, wanting it to both meet their needs and preserve personal relationships. They also want to achieve their goals by using ethical and fair means. Winning through trickery or deception does not seem like a positive outcome to a cooperative negotiator.

Most people perceive cooperative negotiators as fair, sociable, tactful, and friendly. He or she will move away from a position in order to consider another realistic option, and this type of negotiator will not engage in threats or power plays and tends to be sensitive to the needs of others.

What makes this kind of negotiator ineffective? A cooperative negotiator is almost always perceived to be fair, but that isn't necessarily enough. This type of person might disclose too much information too fast, and may not appear professional or organized. If they appear weak, then their positions are not taken seriously and they can be pushed into agreements that aren't in their best interests or the interests of the parties for whom they're negotiating.

Effective cooperative negotiators are never viewed as pushovers, and their competency is usually part of what makes other people comfortable with them. They will use rational and logical positions in order to engage others in the process and mutual trust is assumed. A cooperative negotiator who isn't so effective can be swayed and diverted from the goals presented at the outset.

Since the cooperative negotiator wants to reach an agreement based on the rational and objective analysis of the facts on the table, he or she must be careful not to be exploited by appearing weak. The competitive negotiator will seek concessions from the cooperative party, and if too many positions are given up or altered, there will be little left to concede in the final stages of the process.

Whereas the competitive negotiator may use conciliation and cooperation as a tactic, the cooperative person will be the most comfortable with this style. He or she could experience anxiety in the face of hostility and challenge and be uncomfortable with an atmosphere of entrenchment. An effective cooperative negotiator understands that not everyone shares the desire to reach a win-win outcome. As we've seen, the truly competitive negotiator doesn't believe that such an outcome is even possible.

To be successful, the cooperative negotiator often must rely on the joint efforts of the others involved in the process. If all negotiators are basically cooperative, then the outcome will probably be one with which all parties can live. However, there are negotiators who appear to be cooperative but aren't. These people don't work in unison with others to uncover areas of mutual concern and the outcome can be one-sided.

Let's say you are negotiating with a person who says, "Will these terms meet your needs?" The competitive negotiator will see an opportunity to gain control and perhaps increase demands; the cooperative negotiator will appreciate the gesture to ensure mutual effort to bring the interaction to a conclusion.

Watch for the congruence with which one communicates. Do the words match the body language or do they contradict each other?

Most negotiators fall somewhere in the middle of the spectrum; few people can be extremely cooperative or extremely competitive because it's simply not in their nature.

IT'S NOT A MATTER OF GOOD AND BAD — SKILL IS WHAT COUNTS

There is a natural tendency to want to divide the world into good and bad and right and wrong. But when it comes to negotiation, most people fall somewhere in the middle of the spectrum, and they don't represent an extreme of either style. While Michael may be more or less competitive in his style and Tony and Cathy are more or less cooperative, the question becomes how skilled they are, rather than which one is better.

In addition, a skilled negotiator knows when to employ tactics that reflect their own non-dominant style. For example, Julie may prefer to be a cooperative negotiator, but when dealing with Joe, she may need to adopt a more competitive style. She will do this because she knows that Joe will take advantage of any weakness she displays.

A competitive negotiator may attempt to rely on emotional issues, but a cooperative negotiator doesn't have to "buy in" so to speak. Protecting information and positions is the job of all negotiators, no matter what their style. The cooperative negotiator can use tactics that essentially uncover the weakness of the competitive negotiator's position. Bluster won't compensate for a poorly formed or weak position. Joe may have to watch out for this. Michael, who knew his position was weak, in that it made him appear to be a bully who didn't care about Jackie's feelings, adopted a cooperative manner.

Both styles have value and can be used when the situation warrants it, but in general, we all tend to one style or the other. And it makes no sense to attempt to adopt a style that is completely incompatible with our basic nature. We can't become what we aren't designed to be. When we negotiate in teams, we may find that one negotiator is competitive and the other cooperative, and tactics will emerge based on the two styles. We may find ourselves confronted with a team in which a greater or lesser degree of both styles is also represented.

SHE LOOKS LIKE A COOPERATOR, BUT HOW DO I KNOW FOR SURE?

A logical question involves the ability to discern the style of those with whom you negotiate. If a cooperator can be competitive and a competitor can be cooperative, how is a person supposed to determine who they're up against (if they're natural competitors), or working with (if they're natural cooperators)? This is an important issue, too, because you will be planning your strategy and employing certain tactics based on the basic personalities and styles of your opponents.

In the extreme, you might run up against a competitor who is highly skilled at employing cooperator tactics. You can be lured into talking too much, exposing your positions too early, thereby leaving yourself vulnerable. You just didn't realize that you were dealing with a competitor.

The circumstances surrounding the negotiation setting will also influence your evaluation of the other party's style. What if you are facing a deadline, a time by which an agreement must be reached? How will the parties react? This isn't always easy to determine, but tactics could change. The cooperator may attempt to bring about an agreement by employing a competitor's tactic too, perhaps a touch of anger or impatience. This depends, of course, on what's at stake. The person who has the most to lose — or the least to gain — may not feel the same pressure of the clock. The competitor with a strong position is probably could react by realizing that the opponent is in a weaker position and use pressure tactics to resolve the problem.

The most important thing any negotiator needs to do is monitor the style and tactics as the interactions proceed. Tactics, strategy, and style have a progressive nature, in that we can't rely on one set of circumstances and style to remain static.

All our friends need to think out the tactics that they will use to reach their goals. But they will also need to watch for signs in others that indicate what tactics are, or soon will be, employed. We will next explore the tactics available to us in negotiation.

A LITTLE TECHNIQUE, PLEASE

When we are on the way to reaching agreement in a negotiation our style and tactics begin to become increasingly apparent. It's crucial to stay with a strategy and use tactics that are natural to us, compatible with our personality and character. We could say that if we behave in a way that others know or at least strongly sense isn't authentic then we will be viewed as phony and perhaps not trustworthy. Sometimes, that unnatural behavior can actually halt progress in a negotiation.

Given what we know about Joe, just imagine how Julie would react if he were suddenly gracious and solicitous. A red flag would go up and Julie would immediately respond with suspicion. "Why is he being so nice?", she'd ask herself. "What kind of tactic is he using?" If Tony and Cathy became nasty with the office manager, she'd be very surprised and might even terminate the negotiating session. Their behavior would signal a break down in communication, not mention being profoundly out of character.

When the tactics change, this also alerts others to pay attention to the point on the table at the moment. A quiet negotiator, who suddenly bellows, calls more attention to him — or herself than the person who is loud and belligerent all the time. This can — consciously or unconsciously — lead the listener to focus on the particular point that's at issue at that moment. The behavior is viewed as the effect; the point being discussed is the cause.

On the other hand, a staid negotiator who becomes lively and even humorous, can add interest and may even divert the other party away from an issue. Depending on the situation, this may or may not be a legitimate tactic.

BEING A PROFESSIONAL

No matter what kind of tactics we employ, if we are operating in a professional atmosphere, we should act in a professional manner. An obvious example of unprofessional behavior would be making a promise that we have no intention of keeping.

Eventually, these particular chickens usually come home to roost. If the office manager, Joy, tells Cathy and Tony that she will explore the option of a separate office on another floor, but has no intention of doing so, then she's being unprofessional. If you're negotiating the price of a house and the owner agrees that all appliances stay, knowing all the time that he or she intends to remove them, then unethical behavior becomes involved. If the owner's attorney knows about this but goes along with the negotiating tactic, then he or she is being unprofessional.

Customer service representatives are acutely aware that they must negotiate as professionals even when the customer is extremely upset. In this case, one party is expected to be professional at all times. In fact, the customer service professional is expected to allow opportunities for the customer to save face by backing off from a belligerent attitude. We've probably all been in situations where a professional attitude emerges on the part of someone who is trained to "handle" us. Our challenge is to get satisfaction without becoming personally offensive.

Many of our negotiations are between us and people with whom we're involved in personal relationships. In the best of all possible worlds, we would always have a caring an harmonious attitude when we negotiate with those we love. However, we know this isn't always true. Unfortunately, many people believe that fighting with a partner or family member or a friend over an issue is a form of "personal" negotiation.

While most of these people would never become bullies in the public or professional sphere, they change their behavior with friends or family. However, most people would be better off if they used the same civilized tactics with loved ones—after all, the hostile tactics usually backfire anyway.

HEY, ACT LIKE A LADY

Two people are negotiating a point and won't give an inch. It's an important point in the negotiation. In fact, these two people have caught an opponent in a half-truth. One person gets angry and pounds a fist on the table. Everyone is shocked. What's the big deal? Well, that negotiator is a woman and pounding her fist on the table is not considered appropriate behavior by the three men in the room, including her own negotiating partner. Let's face it, some people are in the dark ages. No matter that one of the other parties does it all the time. He's not judged by the same standard.

On the other hand, some people expect women to behave in a particular way and may assume that tough, competitive tactics will intimidate female negotiators. However, this is often not the case, and skilled female negotiators learn to handle these situations and may come out on top, so to speak, precisely because they adjust their behavior and their tactics to the situation. I don't recommend that anyone let gender stereotyping guide their behavior in negotiating anything. There are too many exceptions to these so-called "rules."

THE COMPETITIVE WAY

As we've said, each negotiation calls for a particular set of tactics, which are compatible with a strategy. Competitive negotiators may, at any point in the negotiation, use one or more of the following tactics. Now, I'm not saying that you will encounter these as a matter of course. I'm simply saying that they could be used, so forewarned is forearmed. Since we're discussing the middle—or the heart—of a negotiation it's possible that a variety of tactics will be used.

Threat and Argument

"If you don't...., then I'll....", is an example of a threat. If Cathy and Tony said, "If you don't give us a new office, we'll quit," they're issuing the ultimate ultimatum. Or, Michael, thinking he's being confident says, "I'll handle the money in the household and I'll divorce you if you keep arguing."

Cathy and Tony could, depending on their value to the company, actually get what they want based on this threat, but what kind of victory would it be? Michael could end up with a divorce he doesn't want when Jackie decides not to be intimidated. Threats are usually not the best way to end up with good will and at times it can mean losing the whole pie.

In this context, argument is different from discussing an actual issue in negotiation. Here, we're referring to argument that moves away from a point of contention and starts getting personal and may include attacks on other parties in the negotiation.

Holding firm on an important point and arguing for its merits is a legitimate and valuable tactic and ethical negotiators expect to use it.

Asymmetrical Time Pressure

You've invited your business partner out to dinner to discuss some important provisions in your partnership contract. You have a drink, you place your order, the entree comes and goes and the coffee is served. You still haven't mentioned the purpose of your meeting. Your partner begins looking at her watch and mentions something about a babysitter. Quickly, you put your proposal on the table, emphasizing that you need an answer immediately. You have prepared to concede two or three points and you concentrate on these — you appear cooperative, but are you? What have you done?

In brief, you've used time pressure to get the concessions you want and you're even offering your own! You've eliminated the possibility for your partner to study the issues carefully. If your partner were a skilled negotiator she might have brought up the purpose of your dinner earlier. But you chatted about all kinds of things, not leaving an opening for her. Usually, this kind of tactic is used when we want last minute concessions. In a boss-employee negotiation, time pressure can be manufactured, usually by the boss. It's wise to watch for this tactic, because it can be used spontaneously.

Belly-Up

One way to control a negotiation is by getting the other party to disclose information. A competitive negotiator might attempt to do this with naive innocence, much like Peter Falk's famous character, Lt. Columbo, who often seemed puzzled, even befuddled. The person from whom he was attempting to elicit information appeared, temporarily, to be the dominant party. The false sense of dominance usually led to disclosing too much information and we all know the outcome.

This can be a valuable tool in any negotiation, and proves, to an extent, the importance of listening and asking questions. If the other party isn't as skilled, you might find yourself with a clear advantage. Tony and Cathy could perhaps use this tactic when they begin to talk with Joy about the company's future plans. Maybe they're trying to find out if the company is planning to relocate to a different suite of offices. Or, perhaps they'll probe a bit to determine if there are cutbacks planned.

Bluffing

Let's say that Joe tells Julie that there is no possibility to have a telecommuting plan and his bosses have said the company will never change this. Julie's response could be to turn around and walk out of the office. Or, she could ask about the city's statute that mandates telecommuting programs. She could keep the subject open to discover if Joe is bluffing.

Bluffing is not a good tactic in most cases, particularly if your bluff can be easily exposed. Generally, bluffing leads to suspicion and the negotiator loses credibility.

"Boulwareism" or Best Offer First

Yes, this is a word, actually a name. Lemuel Boulware once used a particular tactic in labor negotiations. He stated that the company he represented had one proposal and it couldn't be changed or modified. The National Labor Relations Board held this to be an unfair labor practice, because in a sense, it shut down all negotiations. Today, when a negotiator states an offer and says that it's firm, non-negotiable, not subject to revision, and not open for discussion, he or she is said to be employing a Boulwareism. This has come to be known as the "best offer first" tactic, and should be used only by someone who has the power to carry out the promise not to compromise on any point.

This tactic isn't used often, precisely because the logical result is impasse. So, be careful and think before you draw a line in the sand, especially in the middle of a negotiation.

"Brer Rabbit," or Anything But That

Remember the story of Brer Rabbit? The fox traps a rabbit, who pleads for any fate — except being thrown into the brierpatch. Of course, this is what the rabbit really wants. So, after such begging, the fox finally does exactly what the rabbit *claims* not to want.

Sometimes, we end up with what we say we don't want — whether that's true or not. So, be careful if the other party says, "Anything but that!"

Crossroads or Tangled Webs

If Joe begins the negotiating session with Julie by hinting that she may be up for a promotion or a raise, this would begin to confuse the issues on the table at the moment. Mind you, Joe isn't actually offering these things, just hinting. Julie could become confused. Or, let's say that Joe offers her another, bigger office. He expects that she will give up her other requests and be satisfied with a new office.

Sometimes a negotiator will concede on insignificant things, which then leads the other party to make a concession, too. So be careful that you don't concede something significant just because a concession was made to you.

Disassociation

To Arnie, a monetary raise has a distinct value. If Sandra tries to offer other "perks" and attempts to change Arnie's mind about the value he places on an increase in his paycheck, then she is trying to break the association he has between money and achieving his goal. We see this happen in many negotiation settings, and be aware that the other party might attempt to break the psychological connection between your interests and what is required to meet them.

Fait Accompli

If Michael opens a new savings account, in his name only, and then tells Jackie this is done and can't be changed, then he's engaging in a tactic that could backfire. To be presented with a *fait accompli* is always disconcerting for anyone. Jackie might reasonably conclude that Michael is either shutting down negotiations or throwing some power around to intimidate her and show that he can win any argument that involves changing the way family finances are handled. They could end up at an impasse.

Faking it

This is essentially a diversionary tactic meant to move attention away from the real goal or objective at hand. The person could say, for example, "I need more information before I can make any decision here," when both parties know that isn't true. You may or may not comply with the request, depending on the circumstances.

Limits

Sandra could present Arnie with a list of issues she is willing to talk about, thereby limiting what is on the table. She may also introduce a time element that wasn't present before. In other words, she is employing a tactic that can imply that the negotiating session is now under pressure. This could make Arnie vulnerable and he could begin to make ill-advised concessions.

Media or Community Pressure

This tactic is used in high-profile situations. Either party in the baseball strike is vulnerable to media or community pressure. This isn't likely to be brought up in the middle of the typical negotiations most of us will be involved in, but the potential for it is usually known to both sides. An exception could be a community group, for example, that is opposing a toxic waste incinerator proposed for a site in their community. The community group has quietly gone about formulating its goal, which is to build the incinerator in a location outside of town.

When the group met with the parties involved in building the plant it was clear that the incinerator plans were firm and could not — or would not — be changed. At that point the community group said that it had no choice but to go public with the issue.

Mutt and Jeff—Good-Cop/Bad-Cop

This tactic is used when negotiating in teams. One member seems willing to cooperate and engage in give and take. The other member of the team has a stubborn or uncompromising demeanor. When Tony and Cathy negotiate for their new office, Tony might say, "We really appreciate your willingness to talk to us about this issue." He appears yielding and ready to talk. Cathy could physically stand back and indicate both verbally and with body language that she expects something to change — fast.

Limited Authority

Sandra might tell Arnie that anything she agrees to is subject to approval by her supervisor. She is warning Arnie that her authority is limited. Joy or Joe could do the same thing. They could both claim that they don't have the authority to make a decision. They may say this even if it isn't completely true and if the other parties know this, they can change tactics that reflect that they know this. Another way to deal with this tactic is to ask for a time by which the superior can be contacted.

Reversal

Let's say that Michael is listening carefully to Jackie as she talks about changes in the way money is handled in their family. He appears to be cooperative and even a bit on the defensive. But without any specific warning he takes the offensive stance and begins making demands that were previously not on the table. This could throw Jackie a bit because she is not prepared for new issues or a new attitude on Michael's part.

Demonstrate Commitment

Just as it's sometimes difficult for a cooperative negotiator to say no to a proposal, it's sometimes difficult to convince a competitive negotiator that a refusal to accept a proposal is firm. By refusing to accept a "no" as a firm no, the competitive negotiator is attempting to convince the other party that he or she is serious and won't give up. At some point, the other party must end this phase of the negotiation, even if that means physically turning away or preparing to leave.

COOPERATIVE NEGOTIATORS PLAY THE GAME TOO

Cooperative negotiators tend to be problem solvers and they generally use tactics that conform to that style. However, when negotiating with a person using competitive tactics the cooperative person must be on guard. The cooperative negotiator can be manipulated to make concessions if he or she is not on guard. However, there is a set of identified tactics that cooperative negotiators use and it's important to watch for them.

Association

If Jackie tells Michael that her plan for the family finances will improve their long-term security and give them more money to take vacations, then she's framing her positions—what she wants — to play to Michael's objective.

Julie might emphasize the potential for her increased productivity when working at home. Joe doesn't like any waste in his department — of time or money. If she attempts to demonstrate that her desire will benefit the company, then she's using the tactic of association. She's associating her goal with the goals of the other party.

Flexibility

Being flexible doesn't necessarily mean making concessions, but it does indicate a willingness to open up areas of discussion that had been closed. In a sense, it's a way of saying, "Let's take another look at issue B." Sandra might try to convince Arnie to take another look at an agreement about vacation time they'd already reached. Perhaps she'll concede something in that area to avoid a concession in another. On the other hand, she might not consider the concession a big issue and in fact is prepared to be flexible about many areas.

Logrolling

This tactic can be used to break an impasse. A cooperative negotiator will try to put everyone's goals in a hierarchy of sorts and separate out the lesser goals from the higher. Julie might concede that her work-at-home idea is new to the company and that Joe is not inclined to want this change. However, if she acknowledges that Joe's highest goal is productivity, she can appeal to that. She has framed her highest goal with his. She might have problems here, however, because Joe is a competitive negotiator and will see every concession as a sign of weakness. However, she may attempt to keep that higher goal always on the table.

Participation — "Me Too"

Arnie might use a tactic that assumes that fairness is an underlying attitude in the negotiation. Arnie believes that after all, others in the company make certain salaries and have particular perks—he just wants to participate the same way the others do. He's using a cooperative "me too" tactic. This can be used when you make it clear that you want what others have received under similar circumstances.

Romancing

This is not as romantic as it sounds. Rather, it's a way of comparing the situation at hand with similar issues. It's a way to get the other party to jump on a particular bandwagon. It is useful when the current issue reflects the past and will influence the future.

Cutting the Salami

Matyas Rakosi, the former General Secretary of the Hungarian Communist Party, is given credit for naming this tactic. In its basic form, it's a way of saying that if you want the whole salami, it's best to get it slice by slice. Cooperative negotiators will generally not ask for all the concessions at once, but will recover what they want a bit at a time. In some circumstances this will be a powerful tactic. In other situations, it isn't wise to fall back on it. Cathy and Tony can agree to accept a compromise office, but there aren't many small concessions to make along the way.

Changing Viewpoint

If Sandra asks Arnie to look at the issues on the table from the company's point of view, and he agrees, then Arnie is allowing himself to temporarily change viewpoints. This can be effective on either side, especially if the other point of view is another entity or individual outside of the actual setting. It's not Sandra's viewpoint, after all—it's the *company's*.

Splitting the Difference

This is a familiar and popular way to end a negotiation. The sides essentially exchange concessions, presumably of equal value. We usually split the difference when money is involved and the issue has been blocking agreement. We should avoid this 50-50 split arrangement if there are many other issues still on the table. And you aren't obligated to agree to it. Because splitting the difference is a common tactic, however, you are likely to run into it as you negotiate many issues.

ARE WE HAVING FUN YET?

Things are getting tense, perhaps even unpleasant. It may be time for a break, even if only for a few minutes. Others may feel this way, too, and we could be confronted with a couple of scenarios to deal with.

Apparent Withdrawal

Let's say that Arnie insists that something unfair is going on, but actually he just wants a break to think. This is a way to disrupt the proceedings and is not wise if Sandra is being fair and focused. If Jackie tells Michael that he's being a jerk and leaves the room when he's behaving normally, this tactic could shut their conversation down and when it reopens it may not have the same tone. We should never make false claims about problems that don't exist. If we do, we run the risk of permanently altering the atmosphere of the negotiation.

On the other hand, the negotiation could be taking a destructive turn and a break can actually give negotiators a chance to evaluate their behavior and cool down. A temporary halt in a negotiation setting can be like the "time out" tactic parents use to isolate a child who is being obstinate.

Bland Withdrawal

The atmosphere can shift if one negotiator acknowledges the negative turn of the interaction but is nonchalant about it. This can disarm the other party and serve as a kind of mental jolt. It disrupts the flow of the exchange and provides room for the negotiation to revert to the positive tone set in the beginning. Sometimes these breaks can involve refilling coffee cups or indicating that it's time to call for lunch.

A competitive negotiator may resume the same tactics, making this yielding tactic ineffective. On the other hand, the other party may have time to regroup and in some cases, end the negotiation session if it appears that hostility or belligerence will continue.

THAT DOESN'T SOUND RIGHT, BUT WHAT DO I DO?

Sometimes, the tactics of the other party seem to be unfair, sometimes subtly so. It's wise to be prepared to respond at the time and not be forced to wait until after the session. Following are examples of the types of responses to consider.

Question the Source of the Information

We can all be wowed by data and statistics, but we also know that data can be used to support just about any position. If Julie pulls out a lot of data to support work-at-home programs, then Joe is justified in asking for the source of her information. Perhaps he's gathered negative data—news stories or accounts from companies showing that telecommuting programs didn't work. If Julie is well-prepared, she'll be aware of the data and perhaps point out why those stories don't match the situation they're discussing.

In some situations, negotiations can reach an impasse while the other party's data is being evaluated. We must always be wary of a lot of data that seems skewed to support only one position. Remember the tobacco institute and their studies that have never admitted even one tiny link between smoking and health problems?

Momentary Retreat

If Michael says, "I will *never* agree to separate vacations," or, "I'll never agree to separate checking accounts," then Jackie could say, "Let's discuss our retirement accounts." She's not meeting his challenge nor is she acquiescing. She's simply moving the discussion in another direction. She may be allowing Michael a chance to save face, so to speak, by diverting attention away.

When you're confronted with a "never" statement, then consider shifting the conversation to something else. We see this happen in political negotiations all the time. The person who would never yield ultimately accepts a compromise—it may be months — or even years — later, but that's the way legislation works. It can work that way in our businesses or households, too. It most certainly is apparent in international conflicts.

Confront the Matter Directly

If Michael seems firm in his stance, but not hostile, Jackie may decide to say, "Well, I don't agree, but let's look at the issue again later." She's making it clear that she's not going to back down, nor is she willing to fight over it right now. Julie might tell Joe that he should compare his data with hers and they can talk about the statistics later. Meanwhile, they can move on to issues involving their company.

Mutual Testing

This tactic works between two parties of equal authority, but may not work in a boss-employee or business owner-client relationship. For example, Sandra may keep Arnie waiting in her reception room on the day of their appointment. It would not be wise for Arnie to keep Sandra waiting for their next meeting. But two equal parties may exchange this kind of behavioral tactics, just to test one another. This exchange of tactics can also restore the balance of power and perhaps eliminate this kind of game playing in the future.

YOU'LL PICK AND CHOOSE AMONG THESE TACTICS. BE SURE to consider what is natural for you. While you may be surprised at the moment you encounter a particular tactic, your preparation will help you handle it smoothly — like a pro. It is important to understand the stages and process of a negotiation — and that is the next, and nearly last step.

CHAPTER TWELVE

It's Just A Phase You Are Going Through

EVERY NEGOTIATION PROGRESSES THROUGH A SERIES OF phases, each of which you need to understand. Admittedly, people sometimes don't realize that they actually are negotiating, and problems are raised and solved without anyone understanding that the process of negotiation has even taken place. For example, if you and your partner agree to get an apartment together, you might move quickly through the phases of negotiation.

One of you might say, "Since your apartment is closer to my office, why don't I move into your place?" The other might respond, "That's fine I have more room and we could use your furniture. In fact, it's much nicer than my old stuff. I'll just give mine to that charity down the street." But you say, "I like your dining room table, so why don't we keep that?" Your partner agrees, and for now your negotiations are a simple matter of give and take. Down the road, however, the two of you may have trickier issues to discuss.

Assume that you agree to split the rent or whatever and the deal is done. Every once in a while in life things really do go that smoothly. Neither partner would have said that a negotiation was started and completed.

In most situations, negotiations proceed through clearly defined stages, but the transitions might not be smooth or in a straight line toward a goal. In fact, many negotiations may need to backtrack and bring issues back on the table. Perhaps Michael and Jackie agree to a vacation spot that turns out to be full for the season. They may have to revisit the list of acceptable solutions.

The phases of any negotiation are also influenced by some specific conditions, which include:

- **A shared history:** In many situations, we know the people with whom we negotiate. Our group of negotiating friends may not be on intimate terms with their "opponents," but they do know certain things about them. Arnie knows that Sandra is defensive and often appears brusk and rushed. Cathy and Tony know that Joy values them a great deal and she is fair and very efficient, but she's also not particularly creative and her boss intimidates her. They also know that Jason, the co-worker with whom they'd like to trade offices, is very smart and accomplished, but he's a bit shy and reserved.

Michael might walk around with a sense of entitlement, but Jackie knows that he cares about her and doesn't want her to be unhappy. In fact, like many older men, Michael thinks it's his fault if Jackie is dissatisfied—he just doesn't stop to consider why that might be. Julie knows the worst. Joe has a terrible reputation and is not known to be fair or polite. However, he is smart and wants to protect the company, which could work in Julie's favor in the long run.

- **Other history plays a role:** In the situations we're dealing with here, our friends see the other parties in a variety of settings, some personal and some professional. This other history may influence the way negotiations proceed.

- **The nature of the transaction is important:** If one negotiator knows more about the topic at hand than the other party, this added expertise can be an advantage. For example,

Joe knows nothing about trends in telecommuting; but Julie does, which could work in her favor. If Joe lets his guard down and bows to her experience, this could work against his negative position — he might simply run out of arguments.

- **Location:** We know that Michael likes to talk in the kitchen; Tony and Cathy can illustrate their problem in their own space; Sandra can control her environment when she negotiates with Arnie, and he must remain mindful of that. Atmosphere is part of the location. Should Tony and Cathy offer Joy a cup of coffee in their cramped space? Will that help make the atmosphere pleasant despite the cramped conditions?
- **Is this a good or bad day?:** We all have good days and bad days — it's just the way life is. If Arnie has had an argument with his wife before he is supposed to negotiate with Sandra, it is likely that he won't be at his best. If Tony has a terrible headache, he may be unable to adequately play his part.

Sometimes these bad day scenarios are unavoidable, but if we can, we should try to be at our best when we're entering a serious and lengthy negotiation. In fact, it makes no sense to proceed if we're actually ill or so upset about something that we can't concentrate. We should attempt to postpone the session until we're better, unless, of course, time is the most essential element.

IT HAS TO START SOMEWHERE

Let's say that you and I have been assigned to negotiate a contract for our respective companies. Your company is selling a product that my company wants to buy. You fly to my city and we meet in a small conference room in my suite of offices. We don't know each other and although we've talked on the phone, we've never met in person.

In this situation, the two (or more) negotiators evaluate each other, perhaps telling some stories about deals they've made at some point in the past. I will attempt to determine what kind of negotiator you are, and you will do the same. This is called an orientation period and is the first stage in any negotiation.

Even if we know the other party well, we still have an orientation stage. Sandra and Arnie will exchange pleasantries; Joe will wave his hand toward an empty chair, his way of telling Julie that she can have a few minutes of his time; Michael and Jackie will talk about the events of their day.

The orientation phase also serves as a vehicle to anticipate the attitude and positions of the other party. Is the other party a competitive or cooperative negotiator? Cooperative negotiators may not like to negotiate with people they don't know well and therefore, they don't have a sense or a feel about their personalities or character. This person works to establish trust, and is both polite and initially accommodating. The first phase of the session is spent creating rapport. If the other party doesn't do this, the cooperative negotiator might feel uncomfortable. It's important to keep this in mind and prepare for the possibility that the other party may try to establish a dominant position by not establishing rapport.

A competitive negotiator will use the initial conversation to get information about the opponent's resources, and he or she may even make attempts at humor to defuse some tension and to redirect the conversation.

We sometimes have to face the fact that initial conversation can be strained. After all, the competitive negotiator is looking for another win, and the cooperative negotiator is trying to establish common ground and proceed to resolve conflicts. The cooperative negotiator may need to find a place to start the discussion on common ground, while the competitive negotiator may be resisting the concept of mutual interest.

The initial phase may be further complicated by the lack of information on both sides. Sandra doesn't know what Arnie is going to propose, and for his part, Arnie doesn't know what problems Sandra is facing with her budgeting. Joy knows only that Cathy and Tony want to discuss a space problem, and they don't have the same information about the company's future as Joy does.

Julie knows that Joe doesn't much care how she feels or what he will come up with as a reason to turn her proposal down. On the other hand, Joe doesn't have a real clue about how efficient and organized Julie is going to be during their negotiations.

Each party has determined the position they will use to begin the negotiation process. At some point it is put forward, knowing that it is a first step.

In addition, it may be necessary to confront negativity if it's threatening to take over the atmosphere. Let's say that a person with whom you're negotiating starts the conversation by saying, "This is my line in the sand and you can accept it or not—it's up to you." You might respond by saying, "What kind of attitude is that?" Or, you could say, "Are you saying that you intend to be uncooperative?"

When you challenge the behavior, you begin to establish that you are serious about your side in the negotiation; you shift the energy that's developed in the room. You might not even get a response to your question. But you've engaged in what is known as "attitudinal bargaining."

In many cases, you'll find that the attitude shifts when the person is challenged. It's also important to understand that the other negotiator may be searching for the appropriate attitude and may be inexperienced. In the worst case, the person is just socially inept.

If the situation is hostile, it may be necessary to postpone the negotiations. Let's say that Joy has just learned that her staff is being cut and she will lose two key people. If she is angry and upset, and unable to focus or has a belligerent "you think you've got problems" attitude, Cathy and Tony might be wise to suggest meeting at another time.

In most cases, however, the tone and atmosphere becomes more settled; each party understands how the other intends to proceed. If the introductory stage of the first phase is complete, then the parties can proceed to put their opening positions on the table. The following are three types of initial positions:

- **Maximum positioning:** When Tony and Cathy include their idea for a separate office, they are essentially offering a position they don't expect to get. They are doing this because they want to have something to concede, a point from which they can easily move. If Arnie asks for a 15 percent raise, but is willing to settle for 10 percent, he is engaging in maximum positioning, too. In both cases, our friends are willing to shift from their best case, ideal scenario goal. But what if they weren't? Unfortunately, they might become more adamant in their demands, and eventually shift into a win-lose situation. In other words, if they continue to defend this maximum gain position, they will begin to feel that they've lost something if they back down.
- **Equitable Positioning:** The cooperative negotiator will attempt to put a solution on the table that he or she believes will lead to an equitable solution for all involved. The expectation here is that an amicable solution can be found and the negotiators are there to serve that end. These negotiators tend to rely on mutual trust and may make concessions early on. If they are inexperienced, they may misjudge the other party and give ground too soon. This can also be problematic if the other party doesn't have the authority to reach agreement or if the person won't conclude until he or she perceives a "victory."
- **Integrative Positioning:** In this case, the underlying needs and interests are addressed rather than dealing directly with the positions themselves. While the term sounds as if it is a blending of positions, it actually doesn't establish a position at all. Those who take this approach assume that all negotiators will make concessions, and the integrative positioning may begin a negotiation that is by its nature complex or deals with many issues.

We learn from our past successes and failures. Some questions to guide you through this process are discussed at the end of the chapter. You will find these questions of value as you analyze past negotiations or plan for future sessions. The first phase of a negotiation is very important because it sets a tone and allows the early tensions to be noted. Early positions are established and then the actual work can begin.

WHO KNOWS WHAT, AND IS IT IMPORTANT?

Putting it succinctly, we always want to learn as much as possible about our opponents' position. But this second phase, which I call information exchange, is by definition a competitive activity. There is no doubt that Joy wants to know everything that Tony and Cathy are proposing. It's their job to control disclosure, although Joy has an advantage. She might know that the company is planning to move to another floor, perhaps even the same floor that has the office Tony and Cathy want.

On the other hand, she might know that the company is in real trouble, through no fault of the employees. There could be a cutback, meaning that many jobs will be eliminated. But, Joy doesn't know if this will open up some office space or if it means that our friends will lose their jobs. By now, you should be noticing the importance of protecting the disclosure of information.

Julie has to watch out during this initial disclosure stage, especially since she has so much information and Joe does not. In fact, Julie should attempt to get as much information as she can. What is on Joe's mind? Is he really as negative as he first appears? Does he have any documents to support his position? If she can gather information before she discloses her own, she gains control in the negotiation.

Competitive negotiators will attempt to get information about the opponent's "bottom line" early in the interaction. Cooperative negotiators engage in conversation to exchange ideas and statements about interest. If I'm trying to sell you something, then I will talk about mutual interests and how I can meet your needs. If you're buying, then you'll have limits and interests that only you know at this point. Our information exchange will revolve around protection and disclosure, both of which are carefully timed.

Those of us who are cooperative negotiators run the risk of disclosing too much too soon. This is why Tony and Cathy have taken such care to control their documents. The same is true for Julie, and she has to take care to find out what Joe is thinking before she talks too much. Once information is on the table, it can't be taken back. This means that when we negotiate, we need to spend much of the initial time listening to the other negotiator and integrating information into our own minds.

It's clear that we can't refuse to disclose everything—if we do that there can be no negotiation. Think about Cathy and Tony, for example. If they never say what's on their mind, there can be no interaction. They'd all sit and stare at each other without anything actually happening. Wouldn't that be odd? But as a general rule the more information we gather, the more we can control the negotiation procedure. And we need to disclose what is necessary to keep the negotiation flowing.

Communication is important here, because we not only want to state our positions, we want to interject comments that indicate that we understand the other party's information. You can gain information if you keep asking questions. Joy might say, "I understand that you have an obvious space problem, but what do you propose doing about it? I don't see many options." Or, when other information is disclosed, she could ask for clarification, thereby getting more information on the table.

If you find yourself in a situation where you are asked questions, there are a few things you can do to protect information that you aren't ready to disclose. For example, Joe says, "I don't see how people who work at home get anything done." Julie wants to avoid the issue of her productivity just now. So, she could say, "Have you read the reports on productivity and environmental impact that I sent last week?"

This shifts Joe away from the negative and somewhat personal issue and into a general discussion of the future of working at home. If Sandra quickly asks Arnie if he's willing to accept a three percent raise, he can ask if that's the limit of her authority today. In both cases, the focus shifts away from a statement that could shut the negotiations down to one that opens a new area.

We might also answer a different but related question. If Michael says, "Would the Seaside Golf Resort satisfy you?", Jackie might say, "I know I need privacy." Well, Michael has to evaluate in his own mind if the resort he has in mind is even close to what Jackie has in mind.

Sometimes answering incompletely will help shift the focus and avoid making a commitment too early. If Joe asks Julie if she knows the difficulties in changing personnel policies she might simply say yes. In Julie's mind this isn't the issue, so she doesn't dwell on an issue that she knows can be easily handled. She doesn't want to get into an argument over personnel policy, thereby taking her off track.

If Arnie is making his case about competitive salaries, Sandra might say that she has some information in her office that she'll peruse later. She is essentially saying that the information isn't complete now, but she'll review it and get back to Arnie. Arnie could then pursue a different angle, one of his other arguments for a raise.

There are times when we can answer a question only after asking one of our own. Joe asks Julie how she can communicate adequately with her coworkers. Julie then says, "Do you know about our regular Tuesday staff meetings, and have you noticed how often we've used the e-mail system in the last year?" Joe must answer those questions, which makes Julie's response to his question more meaningful.

In many cases, it is possible to avoid disclosing information while answering a question. Julie does this when she asks Joe what he knows about the telecommuting issue. Arnie does this when, without making his own proposal, he asks if Sandra's authority only extends to the three percent. Neither has disclosed information.

Once the initial jockeying for position is over, and the initial information is on the table, then the second discrete phase of negotiation begins.

SOMEBODY HAS TO GO FIRST

In some situations, it is necessary to be the first to put a proposal forward. For example, Cathy and Tony must do this or the purpose of their meeting becomes confused. After all, they have the only proposal and this is why they requested the meeting. (It's always possible that Joy, anticipating the problem, came up with a proposal of her own. We'll see.)

But what's the difference between initial positioning and a real proposal. Cathy and Tony have positioned themselves by illustrating and stating a problem. They tell Joy that they have an office space problem and they have some thoughts about solving it. At this point, Joy knows that a proposal will eventually come through. If she has no proposal of her own, she must proceed to hear the first real position.

Arnie might put part of his proposal on the table first, because he has more than one issue. Jackie might state the problem — the way they handle money, for example—and let Michael offer his ideas, to which she'll respond with her own proposal. Her proposal becomes the most recent idea on the table. Negotiators tend to remember what has been said or proposed most recently. So, she might have an edge because she has a proposal to which Michael must now respond.

It's always a good idea to clarify the ideas in the other party's proposal before presenting a counter-proposal. For example, if Sandra tells Arnie that they can consider a phased-in raise, then he should ask questions about the terms. If Joy tells Tony and Cathy that they can move in six months, they can attempt to understand the time limit she's imposing.

The first real proposal opens a discussion of the issues. It moves the focus from the general to the particular. Clarification gives each party time to consider what's on the table. In some cases, it can lead to many questions. Let's say that Jackie's proposal involves keeping some of their money separate, a departure from their usual way of handling money.

Michael may be confused by this request, which then opens the door to discuss the reasons for Jackie's changed attitude. If she's well prepared, she'll have her reasons clearly outlined and she can state them succinctly. Michael can then react to the information that Jackie is disclosing. If Jackie is listening carefully, she might find that she can add material to her counterproposal.

Sometimes the proposal on the table exceeds what the negotiator expected, giving him or her time to expand the intended initial proposal. Or, other issues could be added. If Sandra offers 8 percent, Arnie might think about a 12 percent raise, with a portion of it phased-in over a period of time. If Julie senses that Joe is willing to try a trial work-at-home program two days a week, she can include a phased-in third day in her proposal. Remember, she was willing to settle for two days, but she now has an opening to ultimately get what she'd really like.

So, the opening proposals are on the table, and now the discussion is open. But what do we concede? What do we question? What is the other party prepared to concede? This is the meat of phase three.

HOW WILL THIS PLAN ACTUALLY WORK?

Cathy and Tony have prepared a time-table to implement their proposals because they know that Joy will want to know how this plan works on a practical basis. Arnie wants more details about the phased-in raise Sandra suggests. He is trying to evaluate what other benefits he can expect to get if he concedes a point or two.

This is a crucial stage of the negotiation and may not be the most pleasant of times. It can be marked by distrust and competition, even among cooperative negotiators. Joy may begin to wonder how she can justify a major move, and she is ready to reject the idea of relocating the office. In fact, she knows that this is a point to which she can't agree. Cathy and Tony must be prepared to argue for their second choice, even though it involves a bit more than moving a few boxes around. Meanwhile Joy is wondering where she'll get even a small moving cost from the reduced budget from which she operates.

Michael is dealing with many issues, one of which involves a perceived loss of power. If they separate some of their money, what does that say about his authority in his home? Why does this rub him the wrong way? His father never had this problem. Why does he have it now? Maybe he needs time. What if he just says no? This is a delicate stage for Michael and Jackie. She might consider conceding time, but she can't take no for an answer. How should they confront these issues?

The second stage requires support of each position. Why does moving into Jason's office solve the problem for Cathy and Tony? How do they know that Jason is willing to move? At what point will he be brought into the discussion? How can Jackie support her need for separate money? Is there a history of differences over money? How can Julie support her contention that telecommuting programs will improve the company — as well as supporting her own needs? Is Arnie's demand for more vacation time in addition to a raise supportable? How will he justify the request?

You can see that the second stage is an important one, which may very well raise many questions, similar to those above. Joe might ask Julie how the company's public relations department can use a work-at-home program to enhance the company's image. Fortunately, as we've seen, Julie has collected facts about this very issue. This may be the time that she discloses it.

This stage also explores the flexibility of the positions. Arnie might ask, "Why is a phased-in raise necessary at this time?" Sandra might have good reasons for this, which she can disclose. She may choose to focus on another issue, conceding something that will cost the company less money.

It's important that this stage avoid personal attack and rancor. If Joe gets testy, or if Michael begins to feel unappreciated and resentful and brings up his own parents unequal marriage as a way to silence Jackie, then this could lead to an immediate breakdown. In fact, Jackie might say, "We can discuss the particulars later, Michael, but why don't we talk tomorrow about the emotional issues this brings up for you." This may defuse the possibility of great misunderstanding and it does give Michael time to think. There is a risk, of course, that Michacl could become further entrenched in his own resentment, but it may be a risk Jackie is willing to take.

In general, this third stage can lead to further cooperation. In order to insure this, keep these points in mind:

1. Focus on the main points of the position presented. Ask questions that deal with the specific content of the position.
2. Listen carefully to each statement and evaluate it for correct information. Question facts that don't seem like facts or which should be tested for their underlying principle.
3. Avoid personal threats and attacks on the other party's character. Negotiations can break down the minute one person feels compelled to leave the room.
4. Patience and silence are your good friends in this stage. So what if it takes longer than you anticipated? Keep your wits about you and maintain a rational attitude. If you repress your need to fill every gap in the conversation, the other party might disclose useful information. This is true in both personal and business settings. Silence can be golden.

At this point, positions are on the table, information continues to be exchanged, and questions go back and forth. The parties begin looking now for a real agreement, a solution that is acceptable to everyone. Ultimately, a successful negotiation will mean uncovering a solution that leads both or all parties to feel good about the negotiation process. Remember, negotiation is a psychological process that only works when all parties believe or feel as though they have been successful or have won.

As the proposals get discussed, the dynamics of style and tactics, discussed in the previous chapter, come into play. The interaction and dynamics continue until a mutually agreeable solution is crafted with which all parties can live. This process can take hours, days, weeks, months—or even years. Clearly, the length of the negotiation is affected by the parties, their needs, and any external deadlines that may exist.

OKAY, THAT'S IT

Almost every problem is eventually solved through negotiation. If only human beings realized this when a conflict first arises. We'd avoid much hardship and pain if we understood that one way or another, an agreement is reached no matter how stubborn we or others may be. For example, when one or both parties refuse to make changes in a marriage contract, then they eventually negotiate the divorce agreement. When two countries refuse to talk, they may used armed force against each other, and eventually they end up negotiating the terms of the surrender. If a boss refuses to negotiate terms of employment with the staff, then one day, sooner or later, the staff members leave and negotiate new terms with another boss.

In most situations, an agreement is reached after a series of concessions or compromises. Rarely do we achieve everything we put forth in our opening position. We can say that the body of the negotiation is concluded when the parties offer statements that indicate closure. Of course, there are often details to work out and issues that will come up later that need further negotiating sessions. But when both parties accept a common resolution, we can say that agreement is reached.

In some situations, the hardest part begins when the negotiation ends. For example, let's say that two large banks have reached a preliminary merger agreement. It's taken months to reach the basic terms — weeks were spent agreeing on a new combined name. In large corporate mergers, it's not unusual for many months or even years to be committed to drafting the final agreement, and during that time many details may come up for further review.

Although the vast majority of negotiations are accomplished in a matter of minutes or hours, they all come to a stage when what the parties agreed to is solidified and confirmed. In some situations, the agreement is reiterated verbally. For example, Jackie might say to Michael: "So, my understanding is that we've agreed to look for a cabin with a golf course nearby. That's our first choice." Michael might say: "Yes, that sounds fine to me — and I think we can find something suitable in the time we have left before our vacation begins." They have confirmed that they are both agreeing to the same thing.

When we make dates to meet for dinner or to go to a movie, and we settle the time and place to meet, we generally don't bother with written communication outlining our agreement. However, if we contract to complete a project for a new client, we might come to mutually satisfactory terms in a face-to-face conversation or over the phone. We then put the terms in writing, usually in the form of a simple letter of agreement. This avoids any misunderstanding between us. If we agree to buy a house, we will always have a written agreement to examine and it's the real estate broker's job to produce the contract for all parties to review.

Confirming our mutual understanding of terms is a crucial stage of negotiation, one that shouldn't be taken lightly or passed off to someone else. If there are misunderstandings about what has been agreed to, it's advantageous to learn about them as soon as possible. You might believe that you agreed to pay $10,000 to a contractor who will be remodeling your house. But when he gives you his written contract, you see that he's allowed for a 15 percent cost overrun. This was not your understanding, so you and the contractor still have an issue that must be resolved before the first tool is in hand. If you hadn't carefully read the contract, you'd could have been in for an unpleasant surprise. This is an example of a common issue that proves the value of consistently confirming the terms reached during the negotiation session.

KEEPING IT SIMPLE

Nowadays, written agreements can be transmitted by standard mail, fax, messenger, overnight delivery, or e-mail. I advise keeping the language simple and straightforward with as little ambiguity as possible. In most situations, "legalese" should be avoided. If your attorney is drafting a complex document, then legal terminology will no doubt enter the picture, because there are specific terms that govern certain kinds of contracts and agreements. However, in written communication between clients, family members, employees and bosses, and so forth, the best language is simple language. Use the following suggestions as guidelines:

1. Organize the document in a logical sequence. A real estate contract, for example, begins with the identity of the house being bought, followed by the price, followed by the items included, and so forth. It doesn't begin by stating the closing date and time. A letter of agreement between clients generally begins with a description of the work being performed, followed by a time-table, and last, the conditions of compensation.
2. In a lengthy document, divide the material into distinct, and perhaps even labeled sections. An employment

agreement might start with the job description, followed by a discussion of salary, with the benefits listed last.

3. Use short declarative sentences constructed with common words and phrases. If you must use a technical term, then include the universally accepted definition of the term so that the interpretation is clear.
4. If there are exceptions to certain items in the agreement, make that list clear and easy to find. This includes the proverbial "small print" consumers often complain about. You've won a free trip, right? Well, not exactly. You have to join a travel club or a time-sharing group that will cost you far more than the trip is worth. That's what the small print told you, but you didn't have your magnifying glass handy so you missed it. Other examples includc: the optional accessories you've negotiated in the price of your car; the items that stay in a house and are included in the sale; the nights that you reserve the use of your family car for yourself, making the car available to your teenager only with prior arrangement, and so forth.
5. Anticipate what issues could reasonably result in a later dispute and carefully draft your agreement with these areas outlined to avoid later misunderstanding. We might say that these include "reserved" items, the details of which may be worked out later. Preliminary agreements between corporations may include many of these clauses, because the spirit of the agreement must be mutually satisfactory before the progression of details can be tackled.
6. Be sure to include supporting documents or notes that bear on the outcome. While this is not necessary in all cases, it's important to keep this step in mind. We don't know yet, but all that information about telecommuting programs that Julie has collected might end up supporting her boss's agreement with the owners of the company. A divorce agreement often includes tax documents, a

bill of sale for property, or other relevant information.

SO, HOW DID YOU DO?

If you're learning to become a better negotiator, then it's imperative that you evaluate how well you are doing. The most experienced negotiators understand that they improve their skills with every negotiation encounter; they may even grow more from those where no agreement is reached and a deadlock results, because a "non-success" offers fertile ground for analysis and feedback. So, if you are feeling down because you didn't "win" this or that time, know that you are no different from those who have been doing it for years. However, you'll find your track record improving if you take time to evaluate how you came out of negotiation sessions.

1. Did you reach your objective completely? You got that raise or your partner has agreed to take over the yard work or you got a new client on the exact terms you asked for. Hey, it can happen like this sometimes. You state your position and it is accepted.
2. Which of your objectives were not met? Were they your most important ones? There are times that you win the battles but the war hasn't ended yet. A friend of mine has consistently increased her employee benefit package, but she can't seem to get more direct cash in her pocket. After two consecutive years of these results, we analyzed the issues and concluded that she'd used these benefits as fall-back positions, but had included too many of them. Next year, she's concentrating on the money, thereby minimizing the areas in which compromise can be offered.
3. Was your preparation adequate? Be honest here. Were you surprised by the other party's information or did you find yourself unable to answer an obvious question? People often do this when they believe their position is so

strong that the other party will not be able to counter it. But don't bank on that—surprises are common. If this happened to you, what can you learn from this experience? Perhaps you moved ahead too quickly, or maybe you hadn't thought through enough possible objections to your position. In any case, benefit from the experience by analyzing it honestly.

4. How do you feel? That sounds like a simple question, but it's an important one. If a person feels bad after a negotiation is over, it's important to note that and work with it. Perhaps you felt tricked or out-matched? On the other hand, you may feel good, even if you didn't achieve some important goals. You felt confident and observed yourself negotiating with the best information you had available to you. You might be able to identify those moments when you didn't react quickly enough or you disclosed information too soon in the process. But you don't feel bad because you exercised your negotiation muscles and have grown from the process. Maybe you gained more than you expected? Why did that happen? Did the other negotiator drop the ball somewhere in the process? Take advantage of the chance to evaluate what happened—what you "won" and what you "lost" and how you feel about it. You might be surprised.
5. Is the agreement enforceable? Have you done your follow-up work? If you negotiated an agreement with your teenager how do you intend to make sure it's carried out? This can be important in contract matters, too. What happens if the work on your house isn't done? What recourse do you have if the company declares bankruptcy before your independent contractor agreement runs its course? Have you written out your understanding of an agreement and double-checked it before you sent it to the other party?

6. What can you learn from the other party? Maybe you were truly out-matched—it happens. Now that you have so much information about communication skills, timing, setting, preparation, and tactics and strategies, measure what you've learned against the behavior of the other party. You might find that he or she was a better listener, asking questions that led to more disclosure than you anticipated. Perhaps you were lulled into believing the other person was a cooperative negotiator when all along the person was intent on a win-lose outcome.

   Likewise, if you did well, examine what the other party did that gave you advantages. You may discover that the other party was careless and assumed too much. Maybe the person misread you or chose to go ahead with a negotiation when he or she didn't feel well or was rushed. Don't stay puzzled about why something happened the way it did—analyze and learn.

NOW THAT YOU HAVE BEEN TAKEN THROUGH THE negotiation process, you may have two thoughts going through your head:

1. All this theory is great, but how does this play out in real life? And,
2. What really did happen to all of these characters I have been reading about? Did they get what they wanted? Were their situations resolved?

I'll address both questions by taking you through the actual negotiations these people experienced. What you will read will be fairly close to how the actual discussions likely played out, but my thoughts and analysis accompany the dialogue so you can get a real-world perspective. This will complete our circle, giving you a sense of how the theory works in actual situations, and most importantly, how your day-to-day can benefit from the theory for the most successful negotiations possible.

CHAPTER THIRTEEN

Turning Theory Into Practice: Looking Behind the Scenes

WE HAVE BEEN FOLLOWING A CAST OF PEOPLE INVOLVED in important negotiations that are likely similar to the kinds of situations we all find ourselves in from time to time. There is no better way to learn to put the theory into practice than by taking a closer look at the actual negotiation interactions of the folks we have been following. Keep in mind that these scenarios are metaphors of sorts for each negotiation we encounter and experience in our own life. Arnie's search for a bigger salary may be equivalent to negotiating a relationship. Open your mind as you read and see how each of these scenarios might fit into your own life.

I have made it clear that nothing may be more important than proper and effective preparation for the negotiation. Let's look in on the last stages of our negotiators' planning. If we were to actually sit in on their conversations or thought processes, what would we hear?

CATHY AND TONY MAKE THEIR PLANS

Cathy and Tony have a simple but important goal, and while they have a preference for their future office, they have some attractive second choices, too. They are cooperative negotiators, but they've been in the business world long enough to know that part of their strategy will be to put the information on the table their way and in their own time. In other words, they intend to control the information.

They would like to move to an empty office on a different floor — that's their first choice. But remember, an interesting thing has happened along the way. Tony and Cathy began to think about leaving the company and opening their own business; some late-night meetings have led these two to believe that this is a viable option. On their own, they've decided not to press strongly for office space on another floor because this may be too tough a position.

That said, Tony and Cathy have decided that the best option is trading offices with Jason, the worker across the hall. Recently, Jason said that he'd sure like to have those big windows in his office. Cathy and Tony filed that information away and they had a strong sense that their colleague would actually like to have their office, even if it is smaller.

So, if Tony and Cathy choose not to press for the separate office space, why are they keeping it on the table? Well, they believe that in a sense, it's a good trading option. Their office manager, Joy, will likely react with surprise when this option is brought up. She knows that this is a rather drastic solution. But, Tony and Cathy know that, too, and at the appropriate time, they can back away from the idea and move to the next one, swapping offices with Jason.

Tony and Cathy have requested a meeting with Joy, which will take place in the afternoon, following a clerical staff meeting. This was Joy's choice, one that she picked from many open appointment times that Tony and Cathy said would also be good for them. They invited Joy to meet in their office, which will work to their advantage. (They also know that Joy likes to get out of her own office in order to avoid constant interruptions.) Joy will surely understand their space problems when she has to sit in the tiny, cramped office. This helps insure that some solution is found.

But, what if Joy doesn't agree to the office-swapping scheme? Or, what if she says they can move to the separate space? Our two professionals have both issues covered. If Joy agrees to rent a separate space, Tony and Cathy will happily move into it, knowing that even if they leave in six months, someone else can likely be found to make use of it. If Joy doesn't like the swapping scheme, then they'll move to their next preference, which involves remodeling their current office space. And if they fail to win that concession, they'll propose storing some of their materials in closets and other offices — they are fairly certain no one else would like that idea.

Cathy and Tony have prepared an initial report that outlines the problem but mentions no solutions. They have another document, however, which discusses the first two options. They also have a separate document with the other options outlined. This is the way they intend to control the information. They may not ever need to use the third document. When Joy meets with them, she may have only a few minutes. They will discuss the problem and then hand Joy the document that discusses their two favorite solutions. They may not be able to control exactly how the negotiations proceed, but they are prepared to carry out the entire negotiation on that day, yet knowing that Joy might ask for more time.

But what about communication and body language? What about other tactics? What is their general strategy? Being cooperative negotiators, Tony and Cathy are using some clever but basically honest tactics; they want to preserve good relations with Joy because that is their style and nature. Tony will sit on the desk while they talk to Joy. The two women will sit on the only two available chairs. They will be physically close to Joy because they don't have another choice, and they aren't attempting to move files out of the way either. They are letting the problem speak for itself—they'll be discussing the problem in the midst of it, so to speak. Shortly, we'll see if their planning pays off.

JULIE PREPARES TO GO HEAD TO HEAD WITH JOE

We know that Joe is not an easy person to deal with and therefore, Julie has done extensive preparation. We've watched as she has put in many requests for meetings, sent memos, and collected research about work-at-home programs at other companies. But, what does Julie really want?

First, she's decided that her ideal is working at home three days a week, using her own computer and one of the company's as a back-up. (She knew that would be one of Joe's concerns.) Julie has prepared sample forms — computer documents — that will serve as her daily work diaries. These diaries will track her hours and the progress she's making. She's also made a diary of her activities in the office. If necessary, she can produce these during her meeting with Joe. She also understands that she is breaking new ground with her company and needs to back up every contention. You'll remember, too, that Julie has researched the current law on the subject and has even gathered environmental impact statements issued by local and federal governmental bodies.

After sending many memos back and forth on the company's e-mail system, Julie has finally landed an appointment with Joe. He's carved out 15 minutes late on a Friday afternoon, not the time that Julie would have chosen, but it was the only time to which Joe would agree.

Julie will bring copies of the initial memos that outlined her idea to the meeting, and she plans to pull out the other written supporting documents as needed. She intends to dress in business attire, meaning that in this case, she'll wear a conservative suit and carry her attache. If this sounds unnecessary, understand that Julie has learned how to "play the game." Conservative clothing emphasize her serious purpose and add credibility to her professional image. It wouldn't be smart to show up in jeans and a casual sweater, the clothes Julie might wear when she works at home. The clothing is part of her strategy, and given who she is dealing with, it's important that she think about these details.

WHAT'S GOING TO HAPPEN WITH MICHAEL AND JACKIE?

As we've seen, Michael and Jackie have gone a long way to solve their immediate problem. They are going to find a vacation spot that satisfies both of their needs and desires. So, what's next? Jackie realizes that Michael has had his way in their household and she's not paid much attention to how decisions were made. But now that their children are grown and she has her own career, there are a few things she'd like to change.

Now that Jackie understands that well-thought-out negotiations can change the way they communicate as a couple, she would like to look at many other issues in their marriage; there's nothing deceitful about this consideration. She isn't playing games with Michael; she's simply stating her case in order to feel better about her relationship. Jackie started with the vacation issue and will move on to money and housework. In each case, she'll think out what she wants and what it will take to get it.

Jackie has picked up on some clues that may help her future negotiations move smoothly. She found that Michael is open to discussion when he's sitting at the kitchen table, usually after their leisurely dinner. He very sensibly doesn't want to discuss these issues when their children are around, nor is he available when a basketball game is on television. Jackie doesn't like to talk about important things when she's tired and ready for sleep, even though Michael tends to be a night owl himself. We'll also find out that Michael has some issues of his own he would like to talk about.

HAS ARNIE LEARNED ANYTHING?

Arnie still wants his raise, but thankfully, he's learned that he can't simply demand it. Instead of storming into Sandra's office, Arnie has done some homework. Since we first met him, Arnie has sorted through all the things he'd like to have, including 30 days paid vacation (he enjoys his time in the Florida sun). Arnie has narrowed down his demands and is prepared to ask for a 15 percent raise, with a fall-back position of 10 percent. This sounds high, but Arnie is underpaid relative to others in the company and in other firms. He knows this because he now understands that he has to do the research and he has documentation to back up his claims of being underpaid. Fortunately, Arnie also has his last performance review, which was very favorable.

Sandra is always rushed, so Arnie had to negotiate a time to talk with her. He decided to wait until she returned from a four-day weekend, when, he hoped, she would be relaxed and not so prone to hurrying the conversation along. Arnie wanted to negotiate in a conference room, but Sandra insisted on staying in her office. He didn't like that, but he had no choice but to go along. Arnie prepared his agenda, a written document that prioritized his discussion points.

In Arnie's case, two or more meetings probably will be necessary. And, to insure that Sandra didn't simply take the document and say, "I'll get back to you on this, Arnie," he had noted a number of open times for a second meeting, while agreeing to accommodate her schedule.

Arnie has learned a lot, but he still doesn't understand how to engage in real give and take. If Arnie were skilled, he might be a competent competitive negotiator, because he has a fear of losing. He's stuck in a model where there has to be a clear loser and a clear winner. This is something Arnie can't quite get past.

We're not sure how he'll fare in actual negotiations, because he isn't prepared to be satisfied with less than the optimal results. Perhaps Arnie will consider a variation on his plan, but he has to keep an open mind during the negotiation setting.

We hope that Arnie will consider how he wants to present himself during the meeting. He has to control his urge to dump the documents on the desk and make his demands, leaving no room for Sandra to think about his side of the issue. This is always a danger, but let's remember that although Arnie is new at this process, he has learned a lot.

WITH THE PREPARATION TIME OVER, OUR CAST OF characters must now put their new-found skills to the test. Let's look in on their interaction . . . and pay attention to my analysis as we go. Remember, my real purpose is to assist you to have more successful negotiations in your own life. Continue to see the application to your issues.

TONY AND CATHY NEGOTIATE FOR NEW SPACE

Joy agreed to meet with Tony and Cathy in their office in the middle of a busy morning. This half hour appointment has been on their calendars for about a week. If you recall, Tony and Cathy sent Joy a memo outlining the problem they face, but they did not include their ideas about solutions. They will attempt to control the information and begin discussing their options after the problem has been explored. Their relationship with Joy is generally positive, and they are considered valuable employees. Since Cathy and Tony know this fact, they begin in a strong position.

Tony offers Joy his chair as she comes in the door and makes some room on his desk for himself.

Cathy: Would you like some coffee or tea, Joy?

Joy: Some tea would be good. I have a headache coming on.

Tony: Oh, sorry to hear that. Are you sure you want to meet today? Would tomorrow be better?

[Tony is confirming that this is indeed a good time. If Joy isn't feeling well, then an offer to postpone can be accepted. This is also part of the exchange of pleasantries that precedes many professional — and personal — negotiations.]

Joy: No, no. Please. Let's do this now. I'm okay. That tea will help.

Tony moves behind Joy and busies himself fixing the tea while Cathy brings out a copy of the memo.

[Notice here that Cathy is starting the actual negotiation. Tony has offered a conciliatory statement offering to postpone the meeting if Joy isn't feeling up to it.]

Cathy: We'll try to be brief Joy — we know you are rushed these days. But we've agreed, and I'm sure you will too, that we're outgrowing our space. That's good news actually. We're each bringing in more business, so naturally there is just more stuff. *(She laughs in a good natured way and lets the "stuff" speak for itself.)*

Joy: Yes, the numbers coming from this office are very good.

[Notice that Joy concedes that point but doesn't globalize any more broadly than necessary. Cathy has posed the problem in the positive way.]

Joy: Unfortunately, everyone is kind of cramped around here. So, how much more space do you foresee needing in the next few months?

[Joy is moving to the information phase, asking questions and expecting answers.]

Tony: We've come up with a couple of ideas that could solve this problem for the foreseeable future.

[Tony avoids answering the "how much" question, the nature of which demands some kind of concrete answer, as in a certain number of square feet or a specific number of added cabinets or chairs.]

Joy: Oh? That's good. At least you have ideas and aren't putting this problem on me.

[This is an example of the advantage of preparation. Tony and Cathy didn't throw the problem out there and expect someone else to come with a plan.]

Cathy: Yes, we prepared a document here, and we'll be glad to discuss the options. Here it is.

Tony: Take a minute or two to look at it. We've thought about these options for several weeks.

Joy: What's this about renting a separate office?

Tony: Would you like to hear about that idea now or would you rather review the other one first.

Joy: Do you have an office in the building in mind?

Cathy: We know that there are several empty spaces, two are one floor above us.

Joy: Really? Well, that's a novel solution. You know I can't make that decision on my own though.

Tony: We understand, Joy. We're just suggesting that as a reasonable solution to our problem. Moving one floor up would be convenient and make this office available to relieve some of the cramped quarters you mentioned.

[Tony is being conciliatory and making his remark based on something Joy had earlier said about the need for space.]

Joy: I see what you mean. It will add expense though.

Cathy: What do you think of our second suggestion?

[Cathy is moving away from the details now, particularly the expense, until the other ideas have been put on the table.]

Joy: I see that you suggest trading offices with Jason. How would that help?

Tony: We know that Jason has often said that he likes our office because of the windows. His office is bigger, you see, so it seemed like a logical option.

Joy: Have you asked him?

Cathy: We wouldn't have done that without talking to you first. We suggest it because we believe strongly that he'd not only agree, he'd probably like the idea.

Tony: While it wouldn't relieve the overall crowding, it would solve the immediate problem here.

[Conciliatory Tony has brought up the general problem in the office, which makes the first option more attractive.]

Joy: Yes, I can see that.

Cathy: Do you know how soon we might be able to resolve this?

[Cathy wants to end the meeting with these options presented. At this point, there is no reason to make further concessions because Joy is open to the two ideas — she hasn't rejected either of them.

Joy: I've got a meeting scheduled with Carl tomorrow. We're discussing some budgeting issues. I'll mention our meeting then.

Tony: So, why don't we talk again the next morning? Can we call you around ten?

Joy: Sounds good. I can see we need to do something.

FROM TONY AND CATHY'S PERSPECTIVE, THE MEETING HAS gone very well. They didn't have to use their fall-back positions, and they gave Joy two ideas to bring to her boss, one of the two owners of the building. They have a time-frame to work with and a commitment to discuss the issue again.

TWO DAYS LATER...

Joy stops by Cathy and Tony's office about 9:45 and sticks her head in the door. She asks if Tony and Cathy can meet with her and Carl at 5:00 in his office. They agree. A few minutes later, Carl stops by to ask a question, but Tony and Cathy note that he seems to be looking around. After he leaves them, he goes across the hall and looks into Jason's office as well, again on the pretense of asking a question.

At 5:00 p.m., Tony and Cathy are in Carl's office. They have brought copies of all the documents they have produced, knowing that Carl may not have seen them all. They also have the fallback position document with them, in case they need it later.

They make small talk when they first enter the office. Cathy casually asks Carl if he's heard about a client who has just renewed a contract for a year of consulting services. Since this has just happened, it's a legitimate question, and not one that could be considered a sign of "grand standing." This was one of the clients Tony and Cathy have worked with for a trial period of six months. Carl nods his head and says that he's heard about that contract from Joy.

Carl: It's late and I need to be going. So I'll be as brief as possible. Joy told me about your space problem and I could see it for myself earlier today. I've been busy and this problem just got away from me. Is everything else okay?

Tony: Fine, Carl, just fine.

Cathy nods her head in agreement.

Joy: Carl sees this space problem as part of a larger issue. That's why we're moving quickly.

Carl: I'm bringing on two more people. One is going to set up a communications office — the position calls for public relations duties and so forth. The other person is going to work with Jason on the accounting and purchasing. I was going to stick that person in Jason's office, but I can see that there's no room. I've decided that I'm going to expand the company anyway, so Joy is going to negotiate with the building manager for two suites of offices upstairs. I see you did some exploring of your own.

Cathy: We wanted to offer some ideas, Carl, rather than just griping about the problem — if you know what I mean.

[Until now, Cathy and Tony have been quiet. Carl is telling his story, so to speak. They speak up only when he makes a direct reference to them.

Carl: Yes, well, that's settled then. You've given me the nudge I need. Jason and the new person will take one of the new suites and the two of you will take the other. Joy and her staff will move into the offices you move out of.

Tony: Is your plan to have this accomplished quickly?

Joy: We'll need six weeks.

Cathy: We'll do our part. Anything we can do to help out?

[Cathy and Tony are signing on to the full program. They have what they want, and they are being part of the larger team. Offering assistance is part of that process.]

Carl: We'll need to discuss some minor remodeling and you'll have to pack up your office. Decide what can be stored and take the rest. It might mean working late a few nights.

Carl stands up and the group knows that the meeting is over. Cathy and Tony offer their thanks to both Joy and Carl for handling the issue quickly.

LATER, OVER DINNER, TONY AND CATHY TALK ABOUT THEIR new office and how they got it. Let's remember that they had many things going for them. They are valuable employees, their problem was obvious, and, unbeknownst to them, the owner was planning an expansion anyway. Right now, they are winners. They got what they wanted and no one else was put at a disadvantage because of them.

It's important to look at what might have happened if they hadn't presented their problem and the solution. Think about this. They might have ended up being among those who got shuffled around in less than optimal offices. By speaking up, they became the recipients of the much larger offices, along with the new employees.

Tony and Cathy illustrate the importance of being proactive and taking initiative on our own behalf. Can you think of times in your life that might have turned out a bit differently if you had spoken up and made your desires known? Could we really have expected Carl or Joy to be mind-readers? As it turned out, asking for what they wanted benefitted others in the office as well.

Right now, their biggest problem is going to be their decision to start their own business. (Ah, but we'll save that for a future book!)

JULIE AND JOE GO HEAD TO HEAD — OR TOE TO TOE

Julie is a valued employee, but Joe has few social skills and offers praise rarely if ever. So far, he's been stubborn about making any kind of change. Julie will bring all her extensive documentation with her, even though she has sent Joe everything by e-mail. She also has some studies about telecommuting and a copy of the local statute mandating work-at-home programs.

Joe agreed to 15 minutes on a Friday afternoon. Julie will do her best. Joe's secretary brings her in after she's been waiting about five minutes.

Julie: Hello Joe. Do you have the rest of your appointment time free?

Joe: Sure. Come in.

Julie: You are clear about what I'm asking for here, aren't you Joe? I'm assuming you've read all the documents I sent. I've detailed how I can accomplish my work for the company by working at home three days a week, and being on-site the other two.

Joe: And you know I feel about that concept; I don't like the idea.

Julie: Well, that's why we're here. To discuss the issue.

Joe: The president won't like it. I told you that.

[Joe is bringing in the higher authority. But Julie knows that this will be Joe's call. The authorities in question are more like silent partners and don't handle this kind of personnel issue. Julie knows this, so she isn't daunted.]

Julie: Well, we can take up that issue later — as I said, we have the local mandates on our side. Besides, that position is probably based on the office set-up prior to our on-line capabilities. Technology has changed the picture. Let's talk about productivity right now.

[Julie is prepared and it is paying off. She's able to direct Joe's attention away from his negativity and back to the issue. She's moving to postpone Joe's discussion of the ultimate authority.]

Julie: As I see it, I can do the most important work at home and be in constant touch with key employees here. Our computer system allows this. I will also be able to work undisturbed — believe me, Joe, my office at home is a lot more quiet than my office here. This is the key issue. I believe I'll be more productive at home. My office time will be reserved for meetings and collaborative work.

[Julie is stating her case. She's listing her key points — and doing it quickly, because she's assuming that Joe will end the meeting after 10 minutes.]

Joe: How will any of us know — that's what I don't like about this. How will we know if you're watching talk shows — or taking care of your kids?

Julie: My work record will reflect that. I think you'll see that my work log will reflect even greater productivity — and my last review was excellent as it is. My children, Lauren and Michael, are in after-school day care. Their father picks them up and brings them home now. That will not change. I think you might want to look at the public relations value of this experiment — and I'm willing to call it that. Many companies are doing it, and to meet local mandates, we're actually required to do it. I'm jumping on the bandwagon here Joe, and I'll work with Ben to see how it can be used in a P.R. campaign.

[Julie handled objections about her personal issues quickly and in straightforward way. She moved into the next area, which focuses on how the company will benefit.]

Joe: How about two half days at home? That way you'll be here every day.

Julie: That doesn't meet the mandate guidelines, which as my supporting documents state, are for the purpose of easing energy consumption and pressure on the freeways caused by increased commuting.

Joe: I don't like this, not this three day stuff.

[Joe is being broken down a bit. He's objecting to the three days. Julie has a chance for a compromise.]

Julie: I'd be willing to start at two days a week, if that would be better for you and the company.

Joe: I still don't like it.

Julie: think you'll see that this move puts us in line with similar companies. In other companies, employees in my position are part of work-at-home programs and the companies are getting civic mileage out of the arrangement.

[Julie is reminding Joe that other companies have employees who do what she does. She could, after all, leave and go to one of those firms. She's also reminding him — again — of the public relations value of such a program.]

Joe: I'll authorize a day and a half — and it's a trial — two months.

Julie: The half day doesn't add to the P.R. benefits. One day a week at home for a month-long trial, followed by a two day, two month trial will give you ample time to assess the program. We can discuss the third day at that time.

[Julie is rejecting the split the difference tactic, because it doesn't benefit her and in fact would be more inconvenient. And while she doesn't belabor the point, the half day is inconsequential to the mandate. She offers a new trial period and states it matter-of-factly. She is speaking authoritatively, as if it's really a settled issue. She's won something. The question is how much.]

Julie: I'll go ahead and draw up a document reflecting our

understanding on this point.

Joe: Do that. I'll look at it and let you know.

[Joe is giving himself a fall-back position. He is opening the way to nix the whole thing.]

Julie: I'll plan to start this during the first week of the month.

[Julie's affirmative statement continues the understanding that this will move forward.]

Joe waves her away and begins to make a phone call, which is how she knows that the conversation is over.

THIS NEGOTIATION PROCEEDED AS IT DID ONLY BECAUSE Julie had prepared for the meeting and Joe had received numerous memos from her. He also had documentation that he probably hadn't bothered to look through too carefully. Many of us wouldn't have tried to get through to Joe, and Julie's strongest point turned out to be something external to both of them, the city's telecommuting mandate. If she had spent too much time justifying herself and going over all the advantages to her, she would have lost. For example:

Julie: You see, Joe, I really like the idea of being able to work from home. It's quiet there and I won't have to dress up and I figure I will save money on gas, wear and tear on the car, lunches, dry cleaning, and clothes. I'll be able to throw a load of wash in after breakfast and switch it to the dryer after lunch.

Joe: I don't like it. There's nothing in it for us and we don't pay you to do your laundry.

Julie: But I just meant that...

Joe: I doubt that people who work at home get as much done and that's why I'm saying no.

Julie: But wait, I'll work just as hard. There won't be any interruptions and anyway, the city has this mandate....

Joe: It won't work. I want you here.

Julie: But you can talk to me any time you want. The computer system....

Joe: Like I said, I'm not going for this.
Julie: But the mandate.
Joe: That's all.

IF JULIE HAD APPROACHED JOE IN THIS SELF-SERVING WAY, she would have ended up with nothing. What Julie outlined are exactly the reasons she wanted to work from home. But Joe — or any other boss — isn't going to care much about those things. They care about the bottom line and the impact on the company. Joe cares about Julie's productivity. The fact is, many people who do like working from home would state reasons sounding much like Julie's. But the companies in question are interested in productivity, not in the lunch money saved by the program. Julie knew this and capitalized on her superior preparation.

Given what we know about Julie, she will no doubt take advantage of her one-day-a-month at-home day and carefully document her work carefully. She'll up-date Joe and let him know when the two-day trial begins. Chances are, Julie will get what she wants because Joe has other issues in front of him. She'll win by determination and by proving her competence. If the third day is never approved, she'll still have two-thirds of her ideal plan. And that's not bad when you're breaking new ground.

MICHAEL AND JACKIE SMOOTH THINGS OUT — IN A MANNER OF SPEAKING

Michael and Jackie have managed to make their way through a tough negotiation over vacation plans. If you recall, Michael assumed that Jackie would go along with his preference and he hadn't given much thought to her wishes to be in a secluded cabin. They compromised and their next vacation will be in a place where Michael can go off and play golf every day at a club near the cabin they will rent. But, the process of negotiating this decision had prompted Jackie to bring up some other issues.

When we see Michael and Jackie now, they are in their kitchen and they have agreed to talk about financial arrangements. Michael is a reluctant negotiator, because he likes things the way they are. He's always handled the money in their household, but Jackie, who has a job and brings in money wants a greater share of the decision-making power in how that money is spent and saved.

Michael: I don't see why we have to do this exercise. Haven't I taken good care of the money — and of you?

Jackie: Yes, Michael, but that's not the point. I'm a grown woman with a responsible job. We're a two-income family and are likely to stay that way for another 15 to 20 years. Until now, you've only told me what you've done with the money — after the fact. Now I want to participate.

Michael: Well, I think you know all the important things. You know about the retirement accounts and the insurance. We have some money put away for the kids' education and you can have anything you want.

[Michael is still in "argument mode." He's making it clear that he'd just as soon not be there at all. The atmosphere will need to change if they are going to get anywhere. They may have to negotiate over the agreement to negotiate.]

Jackie: Having any material thing I want isn't the issue. Surely you can see why I'd like to know more about where the money we make is going. As it is now, I bring money into our household, but just last month, I had to ask you for money to buy a chair for the family room.

Michael: And I said yes, didn't I?

Jackie: Yes, but it's demeaning to have to ask. That's why we're here. This isn't about love or whether you have a generous nature. Let's talk about the specific issues I'd like to deal with — like a vacation home, okay?

Michael: I told you I'd look at the money situation in six

months and see if we can afford it then.

Jackie: Yes, that's what you told me. But I'd like to know how we are doing in terms of the money situation. At this point, I don't know where you've invested our money. I don't know if you have other accounts that don't have my name on them. I only know what's in our joint checking account. Look at this way. I'd just as soon sell this house and move into a smaller one if that means we can have a vacation home. But I don't know if that's necessary because I don't know how much money we have right now.

Michael: You've never mentioned that before — about selling the house. I thought you liked our house.

[Michael is puzzled. Because he believes Jackie generally gets everything she wants, he doesn't understand why she hasn't mentioned selling the house. She hasn't said anything because she doesn't have a framework from which to put proposals on the table. Michael may seem hopelessly old fashioned, but this kind of situation isn't uncommon. Even between business partners, this kind of gap can occur because one partner handles the money and the other handles marketing for new clients, for example.]

Jackie: I do, but I'd give up the house if need be. I need information so that I can be a partner in making this kind of decision. Look, let's talk about some changes about the basic ways we handle these issues. Facts, that's what I need right now. Facts.

Michael: So, you're saying you want an accounting of what we have. And you want to know how I've determined that we can't buy the vacation home now.

Jackie: Exactly. And you need to understand that I'm not accusing you of anything. I'm not suspicious about where the money is going. I just want to know.

[Jackie is speaking in a language Michael can understand. She's moved away from vague issues into gathering information. This is what they're ready for now. She is also reassuring him that she isn't accusing him of wrong doing, which could be the case in some partnerships, both business and personal. She also isn't dealing — at this point — with her feelings, which may be quite hurt by his attitude. Later on, if need be, she can tell him how his control of the money makes her feel.]

Michael: Well it's complicated.

Jackie: That's okay. I'm prepared to learn.

Michael: Well, we have the joint checking — you know that.

Jackie: That's where my check goes — by direct deposit.

Michael: Yes. And my check does too, after my savings and retirement deductions. You can get anything you want from that account.

Jackie: Yes, but what happens after that. This is what I don't know. You pay all the bills out of another account you set up, so I don't really know much about our actual cost of living. And what happens to that savings and retirement money?

Michael: Oh, I set up other accounts.

Jackie: Do you have the paperwork? Can you tell me how much money there is?

Michael: Now?

Jackie: Not necessarily tonight, Michael. I want a regular time where we sit down and look at these issues. That's what I'm after right now.

Michael: Well, I'll gather the stuff together. I'll have to look at it and try to explain it to you. But like I said, it's complex.

[Michael is still being patronizing to Jackie, but he's not refusing all her requests. If she can hang in, she'll win something. She's also being smart about tempering her demands. She wants to win cooperation right now. She doesn't need every fact this evening. She'll need to be sure to get a commitment for a regular financial session before this conversation is over.]

Jackie: What about next Thursday night? A week from today. Will that give you enough time to gather the information? We can sit down again and you can fill me in on the details. I want to learn — if it's complex then I'll study it.

Michael: Okay. Next Thursday.

[It might seem as if Jackie hasn't gotten very far with Michael. She doesn't really know any more than she did when they started. But from her viewpoint, she's achieved an important victory. Michael has agreed to open the books. For Jackie and Michael, that's a good start.

TWO WEEKS LATER...

Michael and Jackie were in for some surprises. They met as planned one week after their first session. During that session, Jackie was very upset because they didn't have nearly as much money as she assumed they had. Yes, there was money for their children's college fees — although from what Jackie knew about tuition, not enough. That money had come mostly from her salary. And the small amount of money in their company retirement funds wouldn't go very far.

Michael had an individual savings account that Jackie hadn't known about, and the mutual funds were in his name, too. He also had a checking account from which he paid many of their household bills. She was the sole beneficiary on these accounts, but she hadn't known about the savings account or the mutual funds. Jackie was upset, because, as she'd said to Michael, she wouldn't have spent so much money over the years if she'd known more about their financial situation.

This third session, suggested by Jackie, was set up to deal with a budget.

Michael: I know you're disappointed about the vacation house, but now you know why we can't do it.

Jackie: That's a minor disappointment to me. Besides, if we handle the money differently, we might be able to have it anyway. I didn't need a new car two years ago or that ring you bought me last Christmas . . . .

Michael: But I wanted you to be happy and I want you to have nice things.

Jackie: I know that, and I appreciate it, but keeping me in the dark hasn't helped. We both know that now. I'd rather pitch in and help us save money rather than spending so much of it the way I do.

[Jackie is conceding that she has spent money on things she didn't need, and she wants to change that. She's offering to work with him, rather than working at cross purposes.]

Jackie: I've been spending so much money because you never told me it wasn't okay with you.

Michael: That's not your fault. I thought it would all turn out all right. I'm due for another raise and your salary keeps going up, so I never said anything.

Jackie: What do you want to do now?

[Jackie is moving the conversation to practical issues.]

Michael: I want to save more of the money we bring in.

Jackie: What will it take to accomplish that goal?

[Jackie may have ideas of her own, but she's asking Michael for his ideas first. In a way, she's conceding to his prior experience.]

Michael: Well, let's start with a moratorium on new purchases of everything but the essentials. I certainly don't need new golf clubs or suits right now. We don't need furniture and our cars are okay.

Jackie: That sounds good to me. What about taking a set amount of our salaries and putting it into a joint money market account?

Michael: Shall we start with 200 dollars a month? Is that okay?

Jackie: I was thinking we could double that. Why don't you close the savings account and we'll open a joint account and start with the two hundred you suggest.

Michael: I don't want to close it. I want some separate

money.

Jackie: Why? Why is that necessary for you?

Michael: I don't know — it's an emotional thing. I just want money I don't have to answer for to anybody. I'm not ready to give it up.

Jackie: Okay. We'll drop it for now. But let's open a new account next week that we can both track.

[Jackie doesn't argue with Michael about his separate account. She takes what he says on face value, and then offers something else.]

Michael: I can agree to that, and I'll put your name on the mutual funds — such as they are.

Jackie: We can add to them as we go along.

Michael: Let's add 100 dollars a month to the mutual funds account. That way we'll be saving 300 dollars a month.

Jackie: I'll go along with that if we agree that this is a start. I want us to keep track of the grocery money and the cash that just seems to slip through our fingers. I think there are many places we can save.

Michael: Well, okay. But let's not go nuts. I don't want to give up our regular life.

Jackie: I'll take responsibility for keeping track of what I spend on the household and myself. I'm not asking you to do anything right now.

[Jackie is taking the initiative for herself, but she's not pushing Michael beyond the place he's ready to go. Again, we may not understand Michael, but Jackie does, and she's achieved a great deal in a short time. Remember, this is the same Michael that didn't want to disclose any financial information and thought it was his prerogative to plan their vacations.]

Michael: And, for now, I don't want to talk about selling the house either.

Jackie: I'll agree to that for now. But I still think that, with or without the vacation house, we don't need this big place. I'd like to discuss that issue in six months.

Michael: We'll see how the savings plan goes first and then decide if the house is an issue.

Jackie: Okay. But let's talk about our basic expenses in a month.

Michael: Agreed.

WHILE THIS PHASE OF THE NEGOTIATION IS OVER AND change is in the air, Jackie will probably need to remind Michael about their next financial session. Michael hasn't really taken any initiative in their negotiations. Jackie is also agreeing to take on more responsibility right now, but that could change as they move along.

This story shows us the importance of information. In many personal relationships, and many businesses, too, misunderstanding comes from lack of information. Jackie assumed that they had plenty of money because Michael gave her lavish gifts and never told her she couldn't have whatever she wanted. Michael assumed that Jackie wanted the things he was giving her and that it was his duty to give them to her. She actually wanted a fuller partnership in their marriage. Communication to clarify these issues was sorely lacking. Putting information on the table led to a greater understanding of each other and probably will enhance their financial security, and therefore, their lives.

In time, Jackie will bring up the housework issue, and that negotiation will probably involve their children. It may seem that if Jackie didn't bring up these issues, nothing would change. Chances are, that's exactly what would have happened — nothing. In this case, Jackie is the one whose discomfort level with the status quo surfaced first. This is not unusual. As far as Michael was concerned, things were going along just fine. Once the truth was exposed, it wasn't as fine as he let himself believe. He thought this part of his life was working well enough on a day-to-day basis.

Millions of families and businesses across the country could benefit from having someone who questions and asks for information. These are people who open up lines of communication and demand facts on which to base important decisions. As basic as are Michael and Jackie's issues, they are not trivial, nor unique. Their quality of life has already improved because of their efforts and willingness to discuss troublesome issues.

DOES ARNIE FINALLY GET A RAISE?

Arnie has an appointment in Sandra's office to discuss his raise. We know that Arnie wants more money — 15 percent more. Sandra, at this point, doesn't know what Arnie will be seeking. She only knows that he's interested in talking about his relationship with the company and his compensation.

Sandra: Come in Arnie—have a seat. It's good to see you. I'm sorry I've been rushed and had to make you wait for an appointment for so long.

Arnie: That's okay. I understand. You're busy. We're all busy around here.

Sandra: Your review isn't due for six months, so I'm assuming this is about something else.

Arnie: Well, not exactly. I've brought a proposal with me. Here's your copy.

Sandra: Tell me what it says, and I can read it in detail later. By the way, you handled that problem very well the other day — you saved us a customer, Mamason, Inc.

Arnie: That technique worked with that other company last month, so I thought it would work again with Amalgamated Tech. Anyway, as you can see, I'm asking for a merit raise now...

Sandra: Do you think you could do some training for new staff about the customer service technique you used?

[Sandra is engaging in a tactic that essentially attempts to take the focus off the issue of the meeting. She's changing the agenda. We'll see how Arnie handles it.]

Arnie: Of course, I'd be willing to do that. I've asked for training opportunities before and I believe I have a lot to offer new reps.

[Arnie is making the point that becoming part of the training team is something he's wanted to do in the past, which establishes that he can take initiative. If he's not careful though, the meeting could be permanently side-tracked.]

The phone rings. Sandra tells the secretary to come in.

Sandra: This will only take a minute. I just have to sign a couple of purchase orders.

Arnie: Fine. No problem.

Sandra chats with the secretary for a few minutes. His 30 minutes are rapidly dwindling.

Sandra: Okay, that's done. Now let's get back to this training issue. I'll pass this information on to Seymour and we'll try to get this moving by next month. What else can you offer the training team?

Arnie: I'll write down my ideas in a memo and send them on to you. I think I can have that done by Friday. Right now, though, I'd like to get back to the compensation issue.

[Arnie acknowledges Sandra's request and offers her a quick solution. Then he tries to get her focus back on his raise. All things considered, he's doing pretty well.]

Sandra: Well, you know that I can't make final decisions. I can pass your proposal on.

Arnie: I'd like to discuss a few issues with you first. I know that the others listen to your recommendations, so I'd like you to be fully informed.

[This is a good response. It will make it difficult for Sandra to just pass the proposal on to her boss. Arnie is expressly telling her that her recommendations will count.]

Sandra: Well, okay. But you will get that memo about the training to me by Friday?

Arnie: Absolutely. So, what I've done here is outline the compensation data from other comparable companies, and . . .

Sandra: What do you mean comparable companies?

Arnie: Well, the data cover other firms in the same industry and of approximately the same size. The graph shows the average salaries for employees holding a comparable position to mine, and the second graph shows entry level salaries and moves on to take years of experience into account.

Sandra looks through the pages, which Arnie has carefully prepared. He's holding his own copy and Sandra is following his lead at this point.

Sandra: What does this all mean, Arnie? What's the bottom line here?

Arnie: If you study the data first, you'll be able to see the reasons for my request.

[Arnie doesn't want to talk about the conclusion until the information is laid out. He wants Sandra to understand the underlying rationale for his request. Remember Arnie is going for 15 percent.]

Sandra: You do know how much we value you around here Arnie, but you must also realize that we're not having the best year ever.

Arnie: We've cut expenses in our department — you've been responsible for some great cost-cutting measures. And the last quarter report showed that sales were way up in our division.

[Sandra always talks this way, so Arnie knows that he doesn't have to take Sandra seriously about the state of the company. He bypasses the negativity by discussing two positive pieces of information, one of which can be credited to Sandra.]

Arnie: So, if you look carefully, you'll see that what I'm proposing is in line with others in this company and in competing firms.

Sandra: Fifteen percent! Arnie, really. That's not going to fly . . .

Arnie: When you look at the full proposal, you'll see...

Sandra: I can't go upstairs with this. Let me think about this for a day. I won't do anything now.

Arnie: So, we'll talk again before you ask for final approval.

Sandra: Yes, we'll see what we can work out.

Arnie: Shall I call you tomorrow afternoon.

Sandra: Yes, yes.

Sandra stands up and starts to walk out of her office with a file in her hand. It's obvious she's ending the meeting now.

Arnie: Well, thank you, Sandra. I'll look forward to talking with you tomorrow.

THE NEXT DAY, ARNIE CALLS SANDRA, BUT SHE'S NOT IN her office. He writes the training memo she asked for and leaves it in her office. He leaves a voice mail message letting her know that it's there. Meanwhile, Arnie continues to do his job. On Monday afternoon, Sandra calls and asks if he can see her right away. They meet in her office.

Arnie: I'm glad you could get back to me.

Sandra: Sorry it wasn't sooner, but everything's upside down.

[This is also typical talk for Sandra. She's always rushed and frantic. Arnie needn't respond.]

Arnie: So, Sandra, do you have any questions about the material?

Sandra: Not really. But I'm wondering if there are other ways you'd like to be compensated. I was thinking about including you in the executive retirement plan, which would increase the company's matching percentage.

Arnie: I'll hear you out on this. Do you have anything written up about it?

Sandra: Here's the brochure. You've exceeded the years of service requirement and we can include you at the first of the year. That would add value to your plan immediately.

Arnie: I'll look it over. You seem certain that this will be acceptable.

Sandra: More acceptable than 15 percent. I'm sure of that.

Arnie: What percentage did you have in mind?

[Arnie has one offer. He hasn't accepted it, and now he's asking for more information. So far, he's holding his own.]

Sandra: I think I could get an immediate three percent, based on your performance.

Arnie: That would leave me well below others in this company and in other firms. As you know, my original 15 percent request would not bring me to parity, but is only a start.

Sandra: Well, that may be true, but it's unrealistic. I can get the retirement fund increase, and I'll try for six percent, but I can't guarantee anything.

Arnie: In the past, I know they generally have gone with your recommendations, and I know you've had a chance to look over my materials, so I think we can get closer. I would be willing to take a ten percent increase now, and talk again in six months. And if the retirement percentage increases at the first of the year, I'll be satisfied with the outcome.

Sandra: I'll tell you that eight percent will probably be the limit, but the retirement issue will compensate for that. I think I can get that.

Arnie: Well, as long as the issue is on the table at my next review, we can go with this.

[Arnie brings in the editorial "we" here, to solidify that they're working as a team on this. Arnie, with Sandra's strong support, will likely get the eight percent.]

Sandra: If we're finished with this for now, let's talk about the training team. They will want to talk with you in about two weeks, and the goal for the next training is..... (That's another book, too.)

WELL, ARNIE DID NOT GET EXACTLY WHAT HE WANTED, but the extra money perk does add value to his full employment package. At this point, Arnie, who must rely on Sandra to negotiate the details for him, is probably doing as well as he can for now. If Arnie had begun this process years before, he'd probably be at parity now. But remember, Arnie waited for others to decide what he deserved and doesn't have a history of speaking up for himself and asking for what he wants. Sandra will know that she is dealing with a new Arnie when his next performance review comes along. His vacation time share may need to wait for now.

Arnie has learned many things, not the least of which is the need to gather information. The old Arnie would have been intimidated by Sandra's tendency to change the subject and by her doom and gloom reports on the company's financial picture. This time he had facts to deal with in crafting his position. The company was not in trouble and when Arnie said as much, Sandra backed off. He was also able to keep Sandra focused on the subject. The old Arnie would have been side-tracked into the training issue and the raise might have become a lost issue. Arnie has learned a lot.

SOME FINAL WORDS

With these scripts in mind, and the keen understanding you now have of the dynamics of the negotiation process, feel comfortable in challenges that lie ahead. Think before you act in future negotiations and realize that every interaction is a new opportunity to learn and grow in your negotiation abilities. From the moment we wake up to the time we negotiate our way to sleep and decide to finish that project in the morning, we constantly negotiate. With ourselves, others we know, and those we do not know, the process of negotiation is ever-present in our interactions.

The scripts presented here represent some fairly typical situations encountered every day by people just like us. Now that you have read through the book, list the kinds of negotiations you regularly engage in. Go back to the Introduction and review the sample list of settings in which negotiations take place. You may find that you are involved in many more negotiations than you once thought. While you may not be negotiating over the best cave, you probably are trying to improve your living conditions, get a better deal from your company or clients, or get that neighbor's dog to quit invading your property.

TAKE ONE OR TWO OF THE SITUATIONS PRESENTED IN THE Introduction that are similar to issues that you are involved with and go through the preparation process. For example, let's say you are a therapist who must negotiate a payment schedule with a new client named Teddy. Imagine yourself as this professional. What steps are involved? Where should you start?

First, what are your options—your goals and objectives? Brainstorm about this. Your list could look something like the following:

1. Teddy's major issues are well on the way to resolution within a 12 month period. Significant progress is made.
2. You believe you should see him at least once a week, preferably twice weekly for the first three months.
3. You would like full compensation each week.
4. The client can take out a personal loan to cover your fees.
5. Teddy can pay what he can afford to each week.
6. The bill is collected in full each month.
7. You can lower your fee for a period of three months and phase in the full fee at that time.

Okay, you've listed what comes to mind. What happens next? What do you know about Teddy? Well, he is deeply in debt already and as far as you know, has no relatives with resources. Anxiety over money is a big issue. But, he is finishing a master's degree program next month and has received a few job offers. Things are looking up. This new client also wants the help and respects your credentials. Good.

When you next meet with Teddy, you raise the issue and explore how he feels about scheduling and fees. You discover that one session a week is what he prefers until he is able to accept a new job with better compensation, and perhaps, insurance benefits. You suggest that Teddy pay you two thirds of your fee at the end of each session, with the agreement that he'll pay the balance in four payments when a new job comes through. He takes a week to think about your offer, and comes back with his own suggestion. He will compensate you by paying a percentage over your fee each week after his job comes through. You won't get your money as quickly, but you will eventually be compensated in full. So, you agree to this arrangement, and at the next session, you present Teddy with a letter of agreement, stating the terms, including a provision that the balance of the fee will be paid even if he terminates therapy. You both sign the letter of agreement, and the financial issue is out of the way. You can now proceed with the real work.

Perhaps this arrangement isn't satisfactory to you. What would you change? Write out a scenario for yourself to see how you might get what you want.

SIMILARLY, TAKE ANOTHER SITUATION OFFERED IN THE Introduction and work with that one. A friend of mine took an issue from her past and reviewed what actually happened. She compared that to what she would do differently now that she had more information. In brief, Cindy's partner left her and went off with another person. She was so distressed that she let John take virtually everything out of the apartment, even those things for which she had paid. Good sense had given way to panic and hurt. Cindy believed that the sooner John was out of her life, the sooner she could put the bad experience behind her. Therefore, John had the power to bull-doze Cindy and my friend ended up losing financially, which caused her self-esteem to plummet, too.

However, when Cindy relived that painful time, she was able to reconstruct the parting of the ways much differently. In her mind, she stood up for herself and her own position by putting new locks on the doors, thereby preventing her apartment from being cleared out. She then presented John with a written list of items that were paid for jointly and suggested a division of the property. She detailed some personal loans and asked for immediate compensation. In other words, if she could go back and do things differently, she would take hold of her emotions and demand more equitable treatment. After reliving the painful events, she concluded that if she should ever take on another live-in partner, she would negotiate the terms of their arrangement. Take Cindy's situation and come up with your own scenario. Sure the past is over and all that. But use it as feedback to help you prepare for the future.

Or, pretend you and some neighbors are attempting to resolve a problem with some other tenants. This family has unruly pets (a cat from hell and the like) and has raucous parties every weekend. The whole building is disgusted with these folks, and as individuals you have approached them and asked for some basic consideration. You have agreed to head up the committee of neighbors who want to change the situation. Where do you start?

Perhaps you make a list of past grievances and if possible, put dates and times on each event. You gather information from other tenants of the building. You check with the neighborhood mediation center and learn about their procedures. Step by step you are preparing to enter into a negotiation— not that you have any guarantees that the troublesome neighbors will respond. But you are gathering facts and looking for solutions.

In this case, the neighbors will not agree to 1) control their pets because they believe dogs should not be muzzled, and 2) their families and friends visit every weekend and they think the other neighbors should loosen up and have more parties themselves. Looks bad, doesn't it? Furthermore, they refuse to mediate. This happens. Mediation can only occur when both parties are willing to try the process.

Fortunately, one of your neighbors knows a good attorney and you and your neighbors decide to take the next step. Aren't you glad you have collected so much information? You didn't want to come to this, but it looks like a court case is inevitable. Unfortunately, situations like this are common in our society. Not everyone will enter into civilized negotiations. But you and your neighbors are doing the best you can and you've hired another party to act on your behalf.

While we like to think we can handle this kind of event by ourselves, there are times when we must call upon institutions to help us. And, that's what they're for; it's why we've collectively agreed to establish our courts and appoint our judges. And, now, our disgruntled tenants will be negotiating with each other over the attorney's fees. But you have made a good start.

SO YOU SEE, THE PROCESS NEVER STOPS. WE MOVE FROM one situation to another, with each presenting its own challenges and opportunities to enrich our lives—or at least make them run a bit more smoothly.

Be assured that each time you enter a negotiation you are offered the chance to learn more about yourself and about others. You will uncover your motivations and desires and you'll evaluate the needs and goals that others present to you. I urge you to use this book as you would a handbook or workbook. Evaluate, prepare, plan, observe, and follow each negotiation through all its stages. You—and everyone you encounter along the way—will be better off for it.

Maintain respect for the others with whom you negotiate and realize that you will gain more by understanding others' view of the world and what they need to get from the negotiation situation. Armed with new sensitivity, awareness and respect, you will find yourself negotiating with greater potential and assuredly, experiencing significant success!